GETTING YOUR
15 MINUTES OF
FAME

AND
MORE!

A Guide to Guaranteeing
Your Business Success

Edward Segal

JOHN WILEY & SONS, INC.

New York ➤ Chichester ➤ Weinheim ➤ Brisbane ➤ Singapore ➤ Toronto

This publication is designed to provide accurate and authoritative
information in regard to the subject matter covered. It is sold with the
understanding that the publisher is not engaged in rendering
professional services. If professional advice or other expert assistance
is required, the services of a competent professional person should
be sought.

Library of Congress Cataloging-in-Publication Data:

Segal, Edward
      Getting your 15 minutes of fame—and more! a guide to
      guaranteeing your business success / Edward Segal.
           p.   cm.
      Includes index.
      ISBN 0-471-37058-4 (paper : alk. paper)
      1. Success in business.   I. Title: Getting your fifteen minutes of
      fame—and more.
      HF5386.S4157   2000
      650.1—dc21   99-053317

Printed in the United States of America.

10   9   8   7   6   5   4   3   2   1

To Pamela Kervin Segal:

My best friend and traveling companion . . .
in life and on the road

Acknowledgments

I've learned many important lessons—whether it was how to do something or how *not* to do something—from the hundreds of clients I've worked for over the years, my friends, colleagues, and coworkers. In a sense, this book is as much a distillation of their collective wisdom as it is the result of my own experiences. But I doubt that this book would have been started or completed without the unfailing support, encouragement, and editing prowess of my wife, Pamela Segal; the generous advice and feedback of Arnold Sanow; and the positive attitude and kind words of Linda Higgison.

A special word of thanks to Michael Larsen who, even before he became my literary agent, shared expertise and insights that strengthened my book proposal; Michael Hamilton, my editor at John Wiley & Sons, for his belief in and support of this project; the dozens of people I interviewed for this book who gladly and unselfishly shared their observations, insights, and recommendations; and my friends at the National Speakers Association for showing me how making speeches and presentations can lead to even greater accomplishments and rewards.

I also want to thank one of my high school English teachers, Phil Martin; a university political science professor, George Henneghan; and three former members of Congress, Glenn Anderson, John Burton, and Mickey Edwards. Each in his own way provided me with opportunities and opened doors that led to surprising destinations.

Last, but certainly not least, I want to thank my parents, Russell and Anita Segal, for their love, support, understanding, and unwavering faith in me.

Contents

Introduction

Andy Warhol said, "In the future, everyone will be famous for 15 minutes." He did not, however, leave behind a guidebook or instruction manual on how to achieve fame or how to handle it once we have it.

This book picks up where Andy Warhol left off. In fact, I like to think that this is the handbook on fame Andy Warhol would have written if, instead of painting pictures of Campbell's soup cans and producing other works of art, he had:

➤ Helped more than 500 individuals, entrepreneurs, corporations, and organizations achieve and manage their 15 minutes of fame.

➤ Provided public relations advice and counsel to clients ranging from start-up entrepreneurs and Fortune 500 companies to government agencies and trade associations such as MCI, Ford Motor Company, Marriott Corporation, Cable & Wireless, the National Park Service, Air Travelers Association, and the Society of the Plastics Industry.

➤ Written more than 1,000 news releases, op-eds, and bylined articles that have resulted in thousands of stories about the products, services, expertise, and activities of individuals, corporations, and organizations. These press releases have generated news coverage by hundreds of news outlets such as *The Wall Street Journal, The New York Times, USA Today, The Washington Post, Time, U.S. News & World Report,* the Associated Press, Reuters, Bloomberg News, Dow Jones, CNN, CBS News, and trade publications in dozens of industries and professions.

➤ Conducted scores of workshops across the country for business executives and government officials on how to understand and work with the media.

Well, Andy Warhol didn't do any of that.

But I have.

I wrote this book to help make your dreams of fame come true and to show how your trip on the road to fame can be easier, faster and, yes, even affordable. The result is the first comprehensive personal marketing handbook with a complete program of tools, information, and expert guidance to catapult you or your company, products, services, accomplishments, or activities into the public eye—and stay there.

This book can also:

➤ Provide a competitive marketing advantage to entrepreneurs such as small business owners, independent contractors, and consultants.

➤ Help those of you who each year unexpectedly or unwillingly find yourselves thrust into the public eye, whether through an appointment to a high-visibility position, involvement in a controversy, or achievements or activities related to your business.

➤ Serve as a useful primer for the thousands of people and companies who hire marketing and public relations agencies, providing them with important basic knowledge of the profession and the tools available to public relations professionals.

➤ Assist the hundreds of thousands of people who study or enter the marketing, public relations, and communications fields every year, and enable them to start their careers one step ahead of their colleagues.

➤ Provide useful insights to managers and employees who are trying to succeed or advance themselves in their workplace, profession, industry, or career.

Here you'll find:

➤ "Hall of Fame" and "Hall of Shame" sidebars. These anecdotes and news reports recount the successes and snafus of people, corporations, and organizations in the public eye and the lessons you can learn from them.

➤ Advice and insights from or about people and organizations in a variety of industries and professions on how they achieved fame, as well as their recommendations on how to handle it.

➤ Proven "real-world" advice and techniques you can use right away to help generate the public recognition you want.

➤ Examples of the news releases and other press materials I and others have prepared that led to local, national, and international news coverage for individuals, corporations, and organizations.

➤ "In Their Own Words"—excerpts from the dozens of interviews I conducted for this book with people who have already achieved their 15 minutes of fame. The interviewees include:

> ➤ Burke Stinson, spokesperson for AT&T. Since 1986, Stinson has been interviewed more than 2,700 times by the media to discuss AT&T's products, services, and workplace issues, ranging from downsizing and strikes to diversity, sexual harassment, and threatened legal action by Richard Nixon.

> ➤ Becky Madeira, senior vice president of public affairs for PepsiCo, Inc. In 1999, *PR Week* named her one of the 50 most powerful women in public relations.

> ➤ Thor Ibsen, Ford Motor Company's manager of Internet and new media. Ibsen is responsible for planning and implementing Ford's brand integration strategy on the Web.

> ➤ Pat Croce, owner and president of the Philadelphia 76ers professional basketball team. Croce has been profiled by magazines ranging from *Sports Illustrated* and *GQ* to *Success* and *Sales and Marketing Management.*

> ➤ Gregory Slayton, president of ClickAction, Inc., a software company in Palo Alto, California. Slayton and his company have been the subject of media coverage by *BusinessWeek, Time, The Wall Street Journal,* CNN, Reuters, and other news organizations.

> ➤ Joyce Oberdorf, vice president, corporate public relations, for Aetna, Inc., a leading provider of health and retirement benefit plans and financial services.

➤ Steven Loueks, public relations director of the Carlson Leisure Group, which has more than 1,000 travel agency locations around the world. Loueks previously served as the spokesperson and communications director of the American Society of Travel Agents.

➤ Dr. John Potter, founder of the Vince Lombardi Cancer Research Center at Georgetown University's Medical Research Center.

➤ William Harlow, spokesperson for the Central Intelligence Agency.

➤ John Gerstner, manager of electronic communications for John Deere & Co.

➤ Mark Wiatrowski, president of the Executive Office Club, which is building a national network of "offices-by-the-hour" in 50 cities across the country.

➤ Karen Friedman, a media and communications expert who has spent two decades in front of the camera. An award-winning TV news reporter, her thousands of stories have been broadcast on stations across the country, and her reports have aired on the ABC, CBS, CNN, and NBC television networks.

➤ Ric Edelman, a national television talk show host and author of *The Truth about Money*. Dow Jones called him "one of the nation's most successful (financial) advisors."

➤ Kathy Collins, director of strategic planning for the Lee Company, which makes a best-selling line of jeans.

➤ Debra Leopold, founder of First Class, Inc., an independently owned nonprofit continuing education center in Washington, DC. Since opening its doors in 1984, more than 300,000 students have attended their classes on different topics and subjects.

➤ David Stempler, president of the Air Travelers Association, an airline passenger advocacy organization. Stempler, an aviation attorney and international authority on airline passenger and travel issues, has been quoted or interviewed by the media more than 3,000 times.

➤ Michael Barnes, a former member of Congress and a partner in the prestigious law firm of Hogan & Hartson.

➤ Michael Saylor, the CEO of MicroStrategy, Inc., a business-intelligence software company in northern Virginia. He and his company have been the subject of hundreds of stories, including profiles by *Fortune,* Dow Jones News Service, *Information Week,* and *The Washington Post.*

➤ John Challenger, CEO of the international out-placement firm of Challenger, Gray & Christmas.

➤ Joe Flynn, international group show director of Advanstar Communications, a global producer of trade shows and publisher of teleconferencing publications.

This book describes many ways for you to achieve and manage the level of fame or recognition you want. But only you can decide which strategies and tactics are a good fit for you, your company, or organization; make sense within the framework of your own personal or business plans; and are appropriate given the time, money, and resources you want to devote to these efforts.

■ HOW TO USE THIS HANDBOOK

While there are several textbook cases on how to become famous, the last thing I wanted to do was *write* a textbook. Instead, this handbook is an "A-to-Z" reference guide to dozens of proven and effective strategies, tactics, and techniques for achieving and managing the level of fame you want.

➤ Would you like to know how much it really costs to become famous? See Chapter 4.

➤ What news hooks and story angles are more likely to capture the attention of the media? Review Chapters 63–83.

➤ Are you afraid to speak in public? Chapter 19 can help.

➤ What's the best way to prepare for a media interview? Take a look at Chapter 27.

➤ Don't know the difference between a news release and an op-ed? Check out Chapters 45 and 51.

➤ Want to prepare a crisis communications plan for your company? Turn to Chapter 85.

The advice is grouped into seven major parts—one part for each of the seven steps for achieving and managing fame:

Part I **How to Get from Here to There: Prepare Your Roadmap to Fame.** Practical information for all readers, no matter why you want to be famous, or how famous you want to become.

Part II **Getting Your Act Together before You Take It on the Road: What Your Mother Never Told You about Being Famous.** Insights about being widely recognized that everyone should know, but may be afraid to ask.

Part III **The Eight Gateways to Fame.** Descriptions of the most frequently used paths to public recognition, and what you should know before you take any of them.

Part IV **So That's How They Do It! The Tools of the Trade and How to Use Them.** Techniques and tactics you can use to tell your story to the public. You'll find some of these recommendations more relevant to your needs than others, depending on your reasons and goals for being famous.

Part V **First, You Have to Get Their Attention: News Hooks and Story Angles.** Examples of dozens of proven strategies and techniques to promote your business, services, activities, accomplishments, or expertise.

Part VI **From Fame to Infamy: When Bad Press Happens to Good People.** How to protect your image and reputation. A good reputation that took years to cultivate can be lost overnight. Learn how to guard yours.

Part VII **"Thanks for Having Me Back, Oprah."** How to measure how famous you've become, and how to keep your fame in perspective so it doesn't go to your head.

In addition, the Resources section lists services to simplify the task of achieving and managing fame.

The recommendations, examples, and mini-case studies in this book are based on the successes and failures of hundreds of persons, organizations, and corporations across the country who have already traveled down the road to fame. Here's hoping that you'll duplicate their achievements—and avoid their mistakes.

Part I

How to Get from Here to There

Prepare Your Roadmap to Fame

1 What's in It for Me?

The Benefits and Advantages of Fame

Ronald L. Culberson wanted to get his 15 minutes of fame so he could attract more customers.

Culberson, a business consultant in northern Virginia, shows companies how humor in the workplace can increase the morale and productivity of their employees.

His efforts to achieve fame paid off handsomely. More than 15 daily newspapers across the country ran stories about the entrepreneur, which helped bring in over a dozen new clients. (To find out how he did it, turn to Chapter 59.)

Culberson was hardly alone in wanting to get his 15 minutes of fame, or in using public recognition to help improve his bottom line.

A recent public opinion poll conducted by the Louis Harris & Associates research organization found that a third of all Americans (more than 60 million people) want to become famous or well known for their accomplishments, activities, abilities, expertise, or opinions.

But most businesspeople, including entrepreneurs and other professionals, never receive their 15 minutes of fame, much less try, since they lack or don't know where to obtain the knowledge, skills, or resources to achieve their goal. And although these people would like to become famous, few would know how to manage fame once they had achieved it.

But that doesn't stop them from wanting renown or lusting after its benefits and advantages.

As the thousands of people who have already enjoyed their 15 minutes of fame will attest, public recognition can:

➤ Provide a tremendous boost to your business and your career or job prospects.

➤ Increase your opportunities for promotions at work or personal financial gains.

➤ Enhance your business or professional reputation.

➤ Put your products, services, expertise, accomplishments, or opinions in the spotlight.

➤ Provide a competitive advantage in promoting your business interests, causes, or activities.

Despite the many benefits of public recognition, fame is not a magic potion that can cure or prevent bad things from happening to you or your business. It's an important truth that one of my clients learned the hard way.

One day I received an urgent call from a national advertising agency that for several months had run an office in Baltimore to serve an important regional client. Company officials told me that, lulled into a false sense of security working for one client, the agency did nothing to publicize its services to the local business community or to aggressively seek new clients. The Baltimore branch office, which had just found out that it was about to lose its largest account, asked me to help place a story in *The Baltimore Sun* daily newspaper about their plight as soon as possible, hoping the coverage would attract new clients and help prevent the office from closing.

As it turned out, the paper was interested in the agency's story and assigned a reporter to spend a day at the firm interviewing the staff and seeing examples of their work. The lengthy article made the front page of the paper's business section, along with a full color photo of the agency's local staff.

The story was positive, upbeat, and did an excellent job explaining the agency's predicament. Despite the great press coverage, the article came too late: the agency's Baltimore office closed a few weeks later.

The moral of the story is that you should not wait too long to publicize yourself or your company; even great media coverage is not an antidote to poor business or marketing decisions.

■ IN THEIR OWN WORDS

Good Stories Can Make People Feel Good

Media coverage has been pretty important to our success. It's definitely a major factor in our recruiting efforts and employee retention, helps with customers and prospects, and is good for the shareholders.

Press coverage is also important to employees, who want to work for an organization that is respected in the community. If you get negative press, that could tend to cause them to want to leave the company. On the other hand, if they pick up the paper and see a story about how great their organization or employer is, then that story can make them feel pretty good.

Michael Saylor, CEO
MicroStrategy, Inc.

2 First Things First

Take This Pop Quiz

Before you can become famous, you must ask yourself three important questions:

1. Why do I want to be famous?
2. What do I want to be famous for?
3. How famous do I want to become?

The answers will provide the foundation for preparing your personal roadmap to fame.

■ WHY DO I WANT TO BE FAMOUS?

Is your motivation for public recognition based on a personal desire or a business or professional goal? In an article called "Is It Time to Start Bragging about Yourself?" *Fortune* magazine noted, "There's nothing like a little positive press to promote yourself . . . the bottom line is that most publicity is good publicity."

Fame can help people advance in their careers and make the task of finding a new job that much easier, according to John Challenger, CEO of the international outplacement firm of Challenger, Gray & Christmas.

Challenger points out, "Employers are much more likely to invite you in for an interview if they have seen or heard about you or read an article or seen a news report about your activities, than if you are an anonymous face in the crowd."

According to Challenger, "As long as what you stand for in the media is positive and progressive, then you can't get too much attention for yourself. That attention can come as a result of a variety of activities, including writing articles about or being interviewed by the media on issues that are relevant to you, your work, or your life; and participating or holding a leadership position in a trade or professional groups. It's all about holding people's attention."

Arnold Sanow, who has written several best-selling books on personal and business effectiveness, says that getting your 15 minutes of fame "can be just the boost you need to help propel yourself and your organization to greater success."

Nido Qubein, a popular figure on the public speaking circuit, believes there are right and wrong reasons for seeking fame. According to Qubein, "The most important kind of fame is that which is in line with your values and achievements. If it is, then you will really cherish the fame, because it will be part and parcel of what you hold most important in your life. But if you are famous for something that is inconsistent with your values and principles, then the recognition you receive will be fame for the sake of fame, and it will never really render measurable value in your life."

Michael Barnes, a former member of Congress who used to be in the public spotlight because of his political activities and congressional duties (see Chapter 87), recognizes the limitations of fame. He says, "If you want to tie your self-image and your life to fame, you are going to have a tough time in life, because fame does not last. Fame is ephemeral. If your sole purpose in life is to be famous, you are not going to be very happy."

It's also crucial for your claim to fame to have substance. Gregory Slayton, CEO of ClickAction (formerly MySoftware Company) in Palo Alto, California, explains, "Some executives in Silicon Valley have engaged in an awful lot of self-promotion, but have not had the corporate results to back it up. That's a big danger. There must be some reality to back up your claims, otherwise people will get upset with you and you are asking for trouble."

A corporate official's image can be important for both the executive and his or her company: A survey conducted by the Burson-Marsteller public relations agency found that 40 percent of a company's reputation is based on how people perceive its chief executive officer, and that 86 percent of surveyed stock analysts said they would purchase the stock based on the CEO's reputation.

Writing in the Conference Board's *Across the Board* magazine, agency officials observed, "A brand name CEO can make a company stand out in a crowd." In addition, they said news organizations "look to a CEO who can clearly and credibly communicate the company's mission and direction."

■ WHAT DO I WANT TO BE FAMOUS FOR?

As much as you'd like to see yourself on television or in the newspaper, there must be a reason news organizations will want to do a story about you in the first place. The possibilities that may constitute your claim to fame are limited only by your activities, accomplishments, and creativity (see Chapter 6).

■ HOW FAMOUS DO I WANT TO BECOME?

Here again, the sky's the limit.

➤ Do you want to be recognized in your neighborhood?
➤ Well known in your city?
➤ A household word in your profession?
➤ Famous throughout the country, and beyond?

Most people aspire to levels of fame based on the following geographic, career, or audience factors:

Geography

Neighborhood.
Community.
City.
Region.
State.
Country.
World.

Career

Job or workplace.
Industry or profession.

Audience

Family.
Friends.
Neighbors.
Peers.
People with similar interests, goals, opinions.
Coworkers and colleagues.
Fellow members of groups or organizations.
Current or future employers.
Competitors.

Current or potential customers or clients.

Investors.

Decision makers (in business, politics, government, etc.).

■ DEGREES OF FAME

Just as there are different levels of fame, there are degrees of public recognition:

➤ Are you seeking newspaper and television profile stories in which you are the star attraction?

➤ Will you be content to simply be quoted within the body of a magazine article?

➤ Perhaps you don't want to be famous at all, but because of circumstances beyond your control (such as a controversy, an accident or event you witnessed, or winning the lottery), you find yourself in the public spotlight against your will or despite your better judgment.

HALL OF FAME: SUCCESS STORIES

How you use your 15 minutes of fame is up to you. Here's how people in different professions and industries have used their public recognition to their personal or professional advantage:

➤ Susan Trivers became famous when a local newspaper profiled her and Café Aurora, the neighborhood restaurant she owned in Alexandria, Virginia. The story resulted in more customers coming through the door and more money in the cash register when they left. Trivers now talks about her entrepreneurial experiences as a public speaker and customer service trainer.

(continued)

HALL OF FAME: SUCCESS STORIES *(Continued)*

➤ Elliot Gold is publisher of TeleSpan, a teleconferencing newsletter he founded in 1981. Gold became a household name in the teleconferencing industry, where he serves as a consultant to corporations and organizations. He capitalized on his fame by raising his hourly rate $100 an hour every time he was quoted in *The Wall Street Journal*. He appeared in the paper so often, however, he had to place a cap on his fees or risk pricing himself out of the market.

➤ Lynda Maddox is well known by both students and colleagues on the campus of George Washington University in Washington, DC. Maddox, an associate professor of marketing and advertising and an expert on buyer behavior, has been interviewed by *USA Today*, *The Washington Post*, ABC's *Good Morning America*, and scores of other news organizations in the United States and overseas. The media coverage has increased her stature within the academic community and reinforced her credibility in the eyes of her students.

➤ Dr. John Potter is a professor of surgery/surgical oncology at Georgetown University's Medical Research Center. Potter says television and newspaper coverage was instrumental in generating awareness of and support for the university's Lombardi Cancer Research Center (which he founded), and for promoting his book, *How to Improve Your Odds against Cancer*.

➤ John Gerstner, manager of electronic communications for John Deere & Co. He notes that news coverage about his work in *PC Week, Financial Executive, Communication World*, and other publications "has very much broadened awareness of who I am and where I work, and has brought me in contact with people I would not otherwise had known about." Gerstner says, "Fame is much like a snowball. If you are careful about forming the first little ball and pushing it down the right slopes, it can gather volume and velocity, and roll into something quite amazing."

➤ Alan Weiss is president of Summit Consulting Group, Inc., a business and management consulting firm. Weiss, who has advised such clients as Hewlett-Packard and

HALL OF FAME: SUCCESS STORIES *(Continued)*

General Electric, has done hundreds of newspaper, radio, and television interviews to promote his expertise. He says that if it were not for his fame, his annual seven-figure income would be cut in half.

➤ Joe Flynn is a leading expert and pioneer in organizing trade shows throughout Latin America; he's delivered scores of speeches and presentations and his expertise, activities, and accomplishments have been chronicled in dozens of stories in industry publications. Flynn has parlayed that visibility into an important job as international group show director with Advanstar Communications, a global producer of trade shows.

➤ Mark Diamond is a leading litigator in the field of indoor pollution. He has conducted hundreds of interviews with reporters from television stations, newspapers, and radio stations and written articles for journals and other publications. The public exposure has led to client referrals and invitations to speak before many groups and organizations.

➤ John Hlinko helped wage a well-publicized satirical campaign against a multimillion-dollar bond proposal to finance construction of a new baseball stadium in downtown San Francisco. Although the measure passed, Hlinko used the local and national media coverage he generated about the campaign to help land a job as a writer/PR strategist with Alexander Ogilvy Public Relations, a premier high-tech agency in the area. "When I was interviewed for the job, I found that a lot of people remembered the campaign, and I used it as proof of my creativity and capabilities."

➤ Nelson Zide, owner of ERA Key Realty Service in Framingham, Massachusetts, sends a regular series of news releases about the activities and accomplishments of his seven offices to about 50 local, national, and trade news organizations. The visibility he has generated for his company has resulted in more business and referrals from across the country. He notes, "Real estate is a people business and a contact sport. The more people I can contact through the news we make, the more business we get."

■ **IN THEIR OWN WORDS**

Fame as a Bully Pulpit

For me, fame is a bully pulpit that you can use to help make people smile. You can really touch people to help them feel great, such as athletes who give fans the autographs or pictures they ask for. Individuals in the public spotlight have the power to add or subtract from the happiness of the people they come in contact with. In this position, more often than not, I get to add to it.

Pat Croce, Owner and President
Philadelphia 76ers professional basketball team

3 Not Yet Ready for Prime Time?

Why Fame May Not Be for Everyone

Not everyone wants to be famous (thus making it easier for those who do), and not everyone may be able to achieve, manage, or handle the public recognition they seek.

Why?

Perhaps they:

➤ Have an exaggerated or distorted opinion as to why they should be well known (see Chapter 2), or how long it will take them to become famous.

➤ Cannot effectively explain or promote the importance or relevance of their products, services, activities, accomplishments, expertise, or opinions (see Chapter 9).

➤ Don't want to give up their privacy. Pat Croce, owner and president of the Philadelphia 76ers, warns, "You will be interrupted in restaurants. You will be interrupted watching a movie at a theatre. You will be interrupted all the time. But if you don't mind dealing with people, then it's okay."

➤ Are unable to spend the time, money, or other resources that are needed to obtain the level of fame they want (see Chapters 4 and 16).

➤ Do not anticipate the toll that fame can take on their personal lives or relationships, or do not know how to manage fame once they achieve it (see Chapter 87).

While no one ever said that the road to fame is free of potholes, you can take steps to ensure that your trip will be a smooth one, which is what the rest of this book is all about.

■ IN THEIR OWN WORDS

The Other Side of Fame

When you do become famous, there can be significant downsides. It can destroy your privacy. It can destroy your personal life. There was a time when I could not go anywhere and not have people stop me or interrupt whatever I was doing. One of the joys of not being famous now is that you have a certain degree of privacy when you are out in public. I feel sorry for movie stars and other people who are so famous that they literally cannot get away from it. For example, I walked into a men's room with Senator Ted Kennedy (D-MA), and as he was trying to do his business, people kept coming up to him to shake his hand.

Michael Barnes
Former member of Congress

4 You Don't Have to Be Rich to Be Famous

Fame on a Shoestring

How much money must you spend to become or stay famous? The cost of a postage stamp, or millions of dollars? One of the biggest misconceptions most people have about fame is that it takes a fortune to become and stay famous.

In 1999, *USA Today* published a story on "the current price of fame" and how much celebrities pay to maintain their status. The newspaper's composite annual budget for these superstars included the following expenses:

Agent	$2,000,000
Business manager	1,000,000
Security	260,000
Private jet	250,000
Personal assistant	65,000
Personal stylist	10,000

Based on an annual salary of $20 million, *USA Today* concluded that it would cost a Hollywood star more than $15 million every year for these and other "necessities" to maintain his or her fame.

The rest of us, however, don't need to make or spend as much as Julia Roberts, Tom Hanks, or the latest Academy Award winner to obtain the level of fame we want. In fact, it can cost nothing more than your creativity, time, and the price of a postage stamp.

Just ask Debra Leopold, founder and president of First Class in Washington, DC, whose company is part of a network of adult continuing education centers with facilities in 14 cities across the country.

Leopold admits that she's never had enough money in her budget to hire an expensive public relations agency. "I was faced with the choice of learning how to do it myself, or not doing it at all."

She decided to learn.

Leopold now prepares and sends news releases about her class offerings to targeted news organizations she thinks will be most interested in doing stories about her company. Sometimes the results have been overwhelming. "Some news releases have created so much media interest in my classes that I've had to prohibit reporters from attending the class so I would have enough room for my students!" she says.

"I've generated thousands of dollars in business because of the stories that have been written about our classes. And all I had to spend was the cost of a postage stamp in order to mail a news release."

The cost of a postage stamp.

That's all you may need to reach the people who have the power to decide who becomes famous in our society: the editors and reporters at television stations, newspapers, magazines, Web sites, and radio stations. In our media-driven society, these men and women are the gatekeepers to fame: it is their stories about the activities or accomplishments of individuals just like you that makes people well known and widely recognized by their neighbors, coworkers, or complete strangers.

Almost every one of the hundreds of public relations clients I have worked for usually have asked two questions about my efforts to make them famous: How much will it cost? How long will it take? And my answer is always the same: it depends.

It depends on:

➤ How much time and effort will be necessary to prepare their story effectively and convincingly for the editors and reporters most interested in covering such news.

➤ Whether I have to do any research to obtain all the facts and figures I'll need to tell their story to the media.

➤ Which "tools of the trade" I will use to tell or show their story, such as news releases, press kits, photographs, and video news releases (see Part IV for more information about methods to promote yourself or your company).

■ A TYPICAL BUDGET

The expense budget for my clients has ranged from less than $100 to $30,000 and up, plus fees of several hundred to tens of thousands of dollars, depending on what they want to accomplish. For many clients who have sought national and trade press coverage about the introduction of a new product or service, the following out-of-pocket expenses are typical:

Research	$ 500
Media lists	225
Telephone/fax	150
Postage	175
PR Newswire	900
Fed-Ex	50
News monitoring service	125
Messengers	75
Total	$2,200

■ BELLS AND WHISTLES

Other clients with more ambitious goals for news coverage— and deeper pockets—often run up additional expenses to achieve their goals:

➤ The production and distribution of a video news release (a prepackaged story that is sent to television stations; see Chapter 53).

➤ Arranging for a client to be interviewed by television reporters across the country without leaving town (satellite media tour; see Chapter 57).

➤ Creating news hooks to capture the attention of the media by commissioning a national public opinion poll and releasing the results to editors, reporters, or columnists (see Chapter 74).

The costs for these and other extras can cover a wide range:

Video news release	$15,000–$20,000
Audio news release	1,000– 5,000
Satellite media tour	5,500– 11,000
Opinion poll	750– 4,000
Press kits	100– 1,800
Mailing house	500– 3,500
Travel	1,000– 4,500

■ CONTROL YOUR BUDGET

How much you'll have to spend to achieve and maintain your fame will depend on three factors:

1. How famous you've decided you want to be.
2. How much effort it will take to get the media interested in doing stories about you.
3. How much of the work you will be able to do yourself.

One way to control costs is to limit the number of reporters you contact. For example, it can cost only a few hundred dollars to distribute a news release via PR Newswire (a private commercial news distribution service) to thousands of news organizations across the country (see Chapter 41).

Or you can mail the news release yourself for the cost of postage.

5 It's a Jungle Out There!

The Opportunities and Competition to Become Famous

News organizations are critical stepping-stones to fame in our society. That's because television stations, radio stations, newsletters, Web sites, magazines, and newspapers are the most effective ways for individuals, companies, and organizations to communicate with the rest of society.

Do you have any idea how many news organizations there are in the United States?

If you were to add up all the news outlets that people read, watch, or listen to, the total would exceed *one million.* The list includes:

750	Television stations that broadcast local shows (plus hundreds of local cable outlets).
1,500	Daily newspapers.
1,500+	Web sites maintained by news organizations.
8,800	Weekly newspapers.
11,000	Radio stations.
11,000	Business, trade, professional, and consumer publications in the United States and Canada.
1,000,000+	Newsletters published by news organizations, corporations, trade associations, consultants, and nonprofit groups.

Each of these news outlets has its own staff of editors, reporters, commentators, or columnists; a defined audience; a list of topics or subjects of interest to that audience; a specific definition of news; and schedules for producing and distributing the product to viewers, listeners, or readers. These outlets also must fill a tremendous vacuum: every year they must find and provide enough information to use up hundreds of thousands of hours of airtime and millions of pages of print.

■ THEIR PROBLEM IS YOUR OPPORTUNITY

The challenge these news organizations have in finding and providing news to their audiences represents a tremendous opportunity for you . . . if you are able to present yourself, product, service, activity, or expertise as news. If you do, then you may have an excellent chance of convincing these news organizations to do a story about you.

Depending on your industry or profession, there are at least a few—and likely scores of—newsletters, magazines, and Web sites that regularly report on the people and activities in your line of work, whether it is marketing, sales, accounting, real estate, travel planning, medicine, law, financial services, education, or any other field.

■ FIRST THE BAD NEWS

The bad news is that you're bound to face competition in your efforts to capture the attention of the media. That competition may come from:

➤ Other persons seeking their 15 minutes of fame.

➤ Hundreds of corporations and organizations that have full-time staff or entire departments to publicize or promote their products and services.

➤ Thousands of public relations and marketing consultants and agencies that try to generate news coverage about their clients.

➤ Current events and late-breaking stories that preempt space in the limited "news hole" filled by news organizations every day.

■ NOW THE GOOD NEWS

Despite all this competition, you are, in fact, trying to become famous on a level playing field that offers everyone the same opportunity. That's because every individual, corporation, or organization seeking public recognition must effectively answer two key questions that, in one form or another, any reporter will ask.

➤ Who cares?
➤ And why?

How you answer these pivotal questions will help determine whether and how you will stand out against your competition.

In the pages that follow, I'll discuss the steps you can take to show the media why you deserve to receive your 15 minutes of fame.

■ NEWS HOOKS THAT WORK

Attracting the attention of the media is like trying to catch a fish. There are any number of hooks, lures, and bait you can use to get the job done:

➤ One of the best ways to convince editors, reporters, or columnists to do stories about you is to identify or create the most effective story angle or news hook you can.

➤ The best story angles are those that affect the most people, impact a news organization's audience, and address the audience's interests, needs, or concerns.

➤ These news hooks vary depending on the nature, needs, and audience of each news organization.

➤ The best news hooks answer the question "who cares?" in a direct, forceful, timely, and compelling manner.

Of the hundreds of clients I have represented and counseled, I've found that the best news hooks usually fall into one of the following 28 major categories. The chances are pretty good that the news hook you use to help publicize yourself, products, or service will fall into one of these areas. If you happen to "invent" a new one, please let me know and I'll include it in the next edition of the book!

1. Starting a company or organization.
2. Introducing a new or improved product.
3. Announcing a new or improved service.
4. Highlighting an interesting or unusual activity of a corporation, organization, or individual.
5. Appointing or promoting employees.
6. Launching a marketing or advertising campaign.
7. Winning or handing out an award.
8. Sponsoring a contest, promotion, or special event.
9. Doing something good for the community.
10. Establishing a scholarship fund.
11. Releasing results, such as sales of a product or quarterly financial earnings.
12. Demonstrating expertise in a particular topic or subject.
13. Setting a record.
14. Celebrating an anniversary or milestone.
15. Distributing helpful or useful advice or information to the public.
16. Piggybacking an announcement on a current event or news development.
17. Warning the public about a problem.
18. Involving one or more celebrities or athletes in a project or activity.

19. Raising or donating money, goods, or services to a worthy cause.

20. Participating at a conference, trade show, workshop, or seminar.

21. Delivering a speech or presentation.

22. Publishing a book or article.

23. Conducting a training program.

24. Serving as the spokesperson for a company, organization, project, or cause.

25. Expressing an opinion or viewpoint.

26. Reacting to a current event or development.

27. Releasing the findings of an opinion poll about what the public thinks on a particular issue.

28. Announcing the result of a survey.

Once you have the news hook, then you're ready to try to attract the attention of the media.

In Part V, you'll find brief case studies of individuals, corporations, and organizations who sought their own 15 minutes of fame about their product, service, expertise, or accomplishment. They range from an entrepreneur who launched a new service and an inventor who introduced a new product, to a survey on airline safety, and the celebration of a corporate anniversary.

Their efforts to tell their stories to the media (or the efforts of the public relations firms or consultants they hired to help tell their story for them) resulted in hundreds of television, newspaper, and magazine stories, and helped achieve their personal, professional, or business goals.

These case studies are excellent examples of the fame that can be achieved when you can tell your story in an effective and attention-getting way, talk in soundbites, use visuals to help show your story, and explain why people should care about your announcement, product, service, or expertise.

6 Your Fame IQ

Take Stock of Your Products, Services, Expertise, and Accomplishments

Once you've decided why you want to be famous, and how famous you want to be, it's time to identify and prioritize which aspects of your business or professional life you want to be famous for, and why.

Ideally, this inventory should not be prepared in a vacuum, but should reflect your career objectives, professional goals, business plan, or organization's marketing strategy. What aspect of your personal or professional life can serve as the reason a news organization would want to do a story about you?

Use the following form, a clean sheet of paper, or a blank computer screen to briefly describe:

➤ What you want to be famous for:

Products

_____

_____

Services

_____

_____

(continued)

Areas of Expertise

_____

_____

Activities

_____

_____

Accomplishments

_____

_____

Opinions and viewpoints

_____

_____

➤ Explain why you or your company should become famous for them.

_____

_____

_____

_____

➤ Prioritize the products, services, and so on you listed above according to the potential value of their fame to you or your organization.

_____

_____

_____

_____

If you haven't already done so, now would be a good time to read Chapters 2, 7, and 14.

Brand Yourself

If It Works for Coke and Disney, It Can Work for You

If I were to hold up an unmarked bottle of brown liquid, you'd have no idea what was in it or what it was for. But if I told you that it was a bottle of Coca-Cola, then you'd know exactly what it was and what you could do with it. Probably, you'd even know how it would taste.

Such is the power of branding, which can immediately communicate the benefits and advantages of a product or company through a name, logo, symbol, or phrase.

Adam Leyland is editor-in-chief of *PRWeek,* a magazine that covers the latest news, trends, and developments in the practice of public relations. He notes that "the same PR strategies and tactics that Fortune 500 companies use to promote their products or brand awareness can be used by individuals to help establish and maintain their own personal or professional brand identity."

Leyland says business professionals and entrepreneurs alike can turn news coverage about their expertise and accomplishments into stepping stones "that may lead to better jobs, bigger salaries, or a competitive advantage in seeking new business."

If branding works for Coca-Cola, IBM, Walt Disney Company, and thousands of other companies and organizations, then it can certainly work for you to help quickly communicate who you are, what you do, and how well you do it.

You need to give careful thought and consideration to what you'd like your reputation or brand to be.

When people hear your name, see your picture, or look at your business card, what words or image do you want them to associate with you?

➤ Smart?   ➤ Talented?

➤ Innovative?   ➤ Shrewd?

➤ Humorous?   ➤ Tough?

➤ Creative?   ➤ Detail-oriented?

➤ Successful?   ➤ Generous?

Whatever "brand" you select for yourself must be communicated in all that you do and say in your business or professional life. But you must ensure that your image or reputation is consistent and reflects the real you. Otherwise, people will start to associate you with brand words like "phony" and "fake."

Sometimes the public imprints its own brand on individuals because of what they say or what they do.

Rep. George Nethercutt (R-Washington) was a leader in the movement to limit congressional terms of service and was elected on a promise not to serve more than three terms in the U.S. House of Representatives. Imagine everyone's surprise when Nethercutt later reversed course, claiming he had made a mistake and that "thousands of people have urged me to run again."

In response, supporters of term limits placed a full-page ad in the *Spokane Spokesman-Review*. They defined "Nethercutt" as a verb meaning "to go back on one's word"; "to say one thing in order to get elected to high political office, and then do the opposite once elected"; and "to be swept off one's feet by the perks and privileges of Washington, DC." The ad went on to say that synonyms of "Nethercutt" included "hypocrite, opportunist, and dishonest."

It's safe to say that's not the brand this politician had in mind for himself.

But it didn't stop there.

➤ In his Doonesbury comic strip, cartoonist Garry Trudeau satirized Nethercutt as the "Weasel King," and someone dressed up in a weasel costume began to show up at the congressman's public appearances to remind voters about the politician's broken promise.

➤ Some of Nethercutt's supporters turned against him, including a popular radio talk show host who said he might run against him in the next election.

■ NOT EVERYONE MAY SHARE YOUR SENSE OF HUMOR

Establishing your brand identity is one thing.

Knowing when not to do something that could tarnish your brand or professional reputation is something else.

The Marriott Corporation may have thought it was poking some good-natured fun at school cafeteria workers when it portrayed them and the food they serve in an unflattering light as part of a series of television commercials to encourage people to eat at its regional chain of Roy Rogers fast-food restaurants. But the labor union that represents the cafeteria workers was not amused, and took steps that led to the offensive TV spots being yanked off the air.

Local and national news organizations reported the fiasco. *Newsweek*'s story about the commercials carried the headline, "Roy Rogers Eats Crow." Even *The New York Times* entered the fray, charging in an editorial, "For Marriott to praise junk food at the expense of nutritious school fare isn't just unfunny. It is cruel to kids for whom that meal may be the best they get all day, and demeaning to those who prepare it."

It was no laughing matter to overweight people in San Francisco when the 24 Hour Fitness club launched what it called a humorous marketing campaign to attract new members. The campaign included a billboard featuring a hungry space alien and the message, "When they come, they will eat the fat ones first." Dozens of overweight men and women protested in front of the health club, carrying picket signs with sayings such as "Bite My Fat Alien Butt."

Exercise: What's Your Brand?

This exercise will help you begin the task of identifying and selecting a brand identity for you or your company.

Since corporate brands are too important to leave in the hands of one person, be sure to consult with all members of your team (marketing, public relations, etc.) in deciding and adopting your brand. If you are seeking your own brand identity, get feedback from your friends, families, and colleagues.

This exercise can start you in the right direction.

➤ In the left-hand column of this page, list all the characteristics you want your target audience to know, understand, or believe about you.

➤ In the right-hand column, jot down the word or phrase that best describes each of these characteristics.

Characteristics   **Short Description**

_____   _____

_____   _____

_____   _____

➤ Now list your services, products, expertise, activities, or accomplishments that support the information in the preceding columns.

_____   _____

_____   _____

_____   _____

➤ Finally, go back through your lists and prioritize the "brand identities" that best represent you, your company, or organization, and are best supported by your products, services, expertise, or activities. Which ones do you feel most comfortable with, and would like to be known for?

_____

_____

_____

_____

8 Hit the Bull's-Eye

Define, Target, and Find Your Audience

You need to tell an editor or reporter only two pieces of information to help convince them to do a story about you: Who cares about it and why:

➤ Who cares about what you have to say, besides your immediate family?

➤ Who cares about the story you have to tell, besides your neighbors?

➤ Who cares why you want to be famous, besides your colleagues at work?

➤ Who cares about your products, services, activities, opinions, or accomplishments besides your friends?

➤ And *why* should they care in the first place?

How will your news affect the way people live or work?

How is your company, product, service, or expertise different or better than the competition?

There's a lot more riding on the answers to these questions than you might think:

➤ As discussed in Chapter 9, news organizations (whether they are newspapers, radio stations, magazines, or television stations) are storytellers. They are in the business of telling stories that affect, impact, or interest their audiences.

➤ If you can convince editors, reporters, or columnists that their viewers, readers, or listeners will care about and be interested in *your* story, then you will be well on your way to fame.

Once you've identified and prioritized what you want to be famous for and why (see Chapters 2, 6, 7, and Part V), you should define, identify, and target the audiences who will be most interested to watch, read, or hear stories about you or your organization.

Using this worksheet, a blank sheet of paper, or a computer screen, answer the following questions about the top priority for which you want to become famous.

Finding Your Audience

➤ Based on your own marketing or other reasons, which target audiences will be the most interested in learning about you or your company?

_____

_____

_____

_____

➤ Why will they want to learn about you or your company?

_____

_____

_____

➤ Which groups and organizations do members of your target audience belong to?

_____

_____

_____

Finding Your Audience *(Continued)*

➤ Where do they live?

_____

_____

_____

➤ What demographic information is available about your target audience (age, sex, education, religion, etc.) that may help you to target and understand them?

_____

_____

_____

HALL OF FAME: HIGH-TECH EXECUTIVE HITS THE TARGET

Michael Saylor, CEO of MicroStrategy, Inc., knew who his audience was and why they would care about his story: potential investors, bankers, financial analysts, and others in the investment community who could help make the initial public offering of stock (IPO) in his young high-tech company a success. And he knew they would care about his story because they'd be interested to learn more about the potential for growing their money as he grew his company.

Saylor knew exactly how to reach his audience: through positive news coverage in a nationally respected daily newspaper. How? By allowing a reporter with *The Washington Post* to follow him around the country as he met with many of the same investors, bankers and financial analysts he hoped to reach—and impress—through the media.

But Saylor said he permitted the *Post* to tag along for another reason: as a public service to other business executives.

(continued)

ALL OF FAME: HIGH-TECH EXECUTIVE
HITS THE TARGET *(Continued)*

"I had gone through the process of applying for an IPO, and found that there was very little useful information in the public domain about it. I thought it would be very useful if a reputable newspaper would cover the process and then share that with other entrepreneurs who may need to know that information in the future," Saylor said.

Most executives might hesitate to allow a news organization to do a behind-the-scenes story such as this. After all, a lot was at stake. Although Saylor said he had no qualms, others around him did, including lawyers, bankers, and investors.

As Saylor recalls:

➤ "Lawyers were concerned because they thought that it might risk some shareholder liability or liability for some future shareholder lawsuits."

➤ "The bankers were concerned because they normally work the IPO process to their benefit; a newspaper that would be actually watching that process unfold might publish something that did not necessarily reflect positively on them."

➤ "Institutional investors were concerned for the same reasons, since they try to get every possible advantage (in connection with an IPO) and they would not welcome the scrutiny."

Allowing *The Washington Post* to see the process in action was similar to the scene in the movie *The Wizard of Oz* when the curtain is pulled back to reveal that it's only an ordinary human being pulling the levers and making the "magic" happen.

As Saylor sees it, "For the most part, the IPO business traditionally has been to the benefit of a set of powerful investors and powerful banks, and not very much to the benefit of the general consumers. That's why a lot of people were not very excited to have a lot of scrutiny from a large newspaper."

It turns out their concerns were groundless.

Saylor liked the story that *The Washington Post* did, which appeared on the front page of the newspaper. "It got our name out there and a lot of people read it. Even today when we meet with people the Washington area, many of them say they remember reading the story. The article was positive all the way around."

9 Once upon a Time . . .

The Importance of Being a Storyteller

The one million news organizations in the United States (see Chapter 5) all have something in common: everyone of them is a storyteller seeking to find and report stories that will be of interest to their audiences.

One of the most important keys to your success in achieving and maintaining fame will be your ability to tell your story—to be, in effect, a storyteller.

Can you tell the story about your accomplishments, activities, products, services or expertise in a way that attracts the interest of news organizations? If you can, then you will likely be able to convince them to tell your story to thousands or millions of their readers, listeners, or viewers.

Even the armed forces and a generally secretive organization such as the Central Intelligence Agency (CIA) know the value of telling good—and true—stories to the public.

CIA spokesperson William Harlow says, "I like to find stories that illustrate the point that we have people here who are doing something extraordinarily brave and courageous or who are successful in their work, whether it's a brilliant analyst, a dedicated scientist, or a technologist who do something which benefits all Americans.

"When I can find a story that can be told, in a way that reflects credit on the entire organization, people here feel good about themselves. To be able to do that is especially satisfying to me."

The importance of storytelling is not lost on the U.S. Army, either. In an *Infantry* magazine article, Captain Christopher C. Graver writes, "Helping media personnel get

their story may seem like a distraction and a drain on resources. But a commander with a well-defined information
strategy will recognize a media event for what it is—a
chance to tell his unit's and the Army's story to the American public."

Telling your own story to the media is truly a classic win-
win opportunity for people who want to be famous:

> ➤ By telling your story to the storytellers, you are help-
> ing them to do their job.

> ➤ And by telling your story to their audiences, those
> news organizations are helping you become famous or
> establish or maintain the image or reputation you want.

Thor Ibsen has seen firsthand the impact that news coverage can have to help promote the services and activities of
a company, and how that visibility can affect the popularity
of its employees. Ibsen, the manager of Internet and new
media for Ford Motor Company, is responsible for planning
and implementing the automaker's brand integration strategy on the Web.

Ford uses media coverage about its Web site (www.ford
.com) to help build and maintain credibility for its Internet
activities with the public, in the auto industry, and within
Ford itself. Ibsen maintains, "Today we are considered to be
one of the automotive leaders, if not the leader, on the Internet, and I attribute that directly to the success of our public
relations efforts."

Ibsen said that news stories about Ford's cyberspace activities have helped the company in some unexpected ways,
including recruitment and staff morale. "The articles have
helped people learn about the exciting things we are doing
and have made them realize that it is somewhat sexy to be in
this part of the auto industry. Our managers are now being
quoted more often in the business and trade press, and that
is very gratifying to all of us."

The public recognition has also made Ibsen and members of his team popular on the speaking circuit: "All of us
are now sought after as experts to speak at trade shows and

HALL OF FAME: TAKE 'EM FOR A TEST DRIVE

You can supply only so many facts and figures about a story to reporters. Even then, they may find it difficult to understand or explain to their audience the significance, nuances, or impact of what's involved. That's when and why it can make sense to have reporters actually try your product or service.

When DaimlerChrysler unveiled the NECAR 4, the first driveable zero emission fuel cell passenger car, their PR firm, Strat@comm, thought it would be important for journalists to drive the car so they could do a better job of reporting the story. Prior to introducing the car at a news conference, the agency arranged for more than 60 journalists from news organizations around the world to participate in a "ride-and-drive" event where they took turns taking the concept car for a 15-minute spin on residential streets in suburban northern Virginia.

Ron Defore, a principal of Strat@comm, said the test drives helped to generate hundreds of favorable television, newspaper, and magazine stories about the new automobile; the TV coverage alone reached more than 70 million viewers across the country.

other events. But we can't do it all, and have to turn down two to three invitations every week."

As you prepare to tell your story to the media, you may want to retain the services of a professional media trainer—a PR specialist (often a former reporter, such as Karen Friedman whose advice appears throughout the book)—who can objectively evaluate your ability to tell your story to journalists and offer recommendations for improvement.

The services of most media trainers include conducting and critiquing videotaped mock interviews, showing how to ensure that your themes and messages are reported by the media, providing tips on how to conduct news interviews, making suggestions on how to prepare and use soundbites/inkbites, offering recommendations on what to wear and how to stand or sit during interviews, and giving advice on how to handle negative questions that are asked by reporters (see Resources section).

■ IN THEIR OWN WORDS

Do Your Homework!

If you do your homework and easily explain your subject to a reporter who faces very strict time constraints, you will have a much better chance of having your story presented in a clear manner. That reporter might have spent just a few minutes with you when he or she gets called away to a breaking story. However, the editor may still want the reporter to finish the story he or she started with you. If you didn't do a good job of boiling down your facts into simple straightforward messages that affect that reporter's audience, either the reporter will get it mixed up or the story may not air at all.

Karen Friedman
Media Trainer and Former TV Reporter

10 Why Not Just Buy an Ad?

The Difference between Advertising and News Coverage

At the seminars and workshops I conduct across the country, people often ask me why can't they just buy the exposure they want by purchasing advertising. They want to know what difference it makes whether their fame comes from commercials or news coverage.

The difference is crucial, and can be summarized in one word: credibility.

➤ If you have enough money, you can buy any amount of advertising, have it say whatever you want, and have it appear almost anywhere or any time you want for as long as you like. But it is impossible to buy favorable news coverage for your company in the business section of your daily newspaper, or charge a human-interest story on your local television station to your credit card.

➤ Knowing that news organizations do not accept payment for the stories they run, the public will place more credibility in an objective news account about you than if you had said the same thing in a full-page ad or 60-second commercial.

Another important difference between advertising and news coverage is that you must *pay* for advertising, but *pray* for news coverage. Unlike advertising, there is no guarantee when, where, how, or if your efforts to generate coverage about yourself or organization will succeed.

Despite that uncertainty, some entrepreneurs are willing to forego advertising altogether and place all their money into efforts that may result in newspaper, magazine, and television stories.

Debra Leopold is the founder of First Class, Inc., an independently owned nonprofit continuing education center in Washington, DC. She says, "I could spend thousands of dollars on a full-page newspaper ad and still not get the name response I've received by simply buying a postage stamp and sending out a news release.

"News releases have more credibility than advertising. I've abandoned all of my advertising efforts and now concentrate entirely on public relations. I simply cannot get the same response with an ad as I can with a one- or two-line mention in a newspaper story."

■ MORE BANG FOR YOUR BUCK

News coverage also provides you with a much larger return on your money than advertising. When IBM staged a chess match between one of its supercomputers and Gary Kasparov, the Russian chess grandmaster, the company estimated that it received $20 in free publicity for every $1 dollar it spent. That's the kind of return on investment that even Warren Buffett would appreciate.

In 1999, a survey of 3,000 company managers conducted by Erdos & Morgan for the American Advertising Federation found that corporate America placed more importance on public relations than advertising. Asked about the "strategic importance" of seven different departments that can help companies meet their marketing and sales goals, public relations came in third, just after product development and strategic marketing. Advertising was rated sixth.

■ IN THEIR OWN WORDS

The PR Megaphone

Advertising is when you tell your own story. Public relations, when done correctly, is when someone else tells your story for you. And that's ten times more valuable. Public relations is the megaphone we use to help tell the world about our new products, services, financial performance, strategic partnerships, et cetera.

Gregory Slayton, CEO
ClickAction, Inc.

11 Keep It Simple, Stupid

Prioritize, Prioritize, Prioritize

When you tell your story to editors, reporters, or columnists, it is important to guard against the tendency to tell them *everything* about the story.

If you tell newspaper reporters 15 reasons your product or service is different or better than anything that's been made or offered before, you'll have no idea which one of those 15 reasons they may use in the story. That's because reporters must confine their story to the length assigned by the editor. To do that, they must decide what information will be most important to pass along to readers.

However, if you don't tell reporters what *you* think are the most important points, then you are leaving the decision about what's important up to them, and you'll have *no idea* which information will wind up in an article. So when the story is printed, you could be upset that the reporter did not include what you thought was the most important information.

Ric Edelman, a national television talk show host and author of *The Truth about Money,* says it's also important that you feel strongly about what you tell the media—and that it shows. Edelman points out, "If you don't believe in what you are saying and don't have a passion for it, then you are not going to accomplish very much. You must be willing to give it the amount of effort that it needs, and to sustain those efforts for as long as necessary. Otherwise, people will see that you don't have the passion and won't believe in your message."

To make sure that your story comes out the way you want:

➤ Prioritize the information you'd like the reporter to include.

➤ Limit the information you tell the reporter to no more than three major points. This will help ensure that the points that are most important to *you* are the ones that will appear in the article.

➤ Keep reinforcing those points if the reporter calls with questions or interviews you for the story.

For additional help in prioritizing the information you provide to reporters, you may wish to consult with a media trainer (see Chapter 9 and the Resources at the end of the book).

■ IN THEIR OWN WORDS

Help Reporters Decide What's Important

Some people give reporters too much information. Sometimes during an interview, a person might rattle off eight or nine talking points. They left it up to me to decide which point was most important. If I picked point number eight, inevitably that person would call me to complain that I missed his point. In reality, he missed his point because if he had focused on one clear message, I would have easily delivered that message for him.

Karen Friedman
Media Trainer and Former TV Reporter

12 Do You Have *Any* Idea What You're Talking About?

The Importance of Research

Most reporters and columnists will not accept anything you tell them at face value. In fact, an editor once told me that he often warned his reporters, "If your Mother says she loves you, check it out!"

When you tell your story to the media, you will face the same skepticism. An effective way to show the media you know what you are talking about is to have and use the most accurate and current facts and figures necessary to prove your points, make your arguments, or bolster your claims.

If you are already an established authority in a particular industry, then you may very well have access to the research you need at work or through your network of colleagues and contacts. Otherwise, you can turn to reference works, magazines and newspapers, the Internet, computer databases, other experts in the field, and brick-and-mortar libraries.

Don't be shy about using your research early and often in your news releases and other efforts to achieve fame. The sooner you can convince reporters you know what you're talking about, the more likely it is that your news release will result in news coverage, and that journalists will contact you for interviews.

Sometimes the best way to get the information you need, such as finding out what the public thinks about a particular topic, is to commission a national public opinion poll. This is not as expensive as it might sound: for example, one polling firm (Market Facts, Inc.) sells questions on its regularly scheduled omnibus survey for about $750 a question. The company polls 1,000 adult Americans by phone, and the results are usually available within a few days. Louis Harris and Associates offers a similar service for a bit more money.

I've often used polls not only to help clients find out what the public is thinking, but as a news hook to get the media's attention (see Chapter 74).

Short of conducting a national public opinion poll, however, there are several faster and certainly more affordable ways to obtain the information you may need to help make your case.

They include a wide range of experts, authorities, and the spokespersons of numerous corporations and organizations that can be found through:

➤ A reference book called (guess what?) *The Yearbook of Experts, Authorities & Spokespersons.* Although it is published annually, there is a regularly updated online version at www.yearbooknews.com that you can search for free using key words and phrases.

➤ *Experts* magazine, or its online counterpart (www.expertsmagazine.com).

➤ The SpeakersVoice Association (www.speakersvoice.com).

➤ Members of the National Speakers Association (www.nsaspeaker.org) or their local chapters around the country.

There are several databases, including:

➤ Dow Jones News Retrieval (www.djnr.com), which has the text of stories from more than 6,000 newspapers, magazines, newsletters, and the transcripts of several news programs. While there is no charge to search for stories, there is a small fee to view or print them.

➤ Vanderbilt University (www.vanderbilt.edu), which maintains a comprehensive library of tapes and abstracts of more than 30,000 major evening network television news shows going back more than 30 years.

➤ The online archives of thousands of news organizations. According to *Editor & Publisher* magazine, more than 11,000 newspapers around the world are now on the Internet.

➤ PR Newswire, Businesswire, and other private newswire services that store copies of previous distributed news releases and other press materials.

➤ The World Wide Web which, by one estimate, has more than one billion home pages, including nearly every imaginable corporation, organization, and news organization. Depending on the capabilities of the search engine you use, it's possible to do a keyword search to locate information about or references to almost anyone or anything.

And don't forget:

➤ The reference librarian and reference works at your local neighborhood library.

➤ Nearby colleges and universities, many of which operate full-time news bureaus to help match the expertise of its faculty to the research needs of corporations, organizations, and the media.

➤ The trusty Yellow Pages which, as one of its TV commercials boasts, is "life, listed alphabetically."

13 Picture This!

Why You Need Visuals

Good storytellers know not just how to tell their story, but how to show it as well. But unless you can show your story, you will only communicate half your story to the media and your target audience. Why?

> Since television is, obviously, a visual medium, your ability to find pictures to help tell your story will make it easier for TV reporters to decide to do a story about you.

> The same holds true for newspapers, where a picture that shows some aspect of your story will make any article they do about you that much longer and eye-catching to readers.

> And since radio reporters are in the business of painting word pictures for their listeners, your ability to provide a visual image that illustrates your story will make the reporter's job easier as well.

As the public relations consultant to the Society of the Plastics Industry, it was my job to generate as much television coverage as possible about their triennial plastics exposition in Chicago. I did it, in part, by going up and down the aisles of the trade show searching for pictures that would capture the attention of the television audience. I found the visuals at the booths of several different exhibitors in the form of, among other things, a graffiti-resistant stop sign, a fire engine made of plastic, and a beverage container that, with the push of a button, almost immediately heats its contents.

In addition to pitching the story about the show, I promoted the pictures to the producers and assignment editors at television stations and networks. The visuals helped to attract just the kind of coverage that show officials wanted, including several stories by CNN, Fox News, and a live appearance by several exhibitors on a local morning news program.

Exercise: Choosing Visuals

List all the visuals you can think of that will help show your story, whether it is a picture of you delivering a speech, a photo of a new product, or a copy of the new logo your company will unveil. Then prioritize the ones that will be most important or effective in helping to promote yourself, or your products, services, accomplishments, activities, expertise, or company.

List of Visuals

_____

_____

_____

_____

_____

_____

_____

_____

_____

_____

_____

_____

_____

_____

_____

_____

_____

_____

_____

HALL OF FAME: A MOVING EXPERIENCE

Instead of razing the historic Empire Theatre in New York City, the 7.4 million-pound structure was moved, inch-by-inch, down the block to a new location for renovation and restoration. In the 1930s, the former burlesque theater was the site of the first performance by the comedy team of Abbott and Costello.

Chances are, few, if any, newspapers would have taken a picture of a building in Manhattan being moved, especially one that took about five hours to relocate. But just before the building was moved, two giant balloons resembling the comedians were positioned to make it appear that they were dragging the structure down the street with a rope. The picture of the Abbott and Costello balloons "pulling" the building was published in newspapers in New York City and across the country.

Sometimes visuals can help effectively publicize political or social causes.

In the 1996 presidential election, "Butt Man," a Democratic protester dressed in a rubber cigarette costume, dogged Republican candidate Bob Dole at several of his campaign appearances across the country. Why? Because Democrats had charged that Dole accepted campaign contributions from the tobacco industry and that he claimed that tobacco is not necessarily addictive for everyone. At the campaign rallies, the 7-foot tall "Butt Man" would wave his arms and pass out phony dollar bills showing Dole smoking a cigarette.

The humorous visual proved irresistible to the Associated Press, CNN, *The New York Times,* and other news organizations, which did stories and published photographs of "Butt Man" on the campaign trail.

And to protest firearms, antigun supporters arranged 109 shoes in front of the building of a gun importer in Alexandria, Virginia. The activists said the shoes symbolized each one of the children who had been killed in Virginia by gunfire over a one-year period. The haunting picture was published by *The Washington Post* along with an article about the demonstration.

14 Plot Your Route to Fame

Prepare Your Plan

If you were planning to drive from one part of the country to another, you probably would take some time to prepare for the trip. Your checklist might include mapping out a route, making sure your car was in good working order, arranging for someone to look out for your house while you were away, and packing the clothes you'd need.

A similar list will come in just as handy as you prepare to start out on the road to fame. Take a few minutes now to familiarize yourself with the following exercise and, as you read through this handbook, go back and fill in each item. The result will be your own personal plan for achieving the level of fame you want. (If you are not reading the chapters in sequence, I've listed where you can find and read up on the information you need to help you fill in the blanks.)

Exercise: Preparing for Fame
_____

Why do you want to be famous? (Chapters 2 and 6)

_____

_____

_____

_____

(continued)

Exercise: Preparing for Fame *(Continued)*

How famous do you want to be? (Chapter 2)

_____

_____

What do you want to be famous for? (Chapter 6 and Part V)

_____

_____

How do you want to use your fame once you've achieved it? (Chapter 1)

_____

_____

How will you know when you've achieved your desired level of fame? (Chapter 86)

_____

_____

What are the three most important things you want to communicate to your target audience? (Chapter 11)

_____

_____

What is your brand identity? (Chapter 7)

_____

_____

Who is your target audience? (Chapter 8)

_____

_____

Exercise: Preparing for Fame *(Continued)*

Where do they live?

_____

_____

Which news organizations do they read, watch, or listen to?

_____

_____

What facts and figures will you need to *tell* your story? (Chapter 12)

_____

_____

What visuals can you use to help *show* your story? (Chapter 13)

_____

_____

What news hooks or story angles will you use to help attract the attention of the media? (Chapters 63–83)

_____

_____

What soundbites will you use during interviews? (Chapter 28)

_____

_____

Who is your competition?

_____

_____

(continued)

Exercise: Preparing for Fame *(Continued)*

How is your story different or better than theirs?

_____

_____

What tactics will you use to communicate your messages?
(Chapters 45–62)

_____

_____

How much time will you need to research, draft, prepare, or
implement these tactics? Following are estimated lead times
for the most frequently used tactics:

Tactic	Lead Time
News releases (Chapter 45)	1–3 days
Fact sheets (Chapter 46)	3–5 days
Press kits (Chapter 47)	1–3 days
News advisories (Chapter 48)	1–2 days
Photos and cutlines (Chapter 49)	1–3 days
Biographical profiles (Chapter 50)	5–7 days
Op-Eds and bylined articles (Chapter 51)	7–10 days
Letters to the editor (Chapter 52)	1–2 days
Video news releases (Chapter 53)	7–21 days
Audio news releases (Chapter 54)	2–4 days
News conferences (Chapter 55)	1–7 days
Photo ops (Chapter 56)	1–3 days
Satellite media tours (Chapter 57)	1–7 days
Multicity media tours (Chapter 58)	7–21 days
Distributing press materials (Chapter 59)	1–3 days
Story pitch calls and letters (Chapter 60)	1–2 days
Newsletters (Chapter 61)	7–14 days
Research editorial calendars (Chapter 62)	1–7 days
Become a resource to the media (Chapter 33)	1–7 days

Exercise: Preparing for Fame *(Continued)*

What resources will you need? (Resources section)

_____

_____

How much will you need to spend? (Chapter 4)

_____

_____

What is your plan in case you, your company or your organization encounter negative publicity or a crisis situation? (Chapter 85)

_____

_____

What approvals, if any, do you need to obtain within your company or organization before you can implement this plan? What is the approval process, and how much time will it take?

_____

_____

If you will not implement this plan yourself, which PR consultant or agency will you work with? (Chapter 16)

_____

_____

Schedule of Activities

Deadline	**Activity**
_____	_____
_____	_____
_____	_____

(continued)

Exercise: Preparing for Fame *(Continued)*

Results

_____

_____

_____

_____

_____

_____

_____

The lessons learned in your efforts to become famous

_____

_____

_____

_____

_____

_____

Recommendations for future activities

_____

_____

_____

_____

_____

_____

15 Before You Begin the Trip . . .

Test Market Your Plan

After you've filled in all the blanks on the worksheet in Chapter 14, you may think you're ready to implement your plan to achieve fame.

Not so fast.

Are you sure that you've answered the questions of who cares and why to the best of your ability? Are you confident that your news hook is the most effective it can be? Are you positive that your news release will make the media sit up and take notice?

There are two ways to find out for sure.

The first way is to simply execute your plan full blast, at warp speed, as soon as possible. Send out those faxes! Distribute those e-mails! Fill the mailboxes with your news releases!

But how will you feel if those releases come back as being undeliverable because of wrong addresses? How will you react if reporters ignore your story? What if your quotes wind up on the cutting room floor?

Most people don't get many opportunities to get their 15 minutes of fame. If you blow it now, it could be a while—if ever—until you can try again.

The best way to help guarantee your success is to do what many Fortune 500 companies do before they launch a multi-million dollar marketing campaign.

They try it on a small scale before unleashing it on the rest of the world.

It's called test marketing.

➤ Instead of sending out hundreds of news releases, send out a handful to see how they are received. Follow up the releases with phone calls to the people who received them, and ask if they are interested in doing a story. If not, why not?

➤ Put yourself in the shoes of the reporter who will receive your news release. If you were the reporter, what questions would you ask?

➤ Arrange for your friends or colleagues to play reporter with you, and see how well you are able to answer their questions.

➤ Are you sending releases to the people who will be most interested in receiving them?

➤ Don't trust whatever sources you used to compile your media list and assume you have the most current or accurate contact information. Call each reporter on the list and make sure that he or she is the best one at that news organization to receive the information you are sending.

➤ Try to arrange at least one interview with a reporter to see how well your news release or soundbites are received.

➤ Are the visuals you selected to show your story hitting a responsive cord? If not, why not?

You get the idea.

Why roll the dice when you could stack the deck and help ensure your success? By taking a little time today to test market your plan, you can take whatever steps may be necessary to make it strong and effective so that you won't be surprised or disappointed tomorrow.

16 Fame Doctors

Find and Work with PR Agencies and Consultants

If you don't have the time, resources, or patience to achieve or manage your 15 minutes of fame, thousands of public relations agencies and consultants can try to do the job for you. I say "try," because no matter how good they say they are or how impressive their list of clients may be, the nature of public relations means there is no guarantee that they will be able to generate the result you want or achieve it when or how you want it (see Chapter 10 on the difference between advertising and public relations).

It is relatively easy to find agencies or individuals to talk to and interview for the job. Among the sources you can consult are friends or colleagues who have used PR agencies or consultants, the national or local chapters of the International Association of Business Communicators or the Public Relations Society of America, *O'Dwyer's Directory of Public Relations Agencies,* and the Internet (see Resources section).

Depending on how famous you want to be and the caliber of the agency you want to hire, the fee for their services can range anywhere from less than $50 an hour to $50,000 a month and more.

It's one thing to find agencies to talk to. It's quite another to select the best one for you. Following is a suggested checklist of questions and issues you should consider as you look for the best agency or consultant to represent you.

Checklist for Choosing an Agency or Consultant

- ☐ What kind of results and news coverage have they achieved for other clients? Ask to see relevant case studies.
- ☐ What awards or recognition have they received for their work?
- ☐ How much turnover do they have in their list of current clients? How long have they worked for their oldest client?
- ☐ How many editors, reporters, and columnists do they know? (This is a trick question, since the number of reporters an agency knows usually has nothing to do with their ability to generate results for you. It is much more important that they know how to find the right reporter who will be interested in your story, and that they know how to pitch your story in such a way as to get the interest of the media.)
- ☐ What do they consider to be their strengths and weaknesses?
- ☐ Have they worked for similar clients in your industry or profession? (This is another trick question. A good PR person should be like a good reporter: with the right facts and information, he or she should be able to create stories for clients no matter what line of business they're in.)
- ☐ Will the people who market their services to you be the same people who will work on your account?
- ☐ What is the background and qualifications of the individuals who would work on your account on a day-to-day basis?
- ☐ Do they charge for their services on an hourly, project, or retainer basis?
- ☐ Do they want a performance bonus as an incentive to meet or exceed your expectations?
- ☐ What is their level of understanding of your own business or profession?
- ☐ Ask to see writing samples from the people who will be working on your account.
- ☐ Do they seem to be overpromising results?

Checklist for Choosing an Agency
or Consultant *(Continued)*

☐ Get everything in writing.

☐ Is there a 30-day cancellation clause in the contract to terminate the relationship with the agency or consultant?

☐ Is there good chemistry between you and the people who will work on the account?

☐ How many turnovers are there among the agency's staff?

☐ How often will they report to you about their activities and results?

☐ Do they work for other clients who would pose a conflict if they worked for you?

☐ Given the work they do for other clients, will they have time to give your account the time, attention, and resources it deserves?

☐ Ask to see a sample of their invoices. Are they clear and easy to understand?

☐ Do they have the ability to provide crisis communications services if you or your company have a public relations problem?

☐ How creative and flexible are they in coming up with new and different ways to achieve results for clients, or in adapting to changing situations? Ask for recent examples.

☐ Ask for references. And call them.

After you've asked your questions of the agency, be prepared to answer some questions they may have for you, including:

☐ Background information about you or your company.

☐ Your goals and objectives.

☐ Your expectations and time frame for results.

☐ How much you are prepared to spend in fees and expenses.

**HALL OF SHAME: IF THEY'RE SO GOOD,
WHY DO THEY HAVE PROBLEMS?**

Although public relations professionals can provide useful and important services for clients, PR people apparently need some help of their own.

A survey released in 1999 by the Public Relations Society of America and the Rockefeller Foundation discovered that publicists have some of the worst credibility problems of any profession. In fact, when measured against the credibility of 44 other people (teachers, military leaders, business executives, etc.), flacks ranked near the bottom of the list.

Who came out on top?

The Chief Justice of the U.S. Supreme Court.

That's certainly a hard act to follow.

■ IN THEIR OWN WORDS

Working with a PR Agency

➤ Find the right PR firm for you.
➤ Prioritize what you want to accomplish.
➤ Understand how public relations works.
➤ Listen closely to the firm's advice.
➤ Have a carefully thought-out plan.
➤ Demand excellent execution of the plan.

Gregory Slayton, CEO
ClickAction, Inc.

Part II

Getting Your Act Together before You Take It on the Road

What Your Mother Never Told You about Being Famous

17 It May Be English, But It's All Greek to Them

Know Your Audience

As important as it is to know what you are talking about (see Chapter 12), it's just as critical that you know your audience.

Failing to be aware of and sensitive to the needs, concerns, and cultural sensitivities of the public is a surefire way to stop your efforts to become famous in its tracks, or convey an image or tarnished reputation that you don't want.

➤ Do you know what they think?

➤ Do you know how they feel?

➤ Do you know what they believe?

➤ Do you know what turns them off or on?

➤ Do you know how to talk to them?

If you don't know the answers to these questions, then you may run the risk of coming down with a severe case of "foot-in-mouth disease."

To remind its faculty about the changing frame of reference of the students they teach, in 1999 Beloit College in Beloit, Wisconsin, issued a list of 43 items that it said students who were born in 1980 may not be aware of.

The list included the following:

➤ They have no meaningful recollection of the Reagan era, and did not know he had ever been shot.

➤ They were 11 when the Soviet Union broke apart, and do not remember the Cold War.

➤ They have never feared a nuclear war. *The Day After* is a pill to them—not a movie.

➤ They are too young to remember the Space Shuttle Challenger blowing up.

➤ Their lifetime has always included AIDS.

➤ They never had a polio shot and, likely, do not know what it is.

➤ Bottle caps have not always been screw off, but have always been plastic.

➤ The expression "you sound like a broken record" means nothing to them.

➤ They have never owned a record player.

➤ They have likely never played Pac Man, and have never heard of "Pong."

➤ *Star Wars* looks very fake to them, and the special effects are pathetic.

➤ They may never have heard of an 8-track, and chances are they've never heard or seen one.

➤ There have always been VCRs, but they have no idea what Beta is.

➤ They cannot fathom what it was like not having a remote control.

➤ They were born the year the Walkman was introduced by Sony.

➤ Roller skating has always meant in-line for them.

➤ The Vietnam War is as ancient history to them as World War I and World War II or even the Civil War.

➤ They never heard the terms "Where's the Beef?" "I'd walk a mile for a Camel," or "De plane! De plane!"

➤ They do not care who shot J.R. and have no idea who J.R. is.

➤ The *Titanic* was found? I thought we always knew where it was.

➤ Kansas, Boston, Chicago, America, and Alabama are all places—not music groups.

➤ McDonald's meals never came in Styrofoam containers.

What do you know about the frames of reference of your target audiences, and how can you use that knowledge to ensure that your story is both heard and understood by them?

18 It's Not What You Say, It's What They Hear

Don't Overestimate the Public's Intelligence

Being on the same cultural wavelength as the public (see Chapter 17) may not be enough to save you from an embarrassing situation. That's because, sad but true, even though the Declaration of Independence says "all men are created equal," not everyone has received the same education or have a complete grasp of the finer points of the English language.

David Howard found that out the hard way.

According to *The Washington Post,* during a budget meeting, Howard, a white aide to the black mayor of Washington, DC, said, "I will have to be niggardly with this fund because it's not a lot of money." People in the meeting took offense at his remarks, thinking he had used a racial slur, and DC Mayor Anthony Williams was forced into asking for and receiving his aide's resignation.

In reality, "niggardly" means "stingy."

Commenting on the incident, Julian Bond, chairman of the NAACP, told the Associated Press, "You hate to think you have to censor your language to meet other people's lack of understanding."

Williams later changed his mind about Howard's resignation, and asked the former aide to rejoin his administration.

The *Dallas Morning News* went through a similar experience with the same word when readers complained that a reviewer had written about "a niggardly hand with seasonings" at a local restaurant. The paper later told readers that it regretted the use of the word.

19 Speechless in Seattle (or Anywhere Else)

Overcoming Your Fear of Speaking in Public

When asked to speak before large audiences, Arnold Sanow always seemed to come up with an acceptable excuse to avoid it: he was either too busy, not feeling well, had a conflicting engagement, was going to be out of town, or was not adequately prepared to make the presentation.

One day his luck ran out. At a companywide staff meeting, Sanow was unexpectedly called on to speak about a project he was working on. By the time he arrived at the podium his mouth was dry, he was sweating profusely, and his stomach felt as if it was full of butterflies. When he opened his mouth to speak, the only sound he could hear was that of his heart, pounding in fear. "This," he reminded himself, "is why I hate to speak in public."

As you climb up the ladder of fame, you may be called on to speak to groups of people about any number of business-related topics. The invitations may range from making informal remarks before a handful of colleagues at a breakfast meeting to delivering a keynote address in front of thousands of people at a national convention. These speaking engagements are golden opportunities for you to establish or enhance your professional reputation; let more people know about your expertise, accomplishments, or opinions; or focus increased public attention on your company, product, or activities. Depending on the audience and topic, reporters or editors from the consumer, business, or trade press may be in attendance or the event's organizers may send out a news release about your remarks. Indeed, you may want to work with the organizers to prepare and distribute your own news release to promote your appearance, or send out a follow-up release summarizing your speech.

Why? Because publicity about your speech can help ensure what you have to say will be communicated to a much larger audience than the one you spoke to (see Chapter 71).

But what can you do if what happened to Sanow happens to you?

Walter Cronkite once said, "It's natural to have butterflies. The secret is to get them to fly in formation."

Arnold Sanow trained his butterflies to fly in formation, and his experience can help you conquer your own fears of speaking in public. For most of his life, Sanow suffered from acute anxiety whenever he had to speak in public. "I was afraid I would look like a fool, did not want to risk being rejected by my peers, and always found excuses not to speak before large groups of people," he says.

But Sanow was determined not to let the butterflies ruin his life. To overcome his fears, he carefully followed a master checklist to help himself prepare, plan, and deliver presentations. The checklist included the following items:

■ PREPARE FOR SUCCESS

> ➤ Rid yourself of beliefs that cause fear, such as:
>
> "I failed before when I spoke in public, so I will probably fail again."

"A survey says that public speaking is the number one fear of most people, so it must be my number one fear."

"The audience wants me to fail. The audience is my enemy."

"I may make a mistake. I want to be perfect."

➤ Replace negative thoughts with positive ones, such as "I am a great speaker."

➤ Practice speaking at every opportunity you can find before groups of people on a variety of topics and in different situations and circumstances.

➤ Join Toastmasters International, a nonprofit organization that helps people master their communication and speaking skills.

➤ Arrive at meetings ahead of time to check out the room, practice your presentation, and get to know the other people who will participate at the event.

➤ Meditate. Before each speech, use a relaxation exercise to tense up different parts of your body and then relax them.

■ RESEARCH YOUR AUDIENCE

Obtain as much information as you can about the audience, including:

➤ Whether they share the same experiences.

➤ If they have any knowledge of the topic.

➤ How many people are expected to attend.

➤ Their preferred learning style (lectures, demonstrations, etc.).

■ PLAN YOUR PRESENTATION

Before you arrive for your presentation, you should know:

➤ How much time you will have for your remarks.

➤ How you will open and close your presentation.

➤ How you will get and keep the group's attention.

➤ What questions the audience will most likely ask you during or after your presentation.

➤ What notes, visuals, and materials you will need.

➤ Schedule breaks during the presentation (one break every one hour and fifteen minutes).

➤ Eliminate all information that is not directly relevant to the central theme of your presentation.

■ DELIVER THE GOODS

When you deliver your remarks:

➤ Put yourself at ease by picturing the audience in their underwear.

➤ Visualize a successful presentation by imagining people smiling, laughing at your humor, applauding at the right times, and then coming up afterward to tell you about the great job you did.

➤ Focus on a friendly face in every audience and keep your eyes on that person until you feel relaxed.

➤ Use a speaking style that reflects your own personality and mannerisms so you come across as genuine, knowledgeable, and sincere.

➤ Tell the audience why your presentation is relevant to them.

➤ Keep your remarks within the allotted time.

➤ Use slides and other visual aids sparingly.

➤ Maintain eye contact with your audience throughout the speech.

➤ Show enthusiasm for your topic.

➤ Keep the attention of the audience.

➤ Use your voice and body language to make your message memorable.

Arnold Sanow's checklist and techniques for preparing, planning, and delivering presentations worked. By thoroughly planning each presentation, knowing his audience, researching his topics, and preparing good outlines, he dramatically decreased the anxiety he felt whenever he got up to talk.

Not only did he get his butterflies to fly in formation, he went on to become a successful full-time professional speaker and president of the Business Source in Vienna, Virginia. Sanow delivers more than 150 paid presentations a year to corporations, organizations, and conferences and is one of only 300 people in the world to be designated a Certified Speaking Professional by the National Speakers Association.

But Sanow is not one to let go of a good thing. He says he still uses his fear-reducing techniques for every presentation he gives. You never know when your butterflies might try to break formation.

20 Boo!

Are There Skeletons in Your Closet?

For the unprepared, fame can be a mixed blessing.

To be sure, it is a tremendous boost to the ego to have people recognize you on the street, in restaurants, or at industry or sporting events. But that recognition can come with a hefty price tag if there are aspects of your personal or professional life you want to keep private or skeletons in your closet that you hope and pray will never see the light of day.

The more you are in the public spotlight, the greater the chance that embarrassing or humiliating aspects of your past may become public knowledge.

You have three options:

Option 1

➤ Stay anonymous.

Option 2

➤ As you climb up the ladder of fame, be sure you have an explanation for your transgression that you can use on a moment's notice if and when your secret is exposed.

➤ Apologize profusely for your mistake when it is discovered.

➤ Promise not to do it again.

➤ Don't do it again!

Option 3

➤ Take the high road by admitting your "sins" before anyone can blame you for covering them up.

➤ Apologize profusely for the error of your ways.

➤ Promise not to do it again.

➤ Don't do it again!

Hidden skeletons have a way of coming out of the closet at the worst possible time.

According to news reports, at speaking engagements across the country, U.S. District Judge James Ware would often tell an emotional and moving story about his childhood: In 1968, two white teenagers on a motorcycle shot and killed his younger brother, Virgil, while the two of them were riding bikes in their hometown of Birmingham, Alabama.

Speaking about the incident in an interview with the *San Jose Mercury News,* the judge said: "When I went through the death of my brother, I came very close to becoming someone who could hate with a passion. What happened to me was a defining experience, a turning point in my life."

It was also a total fabrication, as he admitted when the *Birmingham News* discovered that it was a different man with the same name who had seen his brother killed. The other Ware told the paper, "I couldn't believe a judge would do something like that, being a man of the law. I think it was wrong. He was trying to better himself off someone else's grief."

In addition to embarrassing Judge Ware, the truth also sidetracked his legal career. A few months before, he had been nominated by the president to serve on the U.S. Court of Appeals. After the news accounts surfaced and Ware admitted the lie, the president withdrew the nomination.

Just because lies about your past aren't exposed during your lifetime does not mean that they won't be revealed after you're dead. Take the case of Larry Lawrence, who appeared to have an impressive resume. He was a:

➤ Successful real-estate investor.

➤ Big contributor to Democratic political campaigns.

➤ U.S. ambassador to Switzerland.

➤ Former member of the U.S. Merchant Marine who was wounded when his ship was torpedoed by Germans during World War II.

When Lawrence died in 1996, he was buried in Arlington National Cemetery with full military honors, in recognition of his wartime service.

It was later discovered that Lawrence had lied about his military experience and, in fact, was attending a junior college in Chicago at the time. When the truth came out, Lawrence's widow agreed to have her husband's remains removed from Arlington National Cemetery.

21 Do as I Say, Not as I Do

Setting Good Examples... and Bad

For some people, being in the public spotlight can be another version of the old "good news . . . bad news" jokes.

The good news is that the public listens to everything you say or sees everything you do. The bad news is that the public listens to everything you say and sees everything you do.

As the following anecdotes based on published news reports illustrate, individuals in high-profile positions or those who are famous or widely recognized can never be too careful about what they say or do. People who are in the spotlight and enjoy the trust and confidence of the public should be careful to avoid embarrassing situations that can send the wrong message:

➤ In Newark, New Jersey, the Associated Press reported that one member of a group of firefighters, claiming he was conducting an inspection, cut to the front of a long line to buy tickets to a Bruce Springsteen concert. One of the other firefighters told the people who were standing in the long line, "This is one of the perks of the job." Officials of the Newark Fire Department later confiscated the tickets and said, "There has been violation of our rules and regulations. It wasn't anything criminal. But it was a really stupid mistake."

➤ Days before announcing a campaign to discourage drivers from running red lights in Montgomery County, Maryland, county police chief Carol A. Mehrling ran a red light and hit another car being driven by a fourth-grade teacher. Mehrling, who was driving an unmarked police cruiser at the time, was criticized in news reports for not immediately reporting the accident, and for not receiving a ticket because of the mishap.

➤ Fourteen very able current or former members of a college football team were certainly out of bounds when they were accused of having handicapped parking permits so they could get better parking spots on the campus of the University of California at Los Angeles. The students were each sentenced by the Los Angeles Municipal Court to 200 hours of community service and ordered to pay a fine. One of the former students, Skip Hicks, went on to become a running back for the Washington Redskins. Hicks told *The Washington Post,* "I was young. You do things you regret when you're young. I never parked in a handicapped spot. I shouldn't have had it. I used it to get into lots."

➤ Citing proposed budget cuts by the Clinton administration, the General Accounting Office (the investigative arm of Congress) issued a report saying the Veterans' Administration would have to fire more than eight thousand employees. The need for belt tightening did not seem to faze the Secretary of Veterans' Affairs, however, who ordered a new Cadillac for his official use. A disgruntled employee who noticed the new car parked in a Washington garage called *The Washington Post* to complain about the hypocrisy.

Fortunately, there are those who know when to do the right thing, and how to set a good example for others:

➤ In the aftermath of the tragic shootings at Columbine High School in Colorado, the *Los Angeles Times* reported that the Walt Disney Company had "pulled the plug on several coin-operated arcade games at Disneyland in which players shot at human targets." "We just don't think there's any place for violent video games at Disneyland," park spokesman Ray Gomez said. "This had probably been under consideration for a while, but the events in April brought it to the forefront of our thinking."

➤ *The Washington Post* reported that dozens of brides-to-be who had ordered their bridal gowns were left in the lurch when the Laurel Bridal & Gown shop in Laurel, Maryland, unexpectedly went out of business and closed its doors.

Seeing the story, Steven N. Saidman, owner of Imperial Gown in nearby Fairfax, Virginia, posted signs on the shuttered shop offering the free use of a loaner gown to any woman who could prove she had ordered a dress from the bankrupt merchant. In a follow-up article three days later, Saidman told the paper, "I've been working with brides for 48 years, and I know how anxious they are. When I thought about what these brides must be going through, we thought we had to do something to help."

22 Being Famous Means Always Having to Say You're Sorry

Apologize for Your Mistakes

When you or your company have done something wrong, the best and most effective thing you can do is apologize to the public, your customers or clients, and everyone you may have offended.

The more famous or recognized you or your organization is in your community, profession, or industry, the greater the need that you own up to the mistake. For the sake of your long-term image and reputation, it is imperative that you apologize and put the incident behind you as quickly and gracefully as possible.

To paraphrase the line from *Love Story,* when you screw up, fame means always having to say you're sorry:

➤ Don't agonize over whether you should apologize or not. If it was your fault, take the blame and say you're sorry.

➤ Apologize immediately. Don't delay it any longer than absolutely necessary.

➤ Promise not to do it again, and take steps to ensure you don't.

➤ Then move on with your life.

Depending on the circumstances, you can issue your apology at a news conference, through a news release, or during a series of one-on-one interviews with reporters.

Since "to err is human," there are certainly enough examples of how well or poorly those in the public spotlight have apologized for their transgressions:

➤ When dozens of public television stations were discovered to have given the names of donors to the Democratic and/or Republican parties, the president of the Public Broadcasting Service told Congress: "We blew it." He admitted that it had been an "inappropriate, embarrassing, and downright stupid" thing to do.

➤ Douglas Ivester, chairman of the Coca-Cola Company, told consumers in Belgium he was sorry that some of them had become ill because of his company's product, and gave a free liter of Coke to every Belgian citizen.

➤ Merrill Lynch & Co., Smith Barney, Inc., and Prudential Securities, Inc. sent millions of dollars to irate customers—along with their apologies—for failing to process their stock trades in a timely manner.

HALL OF SHAME: WATCH WHAT YOU SAY!

It's a funny thing about being in the public eye. The public actually watches what you do and listens to what you say. So you'd think that some politicians, radio personalities, sports figures, and others would know better than to say or do anything that is embarrassing, offensive, or in bad taste.

The media continues to show otherwise.

➤ A woman producer was preparing then-Rep. Martin Hoke (R-Ohio) to do a live interview from the U.S. Capitol with television stations in his home state about his reaction to the President's State of the Union message. Before the interview began, but with his mike on and camera rolling, the politician commented about the size of the producer's breasts. His remarks, captured on videotape and reported by *The Washington Post,* instantly became the fodder of critical editorials and articles in dozens of newspapers across the country.

Hoke apologized to the woman and, in a series of interviews with television stations and other news outlets at home, said he was sorry for what he described as "an incredibly dumb thing to do, an incredibly dumb thing to say. If I haven't learned a lesson, I deserve to be smacked on the head by a two-by-four."

➤ Morning radio personality jockey Doug Tracht, a so-called shock jock, was fired by WARW-FM for making a tasteless comment in connection with the torture and murder of a man who was dragged to his death behind a pickup truck in Texas.

➤ After Tiger Woods won the prestigious Masters golf tournament, fellow player Fuzzy Zoeller, who is white, said Woods would want a stereotypical meal of fried chicken and collard greens at a victory dinner. Zoeller, who said he was just joking, later apologized for his remarks.

➤ Invited by legislators to speak on the floor of the Wisconsin state assembly about his urban renewal efforts and race relations, Green Bay Packers defensive lineman player Reggie White (who is black) made several remarks that were widely denounced by the media and community leaders for being insensitive and critical of gays, lesbians, whites, and various ethnic groups.

➤ Several major airlines gave their best customers free frequent flyer miles to apologize for the delays or frustrations they may have experienced flying from or changing planes at Chicago's busy O'Hare International Airport.

➤ MCI WorldCom, Inc. offered 20 days of free service to an estimated 3,000 business customers who, because of technical problems, could not access the company's Internet and e-mail services.

■ IN THEIR OWN WORDS

Don't Be Afraid to Apologize

Don't be afraid to say you're wrong, or that you made a mistake. Apologize, and then fix the mistake. There is no need for doubletalk or backpedaling. Just say: "You're right. We're not." It's amazing how forgiving the media and public are when you put your cards on the table.

Becky Madeira
Senior Vice President for Public Affairs
PepsiCo, Inc.

23 One Size May Not Fit All

The Importance of Tailoring Your Story

The news you want to announce about yourself or your company may be like a new suit: one size may not fit everyone. That's why you may need to target and customize your story to grab the attention of the public and the news organizations they follow.

Sometimes you only need to customize the headline and first paragraphs of a story to help ensure its placement in a particular newspaper.

That's what I did for the American Council of Life Insurance's Life & Health Insurance Medical Research Fund, which sought news coverage about its award of scholarship or grant money to deserving medical researchers across the country.

Rather than send all newspapers a long release with the names of every winner, I prepared a generic release that the client then adapted for each researcher. That release was sent to the hometown news organizations of that particular person. Excerpts from the generic news release follow:

LOCAL STUDENT RECEIVES $80,000 SCHOLARSHIP FROM LIFE & HEALTH INSURANCE MEDICAL RESEARCH FUND

WASHINGTON (June 19) — The Life & Health Insurance Medical Research Fund today announced that it has awarded an $80,000 scholarship to (insert name) of (insert city, state) so he/she can continue his/her work towards an M.D.-Ph.D. degree in (insert general field) at (insert school).

(Insert last name of student)'s scholarship is sponsored by (insert name of company), a participant in the Life & Health Insurance Medical Research Fund. (Insert last name of student) is one of seven students across the country to receive the competitive scholarship this year, according to Fund Chairman Louis G. Lower, II.

Every accredited medical school in the United States was invited to nominate one eligible candidate for this year's scholarship program. Finalists were selected by a scientific advisory panel of eminent scholars and researchers.

Lower noted that students who receive their M.D.-Ph.D. degree, "will be especially equipped to translate the results of basic biomedical research into useable treatment for patients. With the declining number of medical doctors pursuing research careers, people who hold an M.D.-Ph.D. degree are filling an increasingly important niche in biomedical research."
[Used with permission]

The complete generic release can be found on my Web site at www.edwardsegal.com.

24 3...2...1

Timing Is Everything

Have you ever found yourself talking to someone, only to realize that she wasn't really paying full attention to what you were saying? Perhaps you've been guilty of the same thing and haven't paid full and complete attention during a conversation with a friend, family member, or colleague. Maybe you were preoccupied with other matters at the time or simply too busy to listen to what the other person was telling you.

Trying to get the attention of the public and the media to listen to your story is a lot like trying to have a conversation with somebody who's too busy at the time: there are periods during the day, week, or month when you're more likely to have their undivided attention. By waiting until their slow or quiet times, you'll increase the likelihood that journalists and your target audience will show interest in your story and what you have to say about it.

Whatever you do, however, do not become a pest to reporters. If, for example, you leave three or four phone or e-mail messages with a reporter, editor, or columnist and the person doesn't get back to you, take the hint.

The general guidelines for the best and worst times to call reporters include:

Best

➤ Weekday mornings between 10 A.M. and noon, when most reporters and their editors arrive for work and are deciding which stories to cover that day.

➤ Earlier in the week rather than later, when reporters are in the initial stages of stories they may be working on for that week.

Worst

➤ Weekday afternoons after 4 P.M., when most reporters are meeting deadlines for their stories.

➤ Any weekend.

➤ Any national or religious holiday.

➤ The day before or day after Thanksgiving, Christmas, or New Year's Day, when they are likely to be on holiday.

Of course, these guidelines won't apply if you try to contact journalists in ways other than by phone, such as e-mail or fax.

Ironically, some of the best days and times to generate news coverage about yourself may be some of the worst days and times for reaching reporters: slow news days when there is less likely to be competing events or activities that vie for the media's attention, such as Fridays, weekends, and national holidays.

This is not to say that it is impossible to reach reporters during weekends, nights, or holidays: most news organizations have somebody on duty at all times, so if your news is important or urgent enough, you should be able to find somebody to talk to about it.

An effective way to get the media to pay attention to your story is to ride the coattails of a larger news story. For several of my clients this piggyback approach has resulted in news coverage that otherwise would have been difficult to generate, including TV and radio stories, newspaper articles, and wire service stories.

Clarke Consulting Group near San Francisco piggybacked their news release on the return of the U.S. and Russian crews from the historic joint Mir 18 space station mission. The company provided intercultural training to the crews so they would work better together in space. When the U.S. crew returned home, Clarke Consulting issued a news release about their role in the successful mission. You can read the news release on my Web site at www.edwardsegal.com.

News coverage about Clarke Consulting Group's training services included stories by the Associated Press, the BBC, and news organizations in California.

Sometimes the most important part of deciding when to distribute your news release is a heavy dose of common sense. That appeared to be in short supply when the District of Columbia Housing Authority issued a news release about a scheduled drug raid several hours before it happened. News about the raid was broadcast by area radio stations, and heard by the same people the police had planned to arrest on drug charges.

HALL OF FAME: NOT A MATTER OF IF, BUT WHEN

Since it's almost impossible to prevent the media from reporting news that you don't want to get out, sometimes the best you can hope for is to control when and how that news is released.

According to published accounts, that's exactly what happened when movie and TV actor Michael J. Fox learned that the *National Enquirer* was about to break the story that he had Parkinson's disease. Citing family reasons, Fox asked the paper not to print the story. The *Enquirer,* perhaps thinking that Fox would give them the exclusive when he was ready to talk about it, agreed. Fox, fearing that someone else might announce the news, decided to break the story on his own terms by arranging to be interviewed by *People* magazine and Barbara Walters of ABC TV.

The strategy worked. Timing the news to break after he had signed a lucrative TV deal, Fox was the subject of a sympathetic cover story in *People* and an on-air interview with Walters. News organizations across the country followed suit with their own stories about the actor's battle against Parkinson's, often using quotes or excerpts from the magazine and network reports.

The *National Enquirer* never did get an exclusive.

25 Creativity Counts

But Don't Go Overboard

Unless you're able to attract the attention of the media and the public, everything you say about yourself, product, service, activity, or company will fall on deaf ears.

Apparently working on the theory that different is better, many people seek to capture that attention by being as creative or unusual as possible, hoping that their efforts will stand out from the rest of the crowd. And sometimes they succeed—but for all the wrong reasons. That's because in their haste for news coverage, they may have forgotten some important principles—such as good taste, concern for the safety of others, attention to detail, and plain old common sense.

While getting the public's attention is the first step toward fame, it's also true that how you present yourself to the world will determine how the public and media perceive you.

Here are a few examples of some of the best and worst ways people have tried to get the recognition they wanted.

➤ To help mark its first day of trading as a new stock, Parques Reunidos S.A., a company that owns a zoo and several amusement parks in Spain, brought one of its own elephants to the stock market in downtown Madrid. The plan called for several company officials to stand next to the elephant outside the stock exchange for a group photo.

But Clarisa, the two-ton elephant, had other plans. Apparently upset by the busy downtown traffic and the large throngs of people, the pachyderm bolted from the handlers and, according to the Associated Press, "knocked into traffic lights, a lamppost and trash bin, taking swipes at them with her trunk."

Clarisa was later caught, tranquilized, and taken by truck back to her home at the zoo.

➤ The French news agency Agence France-Presse reported that a display window in a Paris department store featured live models wearing lingerie. A government official called on the retailer to close down the display, charging that it reduced women "to the simple status of merchandise and transformed passers-by into voyeurs." News of the incident sparked protests by a feminist group and calls for a boycott by prominent French citizens.

➤ To encourage people to come to its amusement park for the Cinco de Mayo holiday and help raise money for a local charity, Knott's Berry Farm in Buena Park, California, slashed the cost of all-day admission to five cents and heavily publicized the promotion on local radio and TV stations. Local school officials, noting that the holiday fell on a school day, urged Knott's Berry Farm to postpone the event until classes were over.

HALL OF SHAME: STUNTS AND PROMOTIONS CAN BACKFIRE

Some attention-getting stunts and promotions are better left on the drawing board. This was the case when, according to various news accounts, a disc jockey in Fort Worth, Texas, announced on the air that the radio station's staff had hidden $5 and $10 bills in books located in the fiction section of a local public library.

But the radio station, which planned the stunt to help boost public interest in the library, had not bothered to tell the library's staff about the promotion.

Imagine the staff's surprise when 500 people rushed through the doors of the library, stampeded through the book stacks and proceeded to open, tear, destroy, and toss 3,000 books on the floor as they looked desperately for the money. The radio station apologized for the stunt and donated $10,000 to the library to help pay for the damage it had caused.

HALL OF FAME: GIFT-WRAP YOUR PRESENTS

Never underestimate the media's interest in publicizing information that has the potential to make the lives of their viewers, readers, or listeners better, safer, or healthier. Especially if you give that information away.

How you present and package that information, however, can be just as important as the advice you have to offer: the more attractive the "gift wrapping," the more interested the media will be in doing stories about the advice you have to share.

The Greater Washington Board of Trade prepared and formatted tips for driving safely on Washington's Beltway as an owner's manual, similar to the instruction manuals that accompany everything from cars to VCRs. The manual was used by the Board's Develop Outer Interstate Thruways Coalition (DO IT) to help increase public awareness about the need to drive safely and intelligently on the Capital Beltway that surrounds Washington, DC, and to build public support for bypasses to relieve Beltway traffic congestion.

The *Capital Beltway Owner's Manual* was a 32-page booklet designed to fit in a car's glove compartment. The four-color brochure included a map of the Beltway and its trouble spots, tips to make traveling easier, driving recommendations from area traffic reporters, interesting facts and figures about the history and use of the Beltway, and a crossword puzzle with clues based on information in the booklet.

The owner's manual was unveiled at a news conference and publicized through the distribution of a news release to news organizations in the area. Media coverage included stories on Washington's four television stations, scores of newspaper and wire service stories, and several radio stories that reached an estimated audience of three million people in the Washington area.

More than 3,700 individuals contacted the coalition to request copies of the manual; six weeks after the news conference, all 50,000 copies of the *Capital Beltway Owner's Manual* had been distributed free of charge to the public.

Park officials went ahead with the promotion anyway. As feared by education officials, thousands of teenagers skipped school to go to the theme park. So many, in fact, that police shut the gates at 10:00 A.M., denying admission to thousands

of people. Scattered violence in the surrounding neighborhood ensued, and riot police were called to help restore order.

According to the *Los Angeles Times,* a spokesperson for
the park said "the company made a major miscalculation,
and will have to reassess its promotion strategy." He added,
"I think we misunderstood how popular Cinco de Mayo is."

26 They Don't Have Horns or Eat Their Young

Understanding and Getting Along with the Media

After generating thousands of stories for dozens of clients
and dealing with hundreds of editors, reporters, and columnists along the way, I've learned that the most important secret to success in creating news coverage is the ability to
understand and get along with the media.

First and foremost, reporters are looking to satisfy their
own needs, not yours. They wear the shoes of their readers
and viewers. While you want to tell them all about your
product, your company, and its accomplishments, their
task is to gather as much information as possible and produce a story that will hold an audience's attention. They
are storytellers. They are looking for great anecdotes and
simple explanations.

Jerry Brown, a veteran journalist who has worked for the Associated Press, the *Rocky Mountain News,* and other newspapers, notes, "People either bring no agenda or a too self-serving agenda about themselves to the media. The reporter is looking for stories that will be of interest to his audience."

Brown, who now works as a media consultant in Denver, suggests "If you want to get the news media to tell your story, you have to find ways to tell it in such a way that it will be of interest or use to both the reporter and his audience. If you can do that, then you can achieve through the news media the level of public recognition or fame that you want."

To tell your story, however, it helps to step into the shoes of the reporter. Former TV reporter Karen Friedman recommends you take time to understand their needs—and help them to tell your story—by doing the following:

➤ Give accurate and truthful information. If reporters know they can trust you, they'll come back time and time again.

➤ Understand the differences between TV, radio, and print. Readers, audiences, and listeners feel first and think later. That's why reporters want to capture the emotions of the people they interview.

➤ Be sensitive to deadlines. If reporters call and you don't respond quickly, they often don't have time to wait for you. They'll just find someone else.

➤ Accessibility counts. If you agree to a TV interview at your factory, don't tell the photographer he can't take pictures. That's like telling a newspaper reporter not to take notes.

➤ Match your message to the medium. If it's visual, think TV. If it's lengthy and involves audience discussion, perhaps a radio talk show is advisable. If it's filled with facts and details, think print.

➤ The media won't notice you if they don't know about you. If you have an interesting story to tell, call them. Reporters and columnists are always looking for stories. Before you pick up the phone however, remember to think about their audience and their needs. What can you do to help them? How can you personalize your story? How can you make it mean something to their audience? Is your story appropriate for the medium? If you spend a few minutes thinking through these questions, you can make your story stand out (see Chapter 9).

Becky Madeira, vice president of public affairs for PepsiCo, Inc., says, "Arrogance is the single biggest obstacle business people have when they deal with the media. Their attitude is: 'I know my business better than you do, I am very powerful and don't have to win you over or talk with you, so I am not going to work with you.' That attitude does not work, because the reporters will keep on reporting and the news will go on with or without you."

■ THE BOTTOM LINE

The following key truths about working with the media are a summary of the strategies and tactics that are most likely to result in the stories you want about yourself or your company. They are dealt with in greater depth or detail throughout the book:

➤ Reporters and columnists are neither your friends nor your enemies. They are professionals just like you, and are trying to do the best job that they can.

➤ Don't ask reporters to do a story about you. Give them reasons why they should.

➤ Be brief. The average soundbite is nine seconds long (and shrinking!). If you cannot answer a reporter's question in the time it takes to read this paragraph aloud, your interview won't be used by television or radio reporters.

➤ Prioritize the two or three most important things you would like to see in the newspaper about your announcement, and keep your remarks focused on those points.

➤ Reporters will always ask the one question that you don't want to answer.

➤ The most important thing you can tell a reporter about your story is who will care about it and why.

➤ Most reporters hate it when you call them to find out if they received the news release you sent them. But most of them will appreciate it if you let them know ahead of time that you are sending them a story that you think they will be interested in covering.

➤ The easiest way to find out what stories reporters are most interested in covering is to ask them.

➤ There is no such thing as being too prepared for a media interview.

➤ Assume that everything you tell a reporter is on the record and may be used in their story.

➤ If you don't know the answer to a reporter's question, say so. Then tell him or her that you will find out the answer and call them back as soon as possible.

➤ Ask reporters what you can do to help make their job easier.

➤ Never call a reporter when he or she is on deadline.

➤ Never assume that your press list is accurate, complete, or up-to-date.

➤ Never be a pain to a reporter. But always be a resource of information.

➤ The day a reporter sends you a copy of his story for your approval is the day you will win the Publisher's Clearinghouse Sweepstakes.

➤ The best way to help ensure that a reporter will use your press release is to write it as if it's a newspaper story.

What happens when, despite your best efforts, reporters tell you that they are not interested in doing a story about you? Debra Leopold, president of the First Class adult continuing education center in Washington, DC, advises, "When a reporter says no to your story idea, be very polite. Ask if there is anything you can do to make it possible for them to do the story later on. Thank them for their time and keep the door open for the future."

Leopold's company has been the subject of several national and local news articles over the years about its interesting and innovative class offerings. Some stories, such as an article in *The New York Times,* were easier to place than others, like a profile in *Glamour* magazine. She says that one of the keys to success with the media is, "It helps to persevere. If they don't write about you today, maybe they will write about you next week or next month" (see Chapter 36).

When reporters agree to interview you for a story, they will usually assume that they can ask and you will answer any questions they ask. If there are issues that you do not want to discuss or queries that you'd rather avoid, it's best to have a clear understanding with the reporter beforehand about the topics he or she wants to discuss. Otherwise, you may be better off not to do the interview. In your efforts to protect yourself, you also run the risk of offending the reporter, who may decide to simply not do the interview:

➤ According to published reports, actress Calista Flochart, star of TV's *Ally McBeal,* lost an opportunity to be on NBC's *Today Show* when she said she would not answer questions about allegations that she suffers from anorexia, an eating disorder.

➤ Juan Antonio Samaranch, head of the International Olympic Committee, probably wished he'd never agreed to do an interview with CBS's *60 Minutes.* Since CBS televised the games, he assumed that the questions would be friendly. According to the Associated Press, "Samaranch said he was blindsided when reporter Bob Simon asked him about his role in the fascist regime of Spanish dictator Francisco Franco and some touchy Olympic questions."

After the interview, Samaranch said "I was really disappointed because I feel like I was in an ambush."

HALL OF SHAME: THE MICROPHONE
IS ALWAYS ON

When giving radio or television interviews, always assume that the microphone is on and that every word you say may be recorded or broadcast.

Maryland State Senate President Thomas V. Mike Miller, Jr. found this out the hard way when he used profanities to describe Baltimore and its economic problems during an interview with the reporter from WUSA-TV, a Washington television station. The station did not delete his colorful remarks from the story, and several newspapers included the expletives in its coverage about the incident.

Miller later said he had no idea that everything he told the reporter would be recorded or might be broadcast—even though he was wearing a microphone, had gone through voice level checks, and bright television lights were trained on him at the time.

Miller apologized for what he described as his "inappropriate and unsavory" remarks.

News anchors are hardly immune from making the same gaffes as politicians.

Steve Rondinaro, a news anchor for WFTV-TV in Orlando, Florida, found this out the hard way when he narrated a satellite feed of the arrival of First Lady Hillary Rodham Clinton at the Kennedy Space Center. Clinton, who was traveling with her daughter Chelsea, came to watch the scheduled launch of the Columbia space shuttle.

As reported by the *Sun-Sentinel* in Fort Lauderdale, Florida, Rondinaro, not realizing that the microphone was still on, said: "Just moments ago, the First Lady rolled in. There she comes, the old battle-ax. There she is with Chelsea in tow."

Rondinaro quickly apologized to viewers for what he called an "offhand, flippant comment that slipped out on the air."

■ IN THEIR OWN WORDS

Just Doing Their Job

The real rub between journalists and business is that many businesspeople are afraid that reporters will go for the jugular or the negative. As a reporter, I often found that businesspeople were afraid of me and not always ready to provide the kind of information I was looking for. Many business executives think reporters have a hidden agenda. We don't. Reporters are just looking for the information they need to do their job.

Karen Friedman
Media Trainer and Former TV Reporter

27 Your Checklist for Interview Success

What to Do or Say before, during, or after You Meet the Media

The news release you wrote and sent to your media list was well received, and a reporter has just called to interview you.

Like most people, your first reaction may be:

Ohmygoditworkedwhatamigoingtodonow?

First, remain calm.

Second, congratulate yourself on your efforts to convince a reporter to do a story.

Now it's time to take steps to ensure that:

➤ The interview is successful.

➤ Your quotes are used.

➤ The story is accurate.

While there are a lot of things you should do, there are many things you should not do. One of the most important things to avoid at all costs is to agree to do an interview with the reporter right then and there. Instead, delay doing the interview until you've had enough time (whether it's a few minutes or a few hours) to properly prepare for it.

You'd never think to agree to a business meeting without first learning something about the purpose, the participants, and the agenda, would you? Of course not. It's the same principle when it comes to meeting with the media. The more you know before you enter an interview situation, the better off you'll be, and you can decide whether you even want to do the interview in the first place.

Most reporters will understand if you say you're busy just then, but can call them back in a few minutes for the interview. Take that time (or more if you can get it) to review the guidelines and suggestions on the following interview checklist. These recommendations are based on my good and bad experiences, and those of my clients and colleagues, in dealing with hundreds of editors and reporters who have called seeking information or interviews for their stories.

■ INTERVIEW CHECKLIST

Topic

☐ What does the reporter want to talk about?

☐ What questions does the reporter want to ask?

☐ Based on the answers to the preceding questions, is this an interview that you really want to do or should agree to do? Are you the best person in your company or the organization to do this interview? If not, then refer the reporter to the appropriate individual.

Deadline

- [ ] When does the reporter want to do the interview?
- [ ] Can you call him/her back later for the interview?

The Reporter

- [ ] What news organization does the reporter work for?
- [ ] Who is the organization's audience?
- [ ] How much time does the reporter need for the interview?
- [ ] Have you sent relevant background information the reporter needs prior to the interview, such as a copy of your news release, fact sheet, or press kit?
- [ ] Has the reporter received and read the information you sent?
- [ ] Who else is the reporter talking to for the story?
- [ ] Can you research other stories the reporter has done before you do the interview?

Your Message

- [ ] What is the overarching message you want to communicate in the interview?
- [ ] What are the three or four most important points you want to make?
- [ ] Do you have the latest information about the topic?
- [ ] Have you practiced your answers?
- [ ] What visuals can you use to help show your story?

■ GENERAL INTERVIEW GUIDELINES

Length

- [ ] Set a time limit on all interviews: No more than 15–20 minutes for most interviews.
- [ ] Keep your answers short: 20–30 seconds for print interviews, 10–20 seconds for radio and television.

Questions

- ☐ Anticipate all questions that the reporter might ask: the good, the bad, and the ugly.
- ☐ Put yourself in the shoes of the reporter. If you were the journalist, what questions would you ask?

Setting

- ☐ If the interview will be held in your office, make sure any papers or information you don't want the reporter to see have been put safely away; let your colleagues know that a reporter will be in the office so they can act accordingly.
- ☐ If the interview will be conducted over the phone, make sure there are no distracting noises to break your concentration or to be picked up by the phone.

Answers

- ☐ Have an appropriate answer ready for each possible question.
- ☐ Have immediate access to all the information you'll need to answer the questions.
- ☐ Customize your answers for the audience of the news organization.
- ☐ Tell the truth and keep your answers consistent, no matter how many times you are interviewed.
- ☐ Find ways to repeat your key points throughout the interview.
- ☐ Assume *everything* you tell the reporter is on the record.
- ☐ Be prepared to cite the source of any studies, statistics, and so on that you may use in your answers.
- ☐ If you don't know the answer to a question, say so. Then tell the reporter you will have to call back with an answer.
- ☐ Use bridging techniques to avoid giving a direct response to a question you don't want to answer. Jump

from the question he asks to the one you want to answer by saying: "That's an interesting question, but a more important issue is . . ." Then ask and answer your own question.

☐ Explain why you can't give information requested by a reporter, or answer a particular question.

☐ Reply positively to a negative question.

Don't

☐ Answer a question unless you understand what is being asked. If necessary, ask the reporter to repeat or explain the question, or rephrase the question in your own words.

☐ Expect the reporter to ask you the questions you want to answer. Look for ways to include in your answer the points you want to make.

☐ Answer hypothetical questions.

☐ Get mad, defensive, or argue with the reporter.

☐ Say "no comment." Instead, explain why you cannot or will not answer a question.

☐ Talk longer than necessary to answer the question.

☐ Use lots of numbers or statistics in your answers; use them sparingly to make your point.

☐ Agree to talk off the record.

☐ Criticize the competition.

☐ Use jargon, technical terms, or acronyms in your answers.

Listen

☐ Be a good listener to what the reporter is saying, and pay attention to how the reporter is reacting to your answers.

☐ Don't assume you know what the reporter is asking before he or she finishes the question. Be sure you listen and fully understand the question before responding.

Voice

☐ Use a conversational tone—don't give a speech.

☐ Avoid speaking in a monotone.

Attire

☐ Dress appropriately for the interview.

Body Language (for in-person interviews)

☐ Maintain good posture.

☐ Smile.

☐ Use appropriate gestures to express yourself.

☐ Maintain appropriate eye contact with the reporter.

☐ Don't fidget in your seat or do anything that will distract a reporter from your answer.

Feedback

☐ Tape-record your answers for later reference and evaluation. Don't record the reporter without his/her consent.

Attitude

☐ Be positive, upbeat, enthusiastic, and confident in your answers and demeanor.

☐ Be yourself as much as you can. Project self-confidence in the way you dress, your body language, and the tone and manner of your voice.

☐ Appear eager to give honest answers.

☐ Appear friendly, confident, and upbeat.

■ AFTER THE INTERVIEW

How Did You Do?

☐ Being as objective as possible, evaluate how the interview went, and ask yourself what you would do differently the next time.

☐ If you tape-recorded your answers, listen to your responses to make sure you gave the answer you wanted in the most effective way possible. Based on what you hear, how would you respond to the same question the next time?

☐ When the story with your interview is printed or broadcast, evaluate the story to see how your interview was used. Did the reporter accurately report your answers? Are there any mistakes or errors in the story that you should call to the attention of the reporter or editor?

☐ Send a letter or e-mail to the reporter to thank him or her for the interview, and offer to be of assistance on future stories.

For additional help in preparing for and conducting interviews, you may want to consult with a media trainer (see page 35 and the Resources section).

Sometimes a news interview can have unexpected consequences.

The Associated Press reported that a woman was arrested for burglary after a cop recognized the suspect on television. The woman, a Republican mayoral candidate in Baltimore, was spotted by the alert officer as she was doing a live interview on a local TV station talking about—what else?—the police.

She was picked up by the law enforcement officials when she left the station after she finished the interview.

■ IN THEIR OWN WORDS

But That's Not What I Said!

Occasionally reporters will actually write incorrect things about us, either because they just didn't know or because they did not think it through. When they write incorrect facts they create lots of problems and it can actually be quite damaging. When you are working with the press you should try to control the information as best you can and make sure that reporters don't print something that is incorrect.

I've found that about one third of my quotes are not actually my quotes at all. They were actually quotes [prepared] by the writer about something that I might have said or what they would have liked me to have said.

Now when I am around reporters, I think much more carefully about what I am going to say.

Michael Saylor, CEO
MicroStrategy, Inc.

Exercise: Play Reporter

Before you are interviewed by a reporter, take the time to ask questions by the toughest journalist in the world: you. Since you are (or should be) intimately familiar with every detail and nuance of your story, you are also in the best position to come up with the most difficult or embarrassing questions a reporter might ask.

In this exercise, put yourself in the shoes of the reporter, and ask yourself all the possible questions he or she might pose to you in a real interview. Jot down the questions in the left-hand column, and your responses in the right. You'll probably need one or more additional blank pages to complete the exercise, but this page will give you a good start.

Question	Answer
_____	_____
_____	_____
_____	_____
_____	_____
_____	_____
_____	_____
_____	_____
_____	_____

HALL OF SHAME: LEARNING
THE HARD WAY

As strange as it may seem, it is possible to be interviewed by a reporter without your knowledge or consent.

Nancy Kervin worked as a research assistant at *Congressional Quarterly,* a nonpartisan magazine that reports on the activities of Congress. Her responsibilities included responding to telephone inquiries from subscribers and the media.

One day an Associated Press reporter called seeking information about the voting record of Rep. Bob Edgar (D-Pa), who was running for the U.S. Senate at the time. Asked how Edgar's voting record compared with other members of the House of Representatives, Kervin said, "This year, he's definitely in the basement."

It was not until later that Kervin discovered she had done more than simply provide information to the reporter: she had also been interviewed and all her comments were on the record. The realization came when her boss received an angry phone call from Edgar's office, which had read her comments in a story about the Senate campaign in the *Harrisburg Patriot* newspaper:

"According to *Congressional Quarterly,* a Washington-based political journal, Edgar missed 39 percent of the votes taken from Jan. 1 to Aug. 20. 'This year, he's definitely in the basement,' said a research staffer for the magazine."

Edgar's office demanded to know why a member of the magazine's staff was making editorial comments about the lawmaker's voting record to the media. Kervin was counseled by her supervisor about her remarks, and told not to share her personal opinions with reporters.

As Kervin observed later, "I learned the hard way to keep your opinions to yourself, and that you should always assume that anything you tell a reporter may wind up in his story."

28 The Magic Nine Seconds

All about Soundbites and Inkbites

Summarizing the difficulties consumers face in getting airline safety information, David Stempler, founder of the Air Travelers Association, told the Reuters newswire service, "It is easier for travelers to obtain advance information about in-flight meals or movies than it is to find out about the safety record of the airlines they are going to fly."

If you are like most people, you can talk for at least a few minutes on any number of topics, whether it's about a favorite movie or CD, a project you completed at work, or a class you are taking at school. But as you travel the road toward fame, it doesn't matter if you are able to speak for five or ten minutes on any subject. Can you, as David Stempler did, talk about your accomplishments, activities, or opinions—*in nine seconds or less?*

Nine seconds is not a lot of time. (How long is it? Count out loud from 1,001 to 1,009 to see for yourself, or time yourself against a watch with a second hand.) But nine seconds is often all the time a television or radio station will give you in an edited on-air story to talk about your activity or accomplishment, make a statement, give a comment, or react to a news announcement.

These all-too brief remarks are known as *soundbites*— small portions or "bites" from interviews that are inserted in news stories to help enliven, tell, or illustrate news reports.

Inkbites, the printed version of soundbites, can range from 5 to 50 words. As a general rule of thumb, if your response to a reporter's question runs longer than the time it takes to read this sentence aloud, most reporters won't use your quote in their stories. Instead, they will condense, paraphrase, or ignore your answer entirely.

Soundbites were not always so short. In fact, in the 1960s, news programs often allowed people to talk for up to 45 seconds at a time. But three factors helped to shorten soundbites:

> ➤ Pressures on local television stations and national networks to make more money, which led them to sell more advertising time for their news programs.

> ➤ The proliferation of multiple news outlets for consumers to choose from, ranging from cable channels to Internet Web sites.

> ➤ The effect of MTV's popular high-energy, fast-paced programming, which caters to the short-attention spans of youthful audiences.

Faced with the challenge to sell more advertising, attract and keep the attention of viewers, and stay competitive in a crowded media market, broadcast executives began to produce shorter, more visually appealing stories with soundbites to match. These same pressures are forcing the length of soundbites to shrink a bit more with every passing year.

By definition, any soundbite or inkbite is a good one, since it means you said something interesting and short enough to be included in a reporter's story. But good is not good enough. Your comments should also help you to achieve your 15 minutes of fame by meeting the following eight criteria:

1. Creates or enhances the reputation you want.
2. Places you in the best possible light.
3. Conveys the message you want to send to the public.
4. Accurately captures the essence of what you want to say on the topic.
5. Feels right or comfortable for you to say.

6. Offends no one.

7. Is credible and believable.

8. Is interesting enough to encourage the reporter and other members of the media to call on you for future interviews.

With so much riding on what you say to the media and how you say it, the ability to prepare and deliver effective soundbites is one of the most important skills you can have. The challenge is to provide journalists with quotes they can use while serving your best interests.

While hardly anyone points to elected or appointed officials as role models these days, you can learn a lot about soundbites by reading about, listening to, and watching their speeches or interviews. Most politicians do an excellent job of preparing and delivering soundbites to help win votes, explain their stands on issues, or promote various causes—just as you need to effectively promote your own activities, accomplishments, products, services, or expertise.

Politicians are not the only ones who get quoted by the media. Television and radio news broadcasts and newspaper and magazine articles are full of soundbites and inkbites from people in different professions and walks of life. Studying what these newsmakers say and how they say it is one of the best continuing educations you can obtain in the art of preparing and delivering soundbites that will help you to become famous.

After preparing hundreds of quotes for clients and studying thousands of soundbites over the years, I've concluded that effective soundbites are like sandwiches: there are thousands of ways to make them according to your own tastes and preferences.

Here are a few "recipes" for successful soundbites, as offered by a cross-section of corporate spokespeople, newsmakers, former reporters, and public relations experts:

Burke Stinson, AT&T Spokesperson

Since 1986, Burke Stinson has been interviewed more than 2,700 times by the media to discuss AT&T's products, services, and workplace issues, ranging from downsizing and strikes to diversity, sexual harassment, and threatened legal action by Richard Nixon.

➤ Speak plainly, in simple sentences.

➤ Use living room language, not boardroom lingo.

➤ Quote pop stars ("As Elvis might say—").

➤ Refer to body parts ("That was a kick in the ribs—").

➤ Try analogies ("It was like having a big rocket but no fuel").

➤ Appear happy to be in the same room as the interviewer.

David Stempler, President of the Air Travelers Association

David Stempler, president of the Air Travelers Association, an airline passenger advocacy organization in Washington, DC, is an aviation attorney and international authority on airline passenger and travel issues. He has been quoted or interviewed by the media more than 3,000 times.

➤ Identify the heart of the story, and what you can say about it.

➤ Distill and condense your comments into a key point that speaks to the essence of the reporter's question or story.

➤ Use different techniques to help make your point, including analogies and quips.

➤ Watch or read the news stories that contain your interviews to study the kinds of soundbites that get onto the air or are used by newspapers and magazines.

Karen Friedman, Media Trainer

Karen Friedman is a media and communications expert who has spent two decades in front of the camera. As an award-winning TV news reporter, Friedman has broadcast thousands of stories for stations across the country. Her reports have aired on the ABC, CBS, CNN, and NBC television networks.

Friedman says a good soundbite:

➤ Is short and to the point.

➤ Uses real words in plain English. The simpler the better.

➤ Is memorable and drives your point home.

➤ Conveys how you felt when something happened to you; it's the emotion that comes from the heart.

➤ Is a full and complete thought.

In addition, she recommends that you:

➤ Get your message out quickly, without a lot of confusion, in one clear succinct thought. You will reduce the risk of being edited, and your message won't get lost, twisted, or confused.

Timothy John Walker, TJWalker.com

Timothy John Walker is the producer of TJWalker.com, a radio and television news information service. A syndicated columnist and news analyst, Walker frequently appears on the Fox News Channel, MSNBC, and talk radio programs around the country. According to Walker, "Virtually every quote you ever see on TV, hear on radio or read in print" has at least one of the following characteristics, which he spells out using the acronym A BEACH PRO™.

A Analogies.

B Bold action words.
E Emotions, examples.
A Attacks, absolutes.
C Cliches.
H Humor.

P Pop culture references.
R Rhetorical questions.
O Opposition quote.

The soundbite recipes or ingredients you use will depend on what you want to say, how you want to say it, and what you want to accomplish with your remarks. Since quotes can make or break reputations—and sometimes careers—you should choose your words carefully and organize your thoughts before you are interviewed by the media. Although there are no guarantees reporters will include the quotes you want in their stories, you can certainly stack the deck in your favor by using one or more of these methods (for advice on how to prepare for and conduct successful interviews, see Chapter 27).

Just as an athlete does warm-up exercises before a game or race, you should do these warm-up soundbite exercises several hours or days before your interview with the media. List the three most important points you want to make during the interview, as well as every possible question you think you could be asked; and prepare an appropriate soundbite response to each of them.

The more you practice, the more real and natural your soundbite will sound, and the less you have to worry about condensing the most important parts of your story down to the magic nine seconds.

HALL OF SHAME: SOUNDBITE BITES BACK!

It's one thing to come up with an effective soundbite to defend yourself against false accusations. But if your soundbite is a lie, it can come back to bite—and haunt—you. That's what happened to President Clinton, who told reporters, "I did not have sexual relations with that woman, Miss Lewinsky." Seven months later, he admitted that he had an "inappropriate relationship" with the White House intern and apologized for his behavior. The President's earlier quote was immediately repeated and replayed by the media to illustrate how he had deceived his wife, daughter, and the American public.

Exercise: Write Your Own Soundbite

With the possible exception of politicians, it is almost impossible for most people to come up with the perfect soundbite without some degree of preparation and practice. So before you're asked to deliver your first pithy nine-second soundbite by a television reporter, take a few minutes to go through the following exercise:

➤ In 100 words or so, please describe the benefits and advantages of your company, organization, product, service, or expertise.

_____

_____

_____

➤ Now, go over what you just wrote, and eliminate any jargon, buzzwords, or other language that may be unfamiliar to the general public or your target audience; keep the language simple and basic. Take a look at the list of ingredients of the most successful soundbites earlier in this chapter and use at least one of them in your description.

_____

_____

_____

➤ With that out of the way, it's time to shrink your words to a manageable length (about 9 seconds). Rewrite your description one more time, but this time keep the length to no more than 50 words.

_____

_____

_____

(continued)

Exercise: Write Your Own Soundbite *(Continued)*

➤ We're almost done. Take a long hard look at the 50 words you just wrote, and try to say the same thing in 25 words or less. Remember to include at least one of the "soundbite ingredients" from this chapter.

_____

_____

_____

_____

➤ Now it's time for the acid test. Ask a friend, colleague, or family member to play the role of a television reporter, and have them ask you the following question:

"Tell me about your (product) (service) (company) (expertise)." Now, give them your soundbite.

_____

_____

_____

_____

➤ Finally, ask the "reporter" what he or she thought of your answer.

➤ Was your soundbite interesting? Was it short enough? Did it capture the attention of the reporter? Did it adequately convey enough information to provide the audience with a good idea of the benefits and advantages of your company, organization, product, service, or expertise?

➤ If not, reread this chapter, and try this exercise one more time.

■ IN THEIR OWN WORDS

Preparing Your Soundbite

It's important that you prepare your soundbites in advance. If you can come up with a snappy way to say something, such as using an analogy or a quip, then practice it a few times before you say it to a reporter. I've found that coming up with a good soundbite is simply a process of putting your thoughts through a series of finer and finer filters until you can distill or condense your comments into that one brief nine-second statement.

David Stempler, President
Air Travelers Association

29 It's What You Wear and How You Wear It

Dressing for the Press

How you dress for your interviews on television, news conferences, or during one-on-one meetings with newspaper, wire service, and magazine reporters will send certain messages to the media and the public about who you are and how you behave.

Three PR professionals offer their own versions of what is or is not appropriate to wear for TV or other press interviews.

Burke Stinson, AT&T Spokesperson

➤ Watch what television news anchors wear. Use them as your role models.

➤ Men should stay away from ties that demand attention, suits with patterns that "dance," and eyeglasses that are not glare-proof.

➤ Insecure guys with toupees will appear almost clownish; bad hair is distracting.

➤ Pale blue shirts always work; colored silk handkerchiefs never do.

➤ Watch the movie *Broadcast News*. You do look better if you tuck the bottom of your jacket under your butt.

➤ Women should stay away from dangling earrings, clanging jewelry, and "hot" colors.

➤ Too much eye makeup will detract from your message.

➤ Wear a top that can easily accommodate a clip-microphone.

➤ Whether you're a man or woman, it will be your face and expression, not your clothes, that will carry the day. So, don't "dress up."

Melissa Soule of Rossman Martin & Associates (public relations firm in Lansing, Michigan)

Men should wear:

➤ Dark suits (but not black).

➤ Light shirts (no white or thin pinstripes).

➤ Dark ties (red and burgundy are good, avoid those with small dots).

➤ Basic colors.

➤ Natural fabrics (wool and cotton).

Women should wear:

➤ Simple suits and blouses.

➤ Tailored dresses.

➤ Minimal jewelry.

➤ True colors (blues, grays, greens; no whites, blacks, or reds).

➤ Natural fabrics (wool, cotton, and linen).
➤ Minimal prints.

Everyone should avoid:

➤ Red, black, white, and patterns.
➤ Noisy, shiny, or distracting jewelry.
➤ Shiny, slinky materials (silks, satins, and polyesters).
➤ Tinted lenses.
➤ Bulging pockets.

Laura Walcher, Public Relations Consultant to Matthews/Mark (marketing firm) in San Diego, California

Men:

➤ Wear conservative suits or sports jackets.
➤ Choose solid or toned-down (but contrasting) ties.
➤ Solid colors are preferable, except white.
➤ Always carry a handkerchief and mop your brow and forehead before the start of an interview.

Women:

➤ Solid or pinstriped fabrics are good.
➤ Long sleeves and high necklines are more flattering on everyone, regardless of age.
➤ Longer skirts/pants have a pleasing appearance, and a little roominess enables a woman to sit more gracefully.
➤ Modest jewelry is okay, but no dangling earrings.

■ IN THEIR OWN WORDS

You Are What You Wear

The 1990s saw widespread acceptance of casual attire in business offices, an approach long fancied by engineers, scientists, and software companies. But no one who speaks on behalf of a company should appear on TV in "dress-down Friday" garb, unless a laboratory or factory is in the background.

TV editors expect that their crews have taped interviews with company authorities, and classic business wardrobe conveys such a status. Pay close attention to what guests on Meet the Press *wear for interviews: that's the image you want. Nothing flashy. Nothing shiny. Nothing that will distract viewers from your message. Only insecure people hide behind flash.*

Burke Stinson
AT&T Corporate Spokesperson

HALL OF SHAME: ENTREPRENEUR BARES ALL!

Many business executives worry about what clothes and colors to wear for television interviews so they will come off looking their best. Mark Breier, CEO of on-line software seller Beyond.com, solved the problem by appearing to be naked (at least from the waist up) when he was a guest on CNBC's *Squawk Box* show.

According to *USA Today*, "The stunt was a play on the company's television advertising campaign featuring a naked guy working from his home to demonstrate that he can order all the software he needs without having to leave his desk—or get dressed." The stunt apparently worked, resulting in increased sales and visits to the company's Web site.

Sometimes it works. But sometimes it doesn't.

San Francisco Mayor Frank Jordan's "naked grab for publicity" may have cost him his job after he was interviewed live by two radio disc jockeys (and photographed in his birthday suit) while taking a shower in his home. The politician later told the editorial board of the *San Francisco Examiner* that the stunt showed "two things very clearly. One, I've got nothing to hide and, two, I'm squeaky clean."

30 Public Posturing

Right and Wrong Ways to Sit and Stand during Interviews

Your mother probably told you that good posture is important. It turns out she was right for more than one reason.

How you sit or stand during media interviews can send the right or wrong kind of message about who you are, what you think, and how strongly you believe in what you tell the public about your product, service, cause, or company.

Karen Friedman, a 20-year veteran TV reporter who now provides media training to company executives, offers her clients the following advice on the best body language to use during interviews:

Posture

➤ Don't rock, swing, or pace.

➤ Do stand up or sit straight.

Where to Look

➤ Don't stare at the camera.

➤ Do look at the interviewer.

Arms

➤ Don't fold your arms across your chest.

➤ Do keep your arms and hands loose.

Hands

➤ Don't keep your hands in your pockets.

➤ Do gesture to emphasize points.

Sitting

➤ Don't relax too far back in your chair.

➤ Do sit forward and act enthusiastic.

Melissa Soule of Rossman Martin & Associates suggests the following guidelines when you sit during interviews:

Sitting

➤ Uncross your legs.

➤ Move to the edge of your chair.

➤ Lean toward the reporter.

➤ Steeple your hands.

➤ Thrust your chin slightly upward.

➤ Nod your head.

➤ Gesture moderately.

➤ Initiate and maintain eye contact.

➤ Use a loud, clear voice.

➤ Vary your vocal inflections.

➤ Vary your positions.

AT&T spokesperson Burke Stinson offers these recommendations:

Sitting

➤ Stay away from chairs that swivel or rock.

➤ Lean toward the camera.

➤ Sit still.

Standing

➤ Men should not cover their crotches with their hands.

➤ Guys should either place one hand in a jacket (not their pants) pocket—or place both hands at their sides.

➤ Women should never place their hands on their hips. Or bite their lower lip.

Here's one last reminder from your mother: don't slouch!

■ IN THEIR OWN WORDS

The Ins and Outs of Interviews

Given a choice between an exterior stand-up or an interior interview, always choose inside. No wind gusts, sun-glare squints or mussed hair. So, ladies and gentlemen, always consider hair spray before an interview. And if a crew member suggests a dab of makeup, take the advice. Often, in-studio interviews will be preceded by a suggested trip to the makeup room. Never be too proud to accept the offer.

Burke Stinson
AT&T Corporate Spokesperson

31 Overcome Murphy's Law of Fame

Ensure Your Success

Murphy's Law says that "anything that can wrong will go wrong." Based on the experience of my clients, here is a list of the 15 things that will most likely go awry when you deal with the media. The more precautions you take to avoid these mishaps, the less likely they are to happen to you as you seek or manage your 15 minutes of fame.

1. It isn't clear how your story affects audiences of the news organizations that received your releases.
2. Your story was not packaged or presented as a legitimate news story.

3. You are not promoting the most interesting or newsworthy aspects of your story.

4. You did not include relevant facts, figures, or background information that is important to your story.

5. Your news release was too long or the headline did not grab the attention of the reporter.

6. You sent out your release on a busy news day, and it couldn't compete for coverage against the scheduled events and late-breaking announcements made by other individuals, organizations, or corporations.

7. You didn't have any visuals to help show your story; the visuals you had weren't interesting enough.

8. You couldn't explain or tell your story effectively to the reporters.

9. You didn't identify or target the news organizations that would have been the most interested in your story.

10. Your media lists were outdated or inaccurate.

11. You sent your news release to the wrong editors or reporters.

12. You waited too long to return a reporter's phone call.

13. You did a poor job of answering a reporter's questions.

14. You didn't provide the reporter with the additional information he requested.

15. You didn't show why people should care about your story.

32 Oops!

What to Do When News Organizations Make Mistakes

The *Far Eastern Economic Review* reported that after Professor John Wong, the head of surgery at Queen Mary Hospital in Hong Kong, took out a female patient's fallopian tube instead of her appendix, he said: "We all make mistakes."

The news organization ran a correction several weeks later, telling readers that Wong had not performed the operation at all, but was only reacting to the bungled surgical procedure by another doctor at the same hospital.

Well, no one is perfect, especially journalists and, in this case, a certain unnamed doctor in Hong Kong.

Reporters produce anywhere from a handful to hundreds of stories every year, so it may be inevitable that they occasionally get something wrong in their stories. But even if journalists make mistakes less than 1 percent of the time, think of all the stories that are wrong in some way.

If you've noticed mistakes or errors in the newspaper stories you read, you have plenty of company.

In 1998, the American Society of Newspaper Editors' Journalism Credibility Project found that more than 70 percent of the public had found factual errors in their daily newspaper within the last year. Of that number, 9 percent said they found mistakes almost every day, while 14 percent said they noticed errors more than once a week. And of those who found errors, 20 percent said the mistakes were getting more frequent.

What can possibly go wrong when a reporter prepares his story based on an interview with you?

Plenty.

The list of their potential mistakes includes:

➤ Reporting what you said.

➤ Reporting or describing what you did (Dr. Wong in Hong Kong found that out the hard way).

➤ Your name or the names of others who are mentioned or quoted in the story.

➤ The name of your company, division, or organization.

➤ Web site addresses.

➤ Phone numbers, fax numbers, or e-mail addresses.

➤ Job titles.

➤ Your age, sex, race, or physical description.

But even if the reporter gets those basics right, other key details may be wrong:

➤ The name or description of your products or services.

➤ The date, time, location, or details of an event or activity.

➤ Facts, figures, and statistics.

➤ Conclusions, projections, or forecasts.

➤ Interpretation or analysis of the information you provided.

➤ The photo or illustration that accompanies your article.

➤ The caption or cutlines that describe the picture or illustration.

In short, any aspect of the story is subject to error.

What can you do when the media makes these or other mistakes?

Everything you can, as soon as you can do it.

While it's impossible to unring a bell that has been rung, it is possible—and important—that you take steps to have an error in a story corrected as soon as possible. That's because, as with the story about Dr. Wong, everyone who read the original story assumed it was true. But since someone took the time and trouble to contact the news organization about their mistake, now anyone who comes across a media reference about the incident on the Internet (as I did when I went on-line to research this chapter) will know what really happened.

When the media makes a mistake, you should:

➤ Call the reporter who did the story and explain the error.

➤ If you can't reach the reporter right away, ask to speak to an editor about the matter.

➤ Ask that a correction be printed or broadcast as soon as possible.

➤ Monitor the news organization to make sure they make the correction.

PRWeek, an industry publication, recommends against shooting from the hip or lip when a mistake occurs. Instead, plan a strategy, and resist the urge to act on impulse. If you think the matter may lead to a legal action against the news organization, don't contact the reporter until you've had a chance to speak to an attorney.

Getting the media to correct or retract their mistakes can be a lengthy process. For example, it took Mary Rose Oakar, a former member of Congress, seven years and a lawsuit before the *Cleveland Plain Dealer* admitted it had published erroneous information in connection with a story about her.

When called to their attention, newspapers will usually print a correction the next day, and magazines may run a clarification in their next issue.

You have to act fast, however, if the mistake is broadcast on television or radio. If you hurry and call the station immediately, sometimes they will announce the correction during the same newscast, or make note of it on the next broadcast.

Editors and reporters know that factual mistakes in stories affect the credibility of their news organizations. Speaking at a seminar sponsored by the American Society of Newspaper Editors, Allan Siegal, assistant managing editor of the *New York Times* said, "When I see (the *New York Times*) make an obvious mistake in city geography or placing a city in a wrong country, I have to ask myself, 'How are we doing on nuclear physics and astronomy and things that I can't verify?' . . . You don't get back all of the credibility you lost when you run a correction. But you do get back a fraction and I think over time you get back a good chunk."

HALL OF SHAME: ASSUME NOTHING

To accompany a story about National Clown Week, the *Kansas City* (Missouri) *Star* published a picture from its archives of an unidentified clown holding a bunch of balloons. There's no doubt the paper would not have used the photo if it had bothered to check the name of the person dressed up in a "Pogo the Clown" costume: It was John Wayne Gacy, the infamous convicted child serial killer who was executed in the early 1990s. The newspaper apologized to readers for running the photo, saying "It wasn't intentional, it was human error."

---

33 Sometimes It's Not Who You Know, But Who Knows about You

Be a Resource to Editors, Reporters, and Columnists

According to the 1990 U.S. Census, there were 266,543 editors and reporters in the United States. That means if you called 10 of them every weekday to introduce yourself and encourage them to do a story about you, it would take more than 100 years to reach them all (assuming you did not have to play phone tag with them).

While that's a lot of journalists, the number doesn't include hundreds of thousands of other people who perform similar functions for organizations that publish or distribute their own newsletters, magazines, or Web-based information services. The final tally could very well exceed one million people!

You don't have to worry about personally contacting each one of them about your story because:

➤ It's quite unlikely that every reporter in the country will be interested in your story in the first place.

➤ Depending on your audience, story, product, service, or expertise, you may not have to reach more than a handful of reporters to achieve the level of fame you want.

There are usually two reasons a journalist will want to talk to you: either because of something you sent him or her, or because you may have information or insights the reporter needs for a story.

Obviously, if you sent the reporter a news release, he or she would know how to contact you for an interview (assuming you included your phone number or e-mail address).

But what if a reporter is working on an article in which you have some valuable knowledge or expertise, but he or she doesn't know you even exist or how to reach you to arrange an interview?

The answer is for you to become a resource of information to as many editors, reporters, and columnists as possible so that they will know who you are, your areas of expertise, your qualifications, and how to contact you.

Four ways to become a resource to the media are to:

1. Purchase a listing in the *Yearbook of Experts, Authorities & Spokespersons* (www.yearbooknews.com). This annual directory (and its constantly updated on-line version) is like a Yellow Pages of interview sources for thousands of reporters. While the directory is

distributed free to the media, the people who are listed must pay a fee to be included. You can say what you want about yourself, your organization, or your areas of expertise, include a photo of yourself, and include contact information so reporters can reach you when they need to.

I know the *Yearbook* works because I've had a listing in it myself for several years, which has led to interviews with and stories by TV news programs, radio stations, and newspapers across the country.

HALL OF FAME: GET TO KNOW THE MEDIA BEFORE YOU NEED THEM

Carefully targeting the news organizations that you would like to have cover your activities is just as important as customizing the news releases you send them (see Chapter 23). It's a tactic that's paid off in thousands of stories for Steven Loueks. Loueks, public relations director of the Carlson Leisure Group, an international travel agency, previously served as the communications director of the American Society of Travel Agents.

But Loueks takes this approach one step farther by getting to know the media and becoming a resource to them *before* he approaches them with his own story ideas. He says he meets with reporters, writers, and editors at news organizations ahead of time "so they will know who I am, who I work for, and how I can be of assistance to them in the future." In turn, he learns about the stories they are most interested in covering, their likes and dislikes, and establishes the basis for future working relationships with them.

Loueks says the strategy has resulted in top-of-mind awareness among journalists who have called him for quotes, comments, or insights on hundreds of travel-related stories over the years. "Reporters have come back to me over and over and over again for interviews. They realize that I'm a credible source of information. They realize that I can provide information that is vital to their news stories and that I try to provide them with good soundbites" (see Chapter 28).

But Loueks warns, "If you don't make that contact with someone in the media, maybe your competitor will. You want to be the person who is featured, not your competitor. Persistence pays."

2. Join organizations that promote experts and speakers to corporations and the news media. This includes Speakers.com, which also publishes *Experts* magazine (www.expertsmagazine.com), and SpeakersVoice Association (www.speakersvoice.com). Like the *Yearbook*, you can buy listings and say what you want about yourself.

3. Target news organizations that you think would be interested in interviewing you at some point, and send a letter, memo, or e-mail to their editors describing your background, areas of expertise, and topics you can talk about. Ask the editors to forward your information to reporters who cover those subjects.

4. Give good quotes. Reporters are often inclined to interview people who can provide good soundbites and inkbites (see Chapter 28). When reporters see that you've been quoted by one news organization, for example, they may seek to contact you for interviews for their own stories. Consider your quotes to be as much a marketing opportunity to promote yourself to the media as they are a way to promote yourself or company to the public.

34 Insights Served on a Silver Platter

Why and How You Should Study the Media

There's an easy, effective, and affordable way to find out what kind of stories media outlets will cover, the types of quotes they like to use, or how your competition is being portrayed by different news organizations.

All you have to do is:

➤ Read a local or national newspaper.

➤ Subscribe to a newsletter or magazine that covers your industry or profession.

➤ Watch the local and national news.

➤ Listen to news reports on your radio.

➤ Surf the Internet.

➤ Do a keyword search on a computer database.

Too busy to read everything or follow everything you should? Then you can subscribe to a service such as the "Custom Clips" from Dow Jones News Retrieval, which enables subscribers to do keyword searches of more than 6,000 publications. For a few dollars a month, the service will automatically send you via fax or e-mail the text of stories in which the keywords you specify appear. Or, at a greater cost, you can subscribe to a news clipping service that will mail you the actual story as it appeared in the publication, or prepare a transcript of radio or television stories (see the Resources).

To get the most insight about the media from your research, look for the following "clues":

Print Stories

➤ How long are the stories?

➤ In what part of the publication do they appear (business, lifestyle, sports, or the front news section)?

➤ How often do they include quotes?

➤ Who appears to be quoted more often, and why?

➤ How long are their quotes, and what do you think of what they said?

➤ If you had been interviewed for the same story, what would you have told the reporter?

➤ What kind of pictures do they use (color, black-and-white, head-and-shoulder shots, pictures of products, etc.)?

➤ Whose byline usually appears above the stories that are of most interest to you?

Television Stories

➤ How long are the stories?

➤ What time or part of the newscast did the story air?

➤ How often do they include interviews?

➤ Who appears to be quoted more often, and why?

➤ How long are their quotes, and what do you think of what they said?

➤ If you had been interviewed for the same story, what would you have told the reporter?

➤ What kind of pictures do they show during the story?

➤ What is the name of the reporter who did the story?

Radio Stories

➤ How long are the stories?

➤ What time or part of the newscast did the story air?

➤ How often do they include interviews?

➤ Who appears to be quoted more often, and why?

➤ How long are their quotes, and what do you think of what they said?

➤ If you had been interviewed for the same story, what would you have told the reporter?

➤ What is the name of the reporter who did the story?

Internet and Database Stories

➤ How long are the stories?

➤ Do they include interviews?

➤ Who appears to be quoted more often, and why?

➤ How long are their quotes, and what do you think of what they said?

➤ If you had been interviewed for the same story, what would you have told the reporter?

➤ What is the name of the reporter who did the story?

Based on this information, you can then apply your knowledge accordingly by:

➤ Knowing what kinds of stories they cover.

➤ Targeting the most appropriate news organization that will be interested in your story.

➤ Identifying the most appropriate reporter.

➤ Preparing the kinds of soundbites or inkbites they prefer.

➤ Providing the news organization with the best visual to help show your story.

Reading, watching, and listening to news organizations offers one of the best and affordable continuing educations you can obtain on what stories they like to cover and new trends and developments that may affect your own efforts to achieve fame or public recognition. By becoming a student of the media and applying what you learn to your own efforts, you can make the task of achieving your 15 minutes of fame that much more easier, productive, and effective.

35 If You Think *You* Have Problems

Challenges Facing News Organizations, and How You Can Take Advantage of Them

The challenges you face in convincing the media to do stories about you or your company are matched only by the challenges editors and reporters face in gathering and reporting the news.

To produce their final product—whether it's a daily newspaper, nightly TV news program, or hourly radio news segment—editors, producers, and their staff must contend with a never-ending series of daily or continuing hurdles. According to journalists I've met, worked with, and talked to (and based on my own experience), these problems include:

➤ Making decisions on which scheduled events or activities to cover, especially if they will be held at the same time.

➤ Weeding out the truly newsworthy press releases from the hundreds of apparently superfluous, irrelevant, or poorly written ones that cross their desks every week (see Chapter 45).

➤ Ensuring that the stories they cover and people they interview are a true reflection of their community.

➤ Delivering the appropriate blend of local, national, or international news to their audiences.

➤ Fact-checking stories to ensure that there are no errors (see Chapter 32).

➤ Looking for the best available experts to interview, help explain, or provide perspective to technical or complex stories (see Chapter 68).

➤ Taking or locating pictures, graphs, charts, or other illustrations to help explain and show their stories (see Chapter 13).

➤ Maintaining staff morale in the face of budget cutbacks, mergers, and acquisitions among news organizations, and the creeping influence of some advertising departments on the news judgments of editorial personnel.

➤ Finding and keeping good reporters and support staff (a 1999 study by the *Columbia Journalism Review* found that almost 60 percent of surveyed editors and news directors said it is "harder than ever" to find talented people to hire).

➤ Providing enough time and resources so reporters can adequately research a story and be properly prepared to interview people for it.

➤ Ensuring that their reporters, editors, and producers observe the criteria of good journalism in their work.

■ TURN THEIR LEMONS INTO YOUR LEMONADE

How do you turn the media's lemons into your lemonade to ensure that, despite their problems and difficulties, you're able to convince news organizations to do the stories you want about you or your company?

By going the extra mile to help make their jobs—and their decision to do stories about you—as easy as possible.

Here's how:

➤ Help them with their homework.

Provide them with as much background information as you think is appropriate about your story, including news releases, fact sheets, or other stories that have been written about you or the topic. (But don't bury them in paperwork.)

➤ Don't wait until it's too late.

Give editors and reporters as much advance notice as possible about scheduled news such as a news conferences or newsmaking special events.

➤ Show them the story.

Find the best possible visuals that will help show your story as well as tell it (see Chapter 13), and be sure to tell the news organizations about them when you first call.

➤ Give them ideas.

Call editors and reporters with story ideas that you think they may be interested in, even though those ideas may not result in news coverage about you. By showing them you are a resource of information and ideas, they will be more receptive to your calls later when you pitch them a story about yourself.

HALL OF SHAME: JUMPING THE GUN

Thanks to the wonders of technology, important news can be sent around the world within a matter of seconds. But that doesn't mean that it should, especially when the news hasn't actually happened yet.

Like many news organizations, the Associated Press prepares obituaries of famous people to run as soon as they die. Somehow, though, the wire service managed to post on its Web site for news organizations a draft story about the death of Bob Hope, even though the entertainer was alive and well. To make matters worse, the story found its way into the hands of a member of Congress who immediately took to the floor of the House of Representatives to announce that Hope had died. Seeing that the congressman had announced Hope's death, the Reuters news service sent a bulletin with the headline, "Entertainer Bob Hope is dead, lawmaker says." On hearing the news, Linda Hope, the comedian's daughter, began calling journalists to tell them otherwise.

➤ Provide good soundbites (see Chapter 28).

Once you have the media's attention, take full advantage of the opportunity by providing them with the quotes they need to help tell their story to their audiences. The better your quotes, the more likely it is that they'll be used . . . and that the reporters will come back to you in the future for more interviews.

■ IN THEIR OWN WORDS

Fill the Void

TV and radio have more time to fill than ever before. It's relatively inexpensive for an existing news department to put a news show on the air. In some markets today, morning news programming fills up to five hours of airtime, so newsrooms are always looking for stories. News items that would not have received coverage years ago might get that coverage today because there is so much time to fill. That's why you see so much repetition of news stories. Filling time has become a big challenge for these newsrooms.

Karen Friedman
Former TV Reporter

36 I Think I Can ... I Know I Can!

Stay Focused and Be Determined

Anyone seeking fame or recognition is well advised to learn a lesson from *The Little Engine That Could,* a children's story about a train engine that, through persistence and determination, was able to achieve his goal. The moral of that story is that you are more likely to achieve your 15 minutes of fame (and more) if you keep focused and maintain your determination to succeed, no matter what happens or gets in the way.

On the road to fame, you'll likely come across any number of discouraging bumps, potholes, detours, or traffic jams that could delay or prevent you from reaching your destination as quickly as you might wish.

My own files are filled with examples of clients who, through no fault of their own, simply had to wait a while before they were able to get the news coverage they wanted, or until they could convince reporters they were worthy of a story.

Here are four success stories:

1. Group Health Association was an HMO in Washington DC. Even though *The Washington Post* had interviewed

company officials and prepared a multipart feature story about the company, the articles did not appear for more than four months. Why did it take so long? According to the reporter, editors kept deciding to run what they thought were more important or late-breaking stories instead.

2. Medi-Cen Management, Inc., which sought to build a chain of "medical malls" in the mid-Atlantic region. Medi-Cen Management had to wait for several weeks from the time a reporter with *The Wall Street Journal* interviewed the president of the company for a story until that article finally appeared in print.

3. Executive Office Club, which waited several months after it was first contacted by a reporter at *Inc.* magazine who expressed interest in profiling the company before the story finally hit the newsstands.

4. The Federal Home Loan Mortgage Corporation (FreddieMac) had hoped to persuade ABC's *Good Morning America* to do a piece about the organization. Even though the show's staff turned them down, FreddieMac's PR agency, Earle Palmer Brown, would not take no for an answer. The agency's staff found a producer under contract to make business-related segments for the show, which was then obligated to air his stories. The producer liked the story idea, and the story aired several weeks later.

Oh well, better late than never!

■ IN THEIR OWN WORDS

Fame Can Be a Waiting Game

I once wrote to an editor at Glamour *magazine about my company, urging that they do a story about us. She wrote back to say that they were not interested but asked that I keep them posted about our activities.*

Once every three months or so I'd drop her a line about what we were doing, our successes, et cetera. I did not bother

her or complain that the magazine had not yet written about us—I just kept in regular contact with her to let her know how we were doing.

About a year later the editor called to say that they wanted to do the article! Not only did they do that story, but later they published a "where are they now" piece, and I was one of the four women they profiled.

Debra Leopold, President
First Class, Inc.

Part III

The Eight Gateways to Fame

37 It's Black and White and Read All Over

It Must Be True. I Saw It in Writing!

There's something about a newspaper, magazine, or newsletter story that's unlike any other type of news coverage:

➤ You can touch it.

➤ You can feel it.

➤ You can photocopy it and send it to your mother, father, friends, family, and clients.

➤ You can include a copy in your press kit and marketing materials.

➤ You can scan it into your computer and post it on your Web site.

➤ You can hang it on your wall or paste it in your scrapbook with pride.

➤ You can point to it and say (or at least think to yourself), "Hey, I'm famous!"

While every client I've worked for has always appreciated the TV or radio stories I've placed for them, they are usually anxious to get copies of a printed story so they can keep one handy on their desk to look at and show to visitors; pass around to their employees; or hang in the hallway, on their door, or in the company lunchroom or kitchen.

Not only is print coverage tactile and versatile, reprints of it can be seen by many more people than who saw the original when it was published. And depending where it was published, the text of the story may find its way into a computer database library, where future generations of readers, researchers, reporters, and columnists may come across it.

Ironically, many television and radio stations use newspaper and magazine articles as "tip sheets" for their own story ideas, and often quote or refer to those stories in their newscasts. Why? Because the stations' news staffs are often too small or too busy to report or research the same stories themselves. Print stories also differ from other forms of news coverage in several other important ways, as outlined in the accompanying media comparison analysis.

More so than other news organizations, newspapers and magazines tend to deal with topics in greater depth and detail; it is not unusual for them to publish several thousand words, or, run a series of articles over a period of days or months about a particular topic. These longer articles represent tremendous opportunities for experts to be interviewed, since most reporters (or their editors) don't like to rely on just one expert or authority for quotes, opinions, or perspectives in a lengthy article.

Convincing newspaper reporters to do a story about you is no different from trying to get other journalists to cover you. What is different, however, is that the reporter may come to your office or home to interview you for their article.

Newspaper reporters can do more than simply report what you said. As trained observers, they can also convey to readers your demeanor and mannerisms during the interview, how you talked, how you dressed, and how you answered (or evaded) their questions. Just as you'd be on your best behavior for a television interview, realize that everything you say or do during a print interview could be mentioned or reported in the story.

Don't be lulled into a false sense of security or complacency. In an effort to help "loosen you up," the journalist may start the interview by talking about a completely different subject, and then slowly discuss the matter at hand. Always keep in mind the three major points you want to make during the interview, and try not to let the reporter get you off track.

Print reporters can have roving eyes. If they will be coming to your home or office for the interview, make sure that you haven't left any important or embarrassing documents or other materials where the reporter can see them.

Don't assume that reporters can't read upside down, as happened to one client. After an in-office interview with a reporter, the client was surprised to see in the next day's paper excerpts from a confidential memo on the corner of his desk that he assumed the reporter could not read.

For more advice on media interviews, see Chapter 27.

■ MEDIA COMPARISON ANALYSIS

While it's impossible to categorize or describe every one of the one million news organizations in the United States (see Chapter 5), it is possible to make some helpful basic comparisons and generalizations about them. The following charts describe and illustrate the differences among major types of news organizations in terms of frequency, deadlines and so on. For more detailed information, be sure to contact individual news organizations.

Frequency

Papers	Daily (although their on-line editions may be updated on an hourly basis with late-breaking news and headlines from wire services).
Magazines	Weekly, monthly, or quarterly.
Newsletters	Daily, weekly, monthly, or quarterly.
Wires	24 hours a day.
TV	Usually in the morning and evening.
Radio	Can be hourly.
Internet	24 hours a day.

Deadlines

Papers	Usually the day before publication, but some magazine inserts may be printed as much as a week before the rest of the paper.
Magazines	Several days or several weeks before publication.

Newsletters	Depends on individual publication.
Wires	No set deadlines.
TV	Late afternoon for evening newscasts; late evenings for morning shows.
Radio	Can be several minutes prior to the newscast.
Internet	No set deadlines.

Length of Story

Newspapers	300 to 1,500 words.
Magazines	500 to 5,000 words.
Newsletters	50 to 500 words.
Wires	200 to 1,000 words.
TV	90 seconds.
Radio	10 to 60 seconds.
Internet	50 to 500 words.

Expertise of Reporters in the Stories They Cover

Newspapers	Depends on the size and circulation of the paper. At larger dailies, many reporters work the same beat for several months or years and have a greater knowledge of the stories than the people they interview for them.
Magazines	Many magazines rely on freelance writers for stories, so their expertise can vary from naive to expert.
Newsletters	Usually very high.
Wires	Most are specialists or have covered the beat for several months.
TV	Most are general assignment reporters.
Radio	Almost all are general assignment reporters.
Internet	Varies.

Best Time to Reach Them

Newspapers	Before lunch, when journalists first arrive for work. Never call a reporter late in the afternoon when he or she will most likely be finishing a story for the next day's paper. The exception to this rule is that if a reporter calls you in the afternoon or evening, you should try to return the call immediately.
Magazines	Anytime.
Newsletters	Regular business hours.
Wires	Regular business hours.
TV	Up until about an hour before the newscast.
Radio	Up until about 10 minutes prior to the newscast.
Internet	Anytime by e-mail.

Corrections Policies

Newspapers	Usually print corrections the day after the original story was published.
Magazines	Weeks or months after the error was printed.
Newsletters	Usually print corrections in the next issue.
Wires	Almost immediately after the mistake is called to their attention.
TV	While most TV stations do not issue corrections, it's still important that you call as soon as you realize the mistake. Although the station might not issue a correction, they may correct the information for use in the next newscast.
Radio	The next newscast, if you call as soon as you hear the mistake.
Internet	Almost immediately after the mistake is called to their attention.

Length of Quotes They Use in Their Stories

Newspapers	5 to 50 words.
Magazines	5 to 50 words.
TV	9 to 20 seconds (and shrinking).
Radio	5 to 15 seconds.
Internet	5 to 50 words.

Audiences

Newspapers	General public.
Magazines	Readers interested in the topics they cover.
Newsletters	Subscribers interested in the topics they cover.
Wires	General public.
TV	General public.
Radio	General public.
Internet	General public.

Competition

Newspapers	Most metropolitan areas have only one daily newspaper and several noncompeting weekly papers that serve smaller communities or neighborhoods.
Magazines	There are many competing publications on the national level, almost no competition among magazines locally.
Newsletters	Depends on the topics they cover.
Wires	There are five major wire services (AP, Reuters, Bloomberg, Dow Jones, and UPI).
TV	Very competitive, with most areas having between two and five stations.
Radio	The larger the area, the more likely that they will have competing stations. In Southern California, for example, there are more than 100 radio stations.
Internet	Thousands of other Web sites.

■ WHAT I SAY, GOES

Who is likely to have more control over what and when the media writes about them: movie stars or the President of the United States?

Movie stars, hands down.

At many news organizations, having a movie star on the cover of their magazine or as a part of the broadcast adds a tremendous boost to their circulation or ratings. The larger the circulation or ratings, the more they can charge for advertising. That's why, when the movie of a popular actor is about to be released, there can be stiff competition among news organizations for interviews or exclusive stories. And in their efforts to land those stories, news organizations will often agree to or negotiate terms and conditions, including:

➤ Who will write or report the story.

➤ What questions can be asked.

➤ How prominent the story or interview will be in the magazine or broadcast.

➤ When the story will be published or aired.

➤ Whether the star's picture will be on the cover of the magazine.

➤ Who will take the picture.

➤ The right to review or edit the story.

➤ The use of photos or video for the story.

A recent example of Hollywood's successful efforts to control the media is that of PMK, the public relations firm that represents Tom Cruise and other celebrities. According to the *Los Angeles Times,* the agency asked for and got TV shows to agree that "the interview and the program will not show the artist in a negative or derogatory manner."

You have two chances of negotiating similar agreements with the media: slim and none.

Of course, to increase the likelihood that reporters will consent to your demands, you could also change your name to Tom Cruise or Madonna.

38 It's Just like Radio, Except It Has Pictures

How to Do Television News Interviews

Television interviews provide a great opportunity for you to become known by a large number of people in a very short period. In fact, surveys show that more people get their news from television than from any other news source.

So if you think there is a lot riding on your interview with a TV reporter, you're absolutely right. Even though you have an important message or story to talk about, what the public thinks of your message and whether they believe it are often determined by how you dress, how you talk, what you say, and how you say it on television.

Here are 12 tips to help you get the most out of your TV interviews:

1. If you will be interviewed in a studio, arrive early so you can meet the production staff, take a look at the set, make sure you are comfortable in the chair you'll be sitting in, and so on.

2. Know the three or four points you want to make during the interview, and find ways to return to these points throughout the interview.

3. Look at the reporter during the interview, not at the camera.

4. Don't fidget, twitch in your chair, or do anything that will distract viewers from your message.

5. Remove any large, loud, or distracting jewelry.

6. Glance at a mirror before the interview to make sure you look the way you want.

7. Use appropriate gestures to help make or emphasize your points.

8. Be positive, upbeat, and confident in your answers, manner, and demeanor.

9. Smile and keep a pleasant expression on your face at all times.

10. Keep your answers short, usually 20 to 30 seconds.

11. Avoid speaking in a monotone or speaking too fast; vary your voice pitch and tone to help make or emphasize your points and message.

12. Bring or refer the reporter to any visuals that will help show your story or make your point.

Corporate spokespeople, media trainers, and other PR professionals offer additional words of advice.

Karen Friedman, a media trainer and former TV reporter:

Imagine yourself at home watching TV. What would you, a regular average person, care about? Put yourself in the shoes of the viewers if you really want to talk to them.

Burke Stinson, spokesperson for AT&T:

Never let your guard down just because the camera lights have been turned off and the reporter is removing his or her microphone. First, your microphone still might be live and your "off-the-record" remark could find a way to the airwaves! Second, anything you say while in the presence of a reporter—and witnesses—is fair game for the story. Third, reporters are not your friends or neighbors; they have a job to do from the moment they arrive till they depart. Respect that.

David Stempler, president of the Air Travelers Association:

I was nervous about getting things right the first few times I did TV interviews. But I realized that if what I did was successful, then there would be many more interviews in the future. And if I didn't get it right the first time, then I'd get it right the next time. That realization helped me to relax and not to be so worried about getting every word right or making a minor flub. Reporters have told me that they don't mind minor mistakes because it makes you look more like a regular person, not a staged professional. Today, if I'm doing a taped TV or radio interview and do make a mistake, I can always tell the reporter that I wasn't happy with my answer, and ask to do it over again.

All the advice in the world won't be of any help unless you practice using it:

➤ One way to practice is to stand in front of a mirror and pretend you're being interviewed on TV.

➤ A step up from that is to use a video camera to tape your practice interviews.

➤ Finally, you may want to invest the time and money to retain the services of a professional media trainer who can provide important feedback to your mock interviews and provide expert advice on how to craft your message, deliver soundbites, answer a reporter's questions, and so on. A list of media trainers can be found in the Resources at the back of the book.

For additional advice on interviews, see Chapters 27, 39, and 40.

■ IN THEIR OWN WORDS

When You're Hot, You're Hot

I once delivered the Democratic response to one of President Ronald Reagan's televised addresses to the nation. Midway through delivering my speech live to the tens of millions of Americans who had just heard Reagan's speech, the Tele-PrompTer caught on fire. The office filled with smoke and I had to finish my remarks using the back-up text on my desk. As people rushed to put out the electrical fire, I said to myself, "Boy, the Republicans are more powerful than I thought!"

Michael Barnes
Former member of Congress

**HALL OF FAME: GO WHERE
THE CAMERAS ARE**

Every January, Eliot Engel is guaranteed to appear on television screens in millions of homes across the country. Each
year since 1989, Engel, a Democratic congressman from New
York, has expertly positioned himself on the center aisle of
the House chamber so TV cameras will catch him shaking
the hand of the president of the United States as he arrives to
deliver the State of the Union address.

Engel shows up early each year for the speech so he can
claim a good seat within the right camera angle, and says
constituents enjoy seeing him in the limelight on such a pre-
dictable basis, even if it is only for a few seconds.

The New York legislator's annual cameo performance
seems to have been copied by other members of Congress.
Engel says that about 20 other lawmakers now camp out early
with him for good aisle positions so they too can be seen by
TV viewers shaking the president's hand.

---

39 It's Just like Television, But without Pictures

How to Do Radio Interviews

The nice thing about radio interviews is that no one cares
how you look or dress.

And there is absolutely no need to get nervous about it . . . even though your image and reputation are riding on every word you say and how you say it (gulp!).

But seriously, for most people radio interviews can be one of the easiest types of interviews:

> Since most news stories are relatively short (often in the 30–40 second range) your soundbite will be relatively short as well.

> Almost all radio interviews are done by phone, so you can talk to the reporter from the comfort of your home, or even on a cell phone in a parked car.

> You can have as much background information as you need in front of you during the interview and refer to it as often as you need to.

> Most radio interviews are taped, so if you don't like an answer you gave or flubbed a response, simply tell the reporter that you want to give your answer over again.

Here's what you can do to help guarantee your radio interviews go as smoothly as possible:

> Make sure there are no distractions in the room where you will call from, and that there are no street noises, barking dogs, and so on that will be picked up by the phone.

> Jot down on a legal pad the three or four points you want to cover during the interview, and check them off as you make them during the interview.

> Speak in a conversational tone.

> Practice what you want to say ahead of time so your answers don't run more than 10 or 15 seconds.

> Organize any reference materials you may need during the interview so you won't have to shuffle through papers to find the information you need.

> Find out from the reporter whether you are to call him or if he is to call you.

> Make sure you have a phone number where you can reach the reporter prior to the interview. If the reporter

will call you for the interview, be sure to keep your line clear as much as possible prior to the time of the interview.

Finally, use a tape recorder to practice delivering your answers; ask a friend, family member, or colleague to "play reporter" and ask you a combination of easy and difficult questions.

Arrange beforehand to tape-record your radio interview, and then go back to hear how you did. What would you like to do differently or better the next time?

Chapters 27, 38, and 40 provide more advice on conducting interviews.

40 Can You Hear Me? Am I on the Air?

Being a Guest on Radio Call-In Shows

Radio talk shows are important and influential forums for experts, authors, and people in other walks of life to be heard by millions of interested, curious, and oftentimes opinionated listeners. Depending on the format of these shows, guests also may answer questions from, or get into heated disagreements with, the audience.

The number of these radio programs has proliferated in recent years, thanks to the large ratings some of the more popular hosts are able to generate for stations, and the fact that several all-music stations across the country have converted to all-talk formats. As the programs have grown in

number, they have also grown in influence, with hosts sometimes urging listeners to ask their lawmakers to pass or de-
feat legislation.

For all the popularity and impact of these shows, they
may or may not be the best place for you to discuss your company is product, services, accomplishments, or expertise:

➤ Topics and guests are usually decided solely by the
host or his producer. Unlike a newspaper, which may
have scores of reporters to whom you can pitch your
story idea, if you strike out with the host or producer,
there is no one else to turn to.

➤ You must know your topic inside and out. Although
you can bring background or reference material with
you to the studio or keep it in front of you at home, you
may have no chance to use it. Most shows are done live
and you won't have an opportunity to look something up
while millions of people wait for your answer.

➤ Listen to the show several times beforehand to get a
feel for the topics and issues they discuss, the interviewing style of the host, and the kinds of questions callers
ask of guests.

➤ You should have a strong, clear speaking voice that conveys confidence and authority to the listening audience.

➤ While you must prepare for the show as you would for
any other type of interview, radio call-in hosts may be
less willing to share with you the list of questions they'll
ask you. They want their guests to be and sound as spon-
taneous as possible. As a talk show host told me, "I never
interview anyone prior to the program. Occasionally, I
will fax them one or two questions. However, I will
deviate from that line of questioning (in order) to mix
it up. There is nothing worse that a canned, contrived
response!"

➤ You should be able to perform well under pressure. A
lot will be riding on your ability to explain yourself and
answer questions in front of a live audience of up to several million people.

To be a guest on a radio talk show, Joe Shafran, president of PR4U, a media placement agency (www.pr4u.com), says you should be able to talk about at least one of the following topics:

Arts	Medicine
Business	Military
Crime	Movies
Diet	Personalities
Economy	Personal relationships
Entertainment	Politics
Environment	Psychology
Ethics	Scandals
Finance	Science
Fitness	Sex
Foreign affairs	Sports
Gossip	Stock market
Health	Taxes
History	Technology
Law	TV shows
Media	Weather

In addition, Shafran says:

➤ Your subject should provoke controversy or debate.

➤ You should be an acknowledged expert on your subject.

➤ You should be self-confident but not overbearing.

➤ You can be available for an interview by phone at a moment's notice.

41 Sudden Impact

Newswire Services

News organizations receive leads and ideas for stories from several different sources, including their own reporters, current events, viewers, readers, listeners, PR firms, and individuals and companies seeking news coverage about their own activities and accomplishments.

Ironically, an important source of story ideas for news organizations is other news organizations: the Associated Press, Dow Jones, Reuters, Bloomberg News, United Press International, PR Newswire, Businesswire, US Newswire, and other wire services that distribute news and information to subscribers 24 hours a day, seven days a week.

According to Jerry Brown, a former editor with the Associated Press, "The basic mission of wire services is to provide news to other news organizations who cannot gather or report the same information for themselves."

Thousands of major TV stations, radio stations, newspapers, and magazines around the world depend on these services for a steady stream of news reports and feature stories they can use in newscasts or publications, or as the basis from which their reporters can prepare their own stories. Even some Web sites and Internet services, such as America Online, provide visitors and users with excerpts from or full-text versions of selected wire service copy for their own information or entertainment.

Not all news wire services are created equal, however:

➤ The Associated Press carries reports that run the gamut from late-breaking news and movie reviews to sports scores and personality profiles. Its subscribers include 1,700 daily and weekly newspapers in the United

States, 6,000 radio and TV stations, and thousands of international news organizations.

➤ Reuters sends an estimated 10,000 stories and financial market information to over 485,000 users at 58,000 organizations in more than 150 countries. It also provides news to more than 200 Internet sites, such as Yahoo!

➤ Dow Jones distributes business and financial news and information to subscribers and news outlets around the world.

➤ United Press International, which once provided newspapers around the world with stories, now specializes in providing news and information to Internet sites.

➤ Bloomberg News gathers and distributes business and financial stories.

They all have a common problem, however, in determining what information is relevant for their audiences as their editors and writers sift through the hundreds of news releases they receive every day.

For the wannabe famous person, newswire services can be the fastest and most effective way to tell their story to the world, or to help convince other news organizations that their story is worth reporting. Brown, the former editor with the Associated Press (who has also worked for several daily newspapers), says wire services use the following criteria to decide whether to run a story:

1. Will the story be of interest to the news organizations they serve?

2. Will the story be useful or interesting to the audiences of those news organizations?

Some news wire services are easier than others to convince to do stories about you. For three of them (PR Newswire, Businesswire, and U.S. Newswire), all you need is money and a well-written news release on the letterhead of your corporation or organization (they will not accept releases from private individuals).

At a meeting of the Los Angeles chapter of the Public Relations Society of America, officials of the Associated Press,

United Press International, Reuters, and City News Service provided several suggestions for placing stories on their wires and with other news organizations. As reported by *Jack O'Dwyer's Newsletter,* their recommendations included:

➤ Do not send multiple copies of your release to the same person or even to several people at one location.

➤ Use the "who, what, when, where" format to describe the event you want the media to cover.

➤ It's okay to pitch the event via phone, but don't call to ask if a fax has been received.

➤ Don't use e-mail to pitch an idea.

➤ Fax releases by noon so reporters have time to call back later in the day with questions.

➤ Make sure the release is complete, with evening and weekend contact numbers as well as cell phone numbers.

➤ When pitching a bureau, call the one in the city where your company is based.

➤ Feel free to approach business editors with a list of experts who can provide comment on stories.

42 Okay, So It May Not Be *The Wall Street Journal,* But It'll Do

Newsletters

If you tried to raise $1,000, you'd probably have more luck getting the money by asking 100 people for $10 each, instead of asking one person to loan you the entire amount, right?

The same principle holds true when you are trying to become famous or create public awareness about your company, product, services, or accomplishments. Even though *The Wall Street Journal* may not be interested in doing a story about you now, there are lots of newsletters that are read by many of the same people who subscribe to the largest circulation newspaper in the United States.

In fact, according to Howard Penn Hudson, former president of Newsletter Clearinghouse, Inc., there are an estimated one million published newsletters—more than all other news outlets *combined*. If you add the growing number of e-mail newsletters that are sent to Internet users every year, then the opportunities for news coverage by these outlets is almost unlimited. Together, newsletters are read by millions of people who follow certain topics, issues, or stories that are of particular interest to them, ranging from accounting to zoology.

By and large, the strategy for getting newsletters to write about you is the same as for other news organizations:

➤ Do your research to determine the readership and topics they cover.

➤ Read back issues to get a good feel about writing style, editorial preference, and so on.

➤ Customize the information you send to the particular interests or concerns of the subscribers.

➤ Find out and adhere to their deadline for the submission of news releases and story ideas.

➤ If you have any questions or doubts about the kinds of stories they are interested in covering, don't hesitate to call the editorial staff to find out for sure.

Be warned, however, that it may be hard to find back issues of the newsletter for you to study. Most printed newsletters are either too numerous or too expensive for libraries to carry, are not sold in bookstores, or may require a password to view on-line. If you call the publisher to ask for some back issues to review, you may find yourself being solicited for a subscription yourself, or asked to pay a few dollars for the copies you want.

Although newsletters are like other news organizations in many ways, they differ on several counts.

➤ Their stories are often much shorter than articles in any other kind of publication. Depending on their format, style, and topics covered, the length of most articles may be in the 50–200 word range.

➤ Most newsletters carry no advertising, and are financed entirely by subscribers, who may pay several hundred dollars or more each year for the privilege of receiving their daily, weekly, or monthly issues.

➤ Since newsletters cater to a specific clientele, editors are careful to provide their readers only with the particular kinds of news and information that meet their strict criteria as well as the needs or expectations of their subscribers.

Although these may seem like a lot of hoops to jump through to get news coverage, the time and effort can be worthwhile:

➤ The people who read about you represent an important and influential audience.

➤ Subscribers are more likely to read all the articles in their newsletter since they are paying so much money to receive it.

➤ To extend the reach or influence of their newsletter, publishers will often send complimentary copies to editors and reporters. Many times, I've received calls from journalists who, having seen a mention about one of my clients in a newsletter, become interested in doing their own story.

So on your road to fame, don't overlook this important category of news outlets—or the tens of millions of people who read them.

43 Tower of Babel or Great Equalizer?

Using the 'Net to Catch Fame

The Internet is one of the most powerful tools wannabe famous people can use to tell their stories to Web surfers around the planet, not to mention the growing number of reporters who regard the Web as an important source of information and story ideas.

According to a study by News Generation in Bethesda, Maryland, almost every one of the 30 radio stations it surveyed across the country said they turn to cyberspace as a source of information for stories As reported by *Jack O'Dwyer's Newsletter,* the study found that the stations check the Internet more than five times every week.

As more radio stations and other news organizations look to the World Wide Web for information and story ideas, the Internet may very well become the ultimate "level playing field" where everyone has an equal chance to tell their stories to the world.

The numbers are certainly impressive. In 1999:

➤ More than 60 million people in the United States used the Internet for research, entertainment, or communication.

➤ There were more than one billion Web sites to choose from.

➤ Some of the more popular home pages were being visited by hundreds of thousands of people a month.

➤ Internet users sent more than 10 billion e-mail messages to each other.

In the minds of many people, however, the Internet is of questionable use or value:

➤ Pornographic Web sites are one of the most popular destinations for Web surfers.

➤ The Victoria's Secret online catalog of women's lingerie is one of the most frequently visited Web sites.

➤ Anybody can put almost anything they want on the Internet.

➤ There are no protections, filters, or safeguards to ensure that anything you read on Web sites is true or accurate.

➤ Few, if any, search engines include all Web sites in their directories.

➤ There are no surefire methods to ensure that everyone knows about your Web site.

➤ Vandals use the Internet to spread high-tech viruses around the world that can infect or completely destroy important information on your computer.

➤ Hackers can obtain private and confidential information and records about aspects of your personal, professional, and financial life that are stored on your computer, or the computers of companies with which you do business.

Despite the problems and concerns associated with the Internet, a growing number of companies are using cyberspace to communicate with their clients, customers, and audiences.

Among the millions of organizations establishing Web sites there are, ironically, thousands of newspapers and television stations. Seeking to escape the constraints of being able to print their editions once a day or broadcast their news only in the mornings or evenings, these news outlets use the Internet to distribute their news 24-hours a day, seven days a week.

You can take advantage of their expanding need for news by sending the interactive editions of these news organizations copies of your news releases. You might also establish, if you haven't done so already, your own home page so that reporters and editors can read all about you or your company whenever they choose. While you'll face plenty of competition to be noticed in cyberspace, at least you'll be playing on the same level playing fields as such corporate giants as Ford, IBM, Coca-Cola, and General Mills.

To make it as easy as possible for reporters and columnists to find your Web site:

➤ Be sure your Web site and key identifying words are listed with the major Internet search engines.

➤ Include your Web site address on all materials that you send to the media, including news releases, press kits, news advisories, and business cards.

➤ Issue a news release via PR Newswire, Businesswire, or U.S. Newswire announcing your Web site to the media, describing your areas of expertise for media interviews.

➤ Send a copy of the news release to your list of press contacts.

➤ Mention your Web site address during answering machine or voice mail greetings to callers.

As an example of the challenges facing Web sites that want to promote themselves to the largest number of people, several search engines have turned to a low-tech solution: They've posted billboard advertising space along heavily traveled roads and highways, and bought newspaper, magazine, radio, and television ads.

What's next? Handing out flyers on street corners and hiring door-to-door salespeople?

44 The Secret of Eternal Life

Computer Libraries and Databases

Much like the Energizer bunny, thanks to modern technology, it's possible for your fame or recognition to keep "going and going and going" long after you've gotten your 15 minutes of fame.

That's because almost every story that will ever be written about you may be available to everyone with access to the Internet. This includes hundreds of thousands of editors, reporters, and columnists who are working on or researching a story about a topic in which your accomplishments were reported, your company was mentioned, or you were quoted. They can, with a few strokes of the computer keyboard, access computer databases to find those stories or references about you. And once they find your quote or pithy observation, the journalists can recycle them for use in their own article, or track you down for your latest comments or observations on the subject.

In the "olden days" before computers, if you wanted to find out what someone had said or done about something in a particular publication, you'd have to:

➤ Trek down to the neighborhood library during business hours and thumb through the *Reader's Guide to Periodical Literature* for appropriate citations or leads.

➤ Wade through musty stacks of publications to find the magazine you were looking for (unless, of course, the issue you wanted had been stolen, misplaced, or lost).

➤ Then, to check out any relevant newspaper stories, you'd have to hunch over a microfilm machine or go down to the morgue of the daily newspapers.

This inefficient and time-consuming process not only made it hard for you to find out about the work, accomplishments, or opinions of others, it made it just as difficult for millions of others to find out about you.

That was then, this is now.

Today, from free Internet search engines to sophisticated subscription-only commercial databases, reporters and researchers can find out all about you and your activities and 15 minutes of fame through the following databases (some may require users to pay a small fee to retrieve information):

➤ Dow Jones Interactive (www.djnr.com) and Lexis-Nexis (www.lexis-nexis.com), which have the text of stories from thousands of newspapers, magazines, newsletters, and the transcripts of several news programs. While you must subscribe to the Dow Jones service in order to use it, major public libraries have access to Lexis-Nexis, and may be able to conduct the database searches for you.

➤ Vanderbilt University (www.vanderbilt.edu), which maintains a comprehensive library of tapes and abstracts of more than 30,000 major evening network television news shows going back more than 30 years.

➤ The on-line archives of thousands of news organizations. According to *Editor & Publisher* magazine, more than 11,000 newspapers around the world are now on the Internet. How far back you'll be able to research, however, will depend on each newspaper.

➤ PR Newswire, Businesswire, and other private newswire services that store copies of previously distributed news releases and other press materials.

➤ The World Wide Web. By one estimate, the Web has more than one billion home pages of almost every imaginable corporation, organization, and news organization. Depending on the search engine you use, it's possible to do a keyword search to locate information about or references to almost anyone or anything that has ever been in the news.

Part IV

So That's How They Do It!

The Tools of the Trade and How to Use Them

45 A Storyteller's Best Friend

News Releases

Some people think the process of becoming famous is like a TV game show: give the right answer to the questions of who cares and why, and bingo, you win the grand prize, a trip to Fame City! But this is not *Jeopardy,* and your response can't be in the form of a question. But it *should* be in the form of a news release.

The news release represents the cornerstone of your efforts to get your 15 minutes of fame, and the most important and effective way to tell the media and the world who you are, what you are doing, why you are doing it, when you are doing it, and how you are doing it.

These one- to two-page documents can literally become your "ticket to fame" if you:

➤ Answer the all-important question of "who cares and why?" (See Chaper 5.)

➤ Include the who, what, when, where, why, and how of your story (whether it's about the introduction of a new product or service, an announcement of an important activity, award, or achievement, or the expression of your opinion).

Companies spend a lot of time, money, and effort on preparing and distributing news releases. Writing in *PR Week,* Katherine Spellissy, vice president of client services at Ink, Inc., estimates the tab might be as high as $1 billion *every year.* Most of that money appears to be wasted. The magazine surveyed key editors and reporters who said that as many as 99 percent of the materials they receive are trashed because the releases are irrelevant to their needs, void of any real news, or poorly written.

■ THE RECIPE FOR AN EFFECTIVE NEWS RELEASE

The best news releases become self-fulfilling prophecies: the more they *read* like real news stories and are sent to reporters who will be interested in receiving them, the more likely it is that they will *become* news stories.

There is no such thing as a one-size-fits-all, fill-in-the-blanks news release. Rather, you should think of your news release as a custom-made dress or suit that must be carefully tailored to tell your own story in the most effective and attention-getting way possible. You can customize your news release in the following 10 ways:

1. Summarize the announcement with an attention-getting headline.

2. Organize the information in the release as if it were a pyramid, with the most critical information at the top and the least important at the bottom.

3. Write a succinct opening paragraph that captures the who, what, when, where, why, and how of your announcement.

4. Highlight and explain the most interesting or newsworthy aspects of your announcement in the main body of the release. Keep the copy focused and factual.

5. Keep sentences short and limit your paragraphs to one or two sentences each (just as in newspaper or wire service stories).

6. Explain the impact the announcement will have on audiences of the news organizations that receive the release.

7. Include facts, figures, and background information about the new products or services that are being announced.

8. Place your announcement in the context of relevant trends or developments.

9. If appropriate, include a picture that illustrates the announcement, accompanied by a descriptive caption (also called a cutline).

10. Include your name, daytime and evening phone numbers, and e-mail and Web site addresses at the top of the first page if reporters have questions about the release or want to interview you.

■ ENSURE YOUR SUCCESS

While it's impossible to predict how many stories your news release generates, you can take six steps to ensure that your efforts are successful:

1. In addition to writing your releases as if they were newspaper stories, be sure to abide by the same rules for grammar and punctuation that reporters follow when they write their articles. It's all laid out for you in the *Associated Press Stylebook* which can be found at most libraries and bookstores.

2. Send the news release to news organizations that will be most interested in receiving it. If you have any doubts, call editors, reporters, and columnists in advance and ask them if they are interested in the subject of the release.

3. Make sure the list of reporters that receives the release is current and accurate.

4. Fax the news release to reporters on traditionally slow news days, such as Mondays or Saturdays, and send it earlier in the day rather than later (see Chapter 24). Usually, 10 A.M. to noon is best since that's when most editors or reporters decide which stories they will do that day.

5. Return calls from the media as soon as possible.

6. Be prepared to answer any questions reporters may have about the information in the release.

HALL OF SHAME: THE WRONG
KIND OF ATTENTION

Some people are not content to let the merits of a news release speak for itself. In an effort to get the media to take notice of a news release announcing a client's blood-recycling machine that could help control blood-borne diseases such as AIDS, a public relations agency prepared and distributed a news release about the equipment splattered with fake blood.

The release certainly got the attention of at least one news organization. *The Wall Street Journal* ran a story about it with this headline: "'Bloody' Gimmick of PR Firm Leaves Some Seeing Red." The article was about the negative reaction many people had to the stunt and how, in the minds of health officials and public relations experts, using fake blood to get the attention of the press was offensive and in bad taste.

If reporters are interested in doing a story based on the news release, they may call you for an interview or to ask for clarification or more information. Then again, they may not call at all, and write their stories based on the information you've included in the release.

While it is certainly not standard practice, if the release is well-written and meets the criteria of a legitimate news story, sometimes a news organization will simply run the release—or use major excerpts from it—almost exactly as you gave it to them. Now that's my idea of good journalism!

Sample news releases can be found on my Web site at www.edwardsegal.com.

46 Just the Facts, Ma'am, Just the Facts

Fact Sheets

Fact sheets are used to describe essential, complex, or background information reporters or columnists may need in order to fully understand or accurately report an event or news announcement. It may include information that is too long or complex to put into a news release.

■ CHECKLIST

Use the following checklist to ensure that a fact sheet about your project or announcement will help editors and reporters cover your story:

- ☐ If the fact sheet will accompany a news release or press kit, only include background information that is too long or complex to put in a news release.
- ☐ If the fact sheet will not accompany a news release, be sure the information you include is complete and self-explanatory.
- ☐ Cite the source of all information, studies, or research.
- ☐ Limit the length of the fact sheet to five single-spaced pages. The shorter the better.
- ☐ Make the information visually appealing by using boldface headlines, informative subheads, and short paragraphs.
- ☐ Include the name, phone number, e-mail, and Web site for reporters to contact if they have questions about any information in the fact sheet.

A sample fact sheet can be found on my Web site at www.edwardsegal.com.

47 The Whole Enchilada

Press Kits

In telling your story to the media, neatness and organization count.

Reporters and columnists who receive dozens or hundreds of letters and packages from wannabe famous people or companies every week, simply do not have the time, inclination, or patience to wade through all the material in their in box to find those few nuggets of news that will lead them to do interviews or prepare stories.

To help overcome this hurdle, prepare and tell your story in an organized and systematic way that will make it as easy as possible for the reporter to determine the newsworthiness of your story.

A well-written and properly assembled press kit will do just that.

A press kit, usually in the form of a standard two-pocket folder, is a complete package of information that provides reporters with everything they need to know about your story or news announcement.

■ CHECKLIST

While each press kit must be prepared and customized to explain a story or announcement in the most effective way possible, many kits contain the components shown in the following checklist:

- [ ] Cover memo or letter with contact information.
- [ ] News release.
- [ ] Photo and cutline.
- [ ] Fact sheet.
- [ ] Biographical profile (if appropriate).
- [ ] Copies of related news clips.
- [ ] Copies of appropriate additional background information, such as news releases, newsletters, an annual report, or a relevant article that you wrote.

One of the most important ingredients of any press kit, however, is a heavy dose of common sense. Don't:

➤ Stuff the folder with useless or irrelevant information.

➤ Try to put so much material in the kit that the covers will not close.

➤ Jam the kit into an envelope that is so "skin tight" that it's impossible to open without damaging the kit.

➤ Spend a lot of money on designing or producing the kit or its contents.

➤ While it is important for the finished product to look businesslike and professional, reporters will be more interested in being able to find and understand your story quickly, and less interested in looking at fancy or expensive graphics, pictures, or logos that get in the way of finding that story.

48 A Special Invitation

News Advisories

News advisories are used to invite editors and reporters to attend a planned event, activity, or scheduled announcement, such as a news conference. They are best sent several days prior to the event, and once again so they are received a day before the event is held.

■ CHECKLIST

You can take several steps to help ensure that news advisories about your project will result in media coverage:

- ☐ Become familiar with the news organizations that are important to you or your company and write the advisory so it addresses their interests and audiences.
- ☐ Summarize your announcement with an attention-getting headline.
- ☐ Write a succinct opening paragraph that captures the who, what, when, where, why, and how of your announcement.
- ☐ Highlight and explain the most interesting or newsworthy aspects of your project. Keep the copy focused and factual.
- ☐ Explain the significance or impact the announcement may have on the audiences of the news organizations that receive the release.
- ☐ Include appropriate facts, figures, and background information about the project or announcement.

NEWS ADVISORY:
INTERNET PRIVACY AND SECURITY

Event

News conference by Taxsoft, Inc. to announce the results of a national opinion poll which measures the public's concern about keeping personal and financial information private and secure on the Internet. The opinion poll was commissioned by Taxsoft, a software developer in Bethesda, Maryland.

Date/Time/Location

Monday, Nov. 17, 1997/12:00 P.M.
Comdex/Fall '97/Press Conference Room B
Media Facilities Tent, Pavilion #1
Las Vegas Convention Center, Las Vegas, NV

Background Information

➤ The Internet has a proven and continued vulnerability to vandalism, tampering and break-ins which can threaten the privacy and security of the personal and financial information which people place on Web sites.

➤ Hackers have tampered with or illegally accessed information on the Web sites of such security conscious institutions as the Pentagon, CIA, and FBI.

➤ By one estimate, there are more than 1,500 Web sites, on-line bulletin boards, and publications that provide hacking tips, tools, and advice to would be cyber-vandals. (*Source:* Fort Worth Star-Telegram)

➤ A presidential commission recently issued a report warning that the nation's computer networks are vulnerable to attack and sabotage.

➤ Companies around the world are expected to spend more than $6 billion this year to protect their computer networks from internal or external attacks. By the year 2000, that spending is expected to double to more than $12 billion. (*Source:* Dataquest) (Used with permission.)

☐ As needed, place your announcement within the context of trends or developments that affect your target audiences.

☐ Limit the length of the advisory to one single-spaced page.

☐ Include the name and phone number for reporters to call if they have questions about the advisory.

The news advisory on page 169 was used to alert the media about a scheduled news conference. More than a dozen editors and reporters attended the event.

49 It's Worth a Thousand Words

Pictures and Cutlines

In Chapter 13, I discussed the importance of using visuals to help tell your story to the media. When you send information to editors and reporters, what pictures can you provide that will illustrate your product, service, expertise, or announcement?

➤ Are you announcing your appointment to a new position? Enclose a head-and-shoulder shot of yourself with the news release.

➤ Are you seeking to publicize your company's new name or logo? Then send reporters a copy of the new logo as well.

In addition to attracting the attention of the media to your story, including an appropriate photo and descriptive caption (also known as a cutline) can also result in a larger story to accommodate the picture and encourage more people to read the story in the first place, since people are often attracted by pictures and graphics.

Before going to the expense of taking and sending a photo, however, it's wise to check with the publication to make sure they are interested in receiving it and whether they prefer color or black-and-white photos, slides, transparencies, or a digital version on computer disk or via e-mail.

50 I Was Born in a Log Cabin . . .

Biographical Profiles

Do you yearn to be the subject of a personality profile by your hometown newspaper, a national television network, or an important industry publication?

The secret for making it happen can be boiled down to three words: Don't be shy. After all, if you (or your public relations agency) don't tell news organizations why you'd make an interesting story, who will (except maybe your mother)?

Personality profiles are excellent ways to get the media to talk about your company, product, services, or expertise.

Gregory Slayton, the CEO of ClickAction, Inc. (formerly MySoftware Company), has an interesting and varied personal

FROM TIMBUKTU TO SILICON VALLEY: GREGORY SLAYTON HASN'T MET A DYING ORGANIZATION HE COULDN'T BRING BACK TO LIFE

Overview

Supervising a drought relief program for two million people near Timbuktu is the last place most entrepreneurs would think of to learn business management. But Gregory Slayton, 39, credits this experience as the foundation for his success in leading a struggling software company to become the ninth best performing U.S. stock last year.

Between Timbuktu and Silicon Valley, Slayton has learned how to turn dust into gold by successfully overcoming the mismanagement, limited resources, and disillusionment he encountered at a variety of organizations. These challenges provided him with valuable insights on how to turn a culturally diverse group of people into a world class team, and how to handle change and extreme pressure. It is this combination of Third World experience, Ivy league training, and tireless energy that makes Slayton one of the most interesting and successful young CEOs in Silicon Valley.

Formative Experiences

Manila Orphanage—Directed an inner-city orphanage in Manila, Philippines, giving hope to children who lived in and around one of the largest urban garbage dumps in the world (1984).

Timbuktu Drought Relief: Turned around a scandal plagued, multimillion-dollar, multinational drought relief program near Timbuktu for World Vision, an international humanitarian relief organization. Slayton's region won the "most improved country program" award (1985–88).

Life-Threatening Pressure: Slayton notes that "people talk about the pressure and uncertainty of Silicon Valley, where people lose their jobs if a company does badly. Those pressures don't compare to the threats we faced in Africa, where our trucks were frequently highjacked, people were held at gunpoint, and wrong decisions cost people their lives."

Turnaround Successes

MySoftware Company: Joined struggling MySoftware Company as president and CEO in Dec. 1997 and turned it into the

FROM TIMBUKTU TO
SILICON VALLEY *(Continued)*

ninth highest gaining U.S. stock in 1998. Overhauled its strategy, structure, senior team, and operating style. Launched one of the next Internet trends, e-prospecting for new customer leads, and partnered with Intuit, Netscape, Pitney Bowes, and others (1997–Present).

Paragraph International: Joined as president and chief operating officer when Paragraph International was struggling financially. Developed partnerships with Apple, Disney, IBM, Microsoft, and Mitsubishi. In 18 months, took what had been a $5 million company and sold it for $53 million to Silicon Graphics (1996–97).

Business Philosophy

Live and Die By Shareholder Value: Slayton ensures that all employees get sizable stock options, makes all employee bonuses (including his own) contingent upon the company meeting Wall Street's estimates, and makes all managers responsible for their own budgets.

Teach Them To Fish: Slayton believes that providing small business loans and financial incentives to businesspeople is the economic solution for developing countries. This conclusion from his Fulbright thesis has led him to devote significant time and money to such causes as Opportunity International, a nonprofit organization that helps start businesses in 25 Third World countries.

Two-Way Partnerships: Slayton invites key retailers to participate in MySoftware's new product development cycle to discover what will sell best. He also motivates retailers by making incentives increasingly more lucrative at higher volumes. This unique partnership strategy helped MySoftware win Staples' 1998 Partner of the Year award, prevailing over 160 suppliers, including Microsoft, Intuit, and Network Associates.

Sharing Experiences and Lessons Learned: Slayton believes in sharing the lessons he's learned. He has served as the subject of a Harvard Business School (HBS) case study, entitled "The Anatomy of a High-Tech Turnaround," and as a guest speaker for one of HBS's most popular courses, "Running and Growing a Small Company." He has also served as a panelist at MIT's Sloan Business School and at the University of Michigan Business School.

(continued)

FROM TIMBUKTU TO
SILICON VALLEY *(Continued)*

Other Experience

Worlds Inc: Co-founded Worlds Inc. Took company from zero to $80 million market valuation in 18 months. Established partnerships with IBM, Intel, and MGM, making Worlds Inc. the leader of 3D Internet technology (1994–95).

Paramount Studios: Served as vice president of business development and chief financial officer at Paramount's Technology Group. Responsible for sales of $15 million and for Paramount's Venture Capital portfolio, worth tens of millions of dollars (1993–94).

McKinsey & Company: Co-founded McKinsey & Company's Worldwide Multimedia Practice Group to serve the online needs of Fortune 500 firms (1990–93).

Education

Harvard Business School: Graduated with Distinction (1990).

Fulbright Scholarship: Master's in Asian studies. Wrote thesis challenging the International Monetary Fund's approach to lending in Southeast Asia (1984).

Dartmouth College: Graduated Magna Cum Laude with Faculty Honors in Economics (1981).

(Used with permission of ClickAction, Inc.)

---

history and I capitalized on it to help create additional coverage about the company. Working with the staff of his public relations agency, Ogilvy Public Relations Worldwide, we prepared the biographical profile shown on pages 172–174 and sent it to selected news organizations suggesting they do a story about Slayton.

The strategy worked and has led to at least three profile stories, including one by CNN's financial news network and *The Wall Street Journal*.

51 Everyone Is Entitled to My Opinion

Op–Eds and Bylined Articles

Op-eds and bylined articles are opinion pieces published by newspapers and magazines that explain and discuss an individual's viewpoints, observations, or experiences. They are also excellent vehicles for establishing or reinforcing your expertise on a topic and can be used effectively to position yourself as an authority on a particular topic.

It's important to remember, however, that most local newspapers prefer that submissions be made by people living in their readership area. Also, the space that publications reserve for these articles is quite limited, so you should read several issues of the publication to determine which topics they are the most interested in covering, and ask them to send you a copy of their guidelines before you write or submit your article.

■ CHECKLIST

The best op-eds and bylined articles:

- ☐ Provide readers with a new, interesting, or unusual perspective on an issue, cause, or topic.
- ☐ Help educate or inform readers about a topic that concerns them.
- ☐ Provide readers with information or lessons they probably would not receive anywhere else.
- ☐ Help link the topic to local or national events, trends, or developments.

☐ Are based on your experience or expertise.

☐ Address the needs or concerns of the readers of the publication.

☐ Are usually 500 to 1,500 words in length (depends on the publication).

☐ Are subject to editing and condensing with or without your approval.

☐ Are submitted to one publication at a time for their consideration.

The best way to find out the topics and issues that will make the best subjects for an op-ed or bylined article is simply to read through several recent issues of the publication where you'd like to have your article appear, pay close attention to what topics are attracting the attention of other news organizations, or try to get a sense about what the hottest topics may be during the next few days or weeks.

Once you've chosen a topic, however, don't delay preparing a draft and sending it to the editor: your timing can be crucial. As the saying goes, nothing is as boring as yesterday's news.

After your op-ed has been published, don't be shy about making people aware about it.

➤ Tell your friends, family coworkers, clients, and customers.

➤ Send copies of the article to people who might have missed it when it came out.

➤ If appropriate, include it in the press kit that you send to journalists, and in the marketing materials you send to new business prospects. You also can place it on your Web site, mention it in your bio, and so forth. [See the Resources section for a sample byline article.]

52 Dear Sir:

Letters to the Editor

Writing letters to the editor is a time-honored way to express views, comment on current events, seek to correct mistakes by the media, and respond to the opinions of editors and other readers.

The correspondence is also an easy and affordable way to establish or reinforce your credibility or expertise on an issue while getting free publicity for yourself or your company.

For example, shortly after *BusinessWeek* ran an article about the benefits and advantages of buying insurance on-line, the magazine published a letter in its "Readers Report" from Michael P. Hanley, a founding principal of First Financial Resources in Walnut Creek, California.

Hanley took issue with the publication, writing that "Buying insurance on the Web is no less costly than buying from a broker or an agent who has access to the same carrier."

He noted that his company offers the same products as online companies at the same price. According to Hanley, however, "the difference is that we follow through and the customers can rest knowing that ownership, premium payment, and beneficiary are properly coordinated with their wills and estate plans."

Given the volume of mail that newspapers and magazine receive (*The New York Times* gets about 1,700 letters, faxes, and e-mail every day), there is no guarantee that any letter you send will be used and, even if it is selected for publication, it can be edited and condensed without your approval.

■ CHECKLIST

Follow these suggestions to help ensure that your letter is used and printed the way you wrote it:

☐ Respond as quickly as possible to the story or event you are writing about. Check with the publication on how they prefer to receive letters from readers—mail, fax, e-mail, overnight delivery, or by messenger.

☐ Keep it short, from 25 to 250 words depending on the publication.

☐ Remember that whatever you write may be edited or shortened by the editor before it is printed.

☐ Keep your comments focused on the story or event you are responding to.

☐ While it can be appropriate to refer to your expertise or experience, do not turn your letter into a commercial for you or your company.

☐ Read the letters or comments in recent issues of the publication so you can review the style, format, length, and content of the letters they publish.

☐ Before you send your letter, be sure to read it out loud to help you catch any grammatical or other errors.

☐ Check with the newspaper or magazine for their submission guidelines.

53 Lights, Camera, Action!

Video News Releases

If you watch the local news on television with any regularity, the chances are pretty good you've seen a video news release and did not realize what it was.

Video news releases (or VNRs) appear to be just like any one of the hundreds of other news reports you've seen on the television station. They are complete 90-second stories that hundreds of TV stations across the country air in whole or in part during their regular local newscasts.

But there are several important differences between a VNR and other TV news reports:

➤ The story is usually about some aspect of the products, services, or activities of a corporation or organization.

➤ You probably don't recognize the name of the reporter, or have never seen him or her on screen.

➤ Every aspect of the story, including research, preparation of the script, and producing and editing the report, was handled not by the news department at the TV station that broadcast the story, but by a private company that produced the VNR.

➤ The news report has been paid for by a corporation or organization, usually to help publicize the product, service, or activity that was the subject of the video news release.

Karen Friedman, who was a TV reporter with a major network affiliate in Philadelphia, notes that VNRs are most often used by small or midsized newsrooms with limited staffs and resources, while bigger newsrooms shoot their own videos and tend to rely on stories that are sent to them from the TV networks and satellite news feeds. The larger stations, however, may incorporate portions of a VNR into their stories, or delete and replace the reporter who appears on the VNR with one of their own.

■ CHECKLIST

A VNR can help tell your story to television audiences across the country, if you have:

☐ A story of interest to millions of people that can be localized for specific television audiences.

☐ Good pictures to help show your story. Remember, this is television, which depends on visuals.

☐ Enough money. Typical VNRs can cost anywhere from $15,000 to $20,000 to produce and distribute.

☐ Enough time and patience. Allowing for research, script preparation, shooting schedules, and editing time, it can take either several days to several weeks to produce and complete the finished piece.

To the uninitiated, the whole process of putting together a VNR may sound interesting and exciting, and as close to being a Hollywood director as we mere mortals are ever likely to get. Frankly, I felt that same anticipation, sense of excitement, and visions of video grandeur until I produced a VNR for a client.

The novelty quickly wore off as I tried to resolve differences between what the client wanted to show and what the video production company said was newsworthy footage. I sat for several hours in an editing booth working with producers and directors to select the best pictures while ensuring the finished piece did not run over its allotted time of 90 seconds.

In the end, I found that helping to direct, produce, and edit a VNR is much like hitting your head against a wall: it feels so good when you're done!

But for all the frustrations and aggravations, there was also a tremendous sense of accomplishment and fulfillment, knowing that the story I had worked on would be sent to TV newsrooms across the country and might be seen by millions of viewers. More often than not, that's exactly what happened with several of the VNRs I have done for clients, including:

➤ MCI, which wanted to publicize its role in the growing telecommuting trend.

➤ The American Association of Blood Banks, which sought to explain to the public the steps it was taking to help guard the nation's blood supply against the AIDS epidemic.

➤ The Society of Manufacturing Engineers, which launched a nationwide campaign to encourage students to consider an engineering career.

In addition to providing you with a polished, broadcast-quality video news report, most VNR production or distribution companies can make arrangements to track the usage of the report; provide you with documentation about which stations aired all or parts of the VNR, when the story was broadcast; and tell you the estimated number of people who saw it. For an additional fee, some firms can also get you copies of the "air checks"—copies of the story as it was used on each TV station.

VNRs not only promote corporations and organizations, but also are important to the television stations that receive them. These packaged reports serve as a valuable and free source of news programming for budget-strapped stations that cannot afford the time or staff to produce the same stories on their own, or as a source of story ideas for their own reporters.

Indeed, if properly and effectively done, VNRs have something to offer everyone: news coverage for the companies that sponsor them, a key source of programming for the TV stations that get them; and news information for the audiences that watch them. (To see a sample script of a VNR, please visit my Web site at www.edwardsegal.com.)

54 All News, All the Time

Audio News Releases

An audio news release (ANR) is similar to a video news release (see Chapter 53), but is produced and distributed for use on radio stations. Instead of using pictures, the ANR relies on narration and soundbites. The finished piece is nearly identical to a "real" news report you'd hear on your local radio station.

The cost to produce and distribute an audio news release is about $4,500, according to North American Networks, Inc, which includes editing, narration, and soundbites of you or your spokesperson.

Following is the transcript of an ANR that was produced and distributed by North American Network, Inc., for Ford and the American Automobile Association concerning their jointly sponsored student auto skills competition.

(WEINER OPEN):

With cars becoming ever-more high-tech, the skills required to service them are changing dramatically. Given the trend, tomorrow's technicians will need more math and computer smarts than elbow grease. Yesterday [Monday, June 21], one-hundred of America's top auto-service students faced off in Washington, DC in the National Finals of the 1999 Ford/ AAA Student Auto Skills contest—the "national spelling bee" of the auto-service world. Jim Kolstad, Vice President of Public and Government Affairs for AAA, explains . . .

(KOLSTAD):

ACCORDING TO THE LABOR STATISTICS, WE'VE GOT A SHORTAGE OF ABOUT 60-THOUSAND TRAINED AUTOMOTIVE TECHNICIANS. THE PEOPLE THAT ARE AT THIS CONTEST WILL FILL SOME OF THAT GAP. BUT HOPEFULLY, THERE ARE GOING TO BE MANY OTHER YOUNGSTERS THAT ARE INCENTIVIZED BY THE CHALLENGE, BUT ALSO BY THE SCHOLARSHIPS AND PRIZES THAT ARE ASSOCIATED WITH THE FORD/AAA CONTEST.

(WEINER BRIDGE):

Also involved with the contest was Tom Eastman, Technical Training Manager for the Ford Customer Service Division . . .

(continued)

(EASTMAN):

FORD/AAA STUDENT AUTO SKILLS COMPETITION GOES A LONG WAY TO HELP MEET THE DEMANDS FOR TECHNICIANS. THESE STUDENTS ARE ALL STATE CHAMPIONS; THEY'VE ALL BEEN GIVEN SCHOLARSHIPS FOR EDUCATIONAL INSTITUTIONS THAT HAVE AUTOMOTIVE PROGRAMS.

(WEINER CLOSE):

This year's winning team was Mark Jones and Shawn Upchurch of North Lamar High School in Paris, Texas; they will receive over 65-thousand dollars in scholarships and prizes. In Washington, this is Mike Weiner reporting.
[Used with permission.]

55 You're Probably Wondering Why I Called You Here Today

News Conferences

News conferences can be the easiest and most effective way to meet with and answer the questions of as many reporters as possible at one time about a story or news announcement. Indeed, the very fact that you've scheduled a news conference can help raise the media's interest in covering your story since they assume you'd schedule the event only if you had important news to discuss.

News conferences are also one of the riskiest way to generate news coverage, since any number of late-breaking or more important stories may prevent reporters from attending.

A case in point is a news conference that I arranged in Washington concerning an important local transportation project; it promised to be one of the best-covered news stories that day:

> ➤ The Associated Press had listed the conference on its daily calendar of scheduled news events.

> ➤ Every major television station in the region had agreed to send a reporter and news crew.

> ➤ The two daily newspapers had given me the names of the journalists who would attend.

> ➤ Several radio stations promised they would send reporters.

> ➤ But when it came time for the news conference to start, none of the reporters who said they'd attend were in the room.

Tragically, earlier that morning a Maryland state trooper had been gunned down during a routine traffic stop, and every news organization in the region was, understandably, covering the story.

While I scrambled to send information about our announcement to the reporters who had been scheduled to attend our event, my efforts were to no avail. The murder of the state trooper was big news for several days, dominating all local news coverage. It was impossible to get the media to focus on anything else.

Sometimes the best way to ensure reporters will attend a news conference is to take the news conference to the reporters.

One of my high-tech clients was scheduled to unveil a new version of its software at COMDEX, the prestigious computer show in Las Vegas that attracts tens of thousands of visitors and hundreds of editors and reporters. Working with show officials, I scheduled and promoted a news conference at the COMDEX press center to discuss the software. [See Chapter 48.] The event was held in a room adjacent to where reporters picked up press passes, press kits, free food, and wrote their stories.

When I entered the room to begin the press conference, more than a dozen editors and reporters were in their seats, ready to listen to my opening remarks and to ask questions about the announcement.

While it is impossible to guard against the unexpected, you can take steps to ensure that your news conference goes off without a hitch:

➤ Make sure your topic is newsworthy enough to warrant a full-scale news conference, and that it concerns a timely topic of interest to a large audience.

➤ Select a location that is easily accessible by reporters.

➤ Bring or have access to good visuals (charts, graphs, etc.) to show your story or demonstrate your announcement.

➤ Schedule the conference early in the day: Between 10 A.M. and noon is best.

➤ Shorter is always better: the conference should not last more than 15 or 20 minutes.

➤ Have refreshments available for reporters.

➤ If possible, notify the media about the conference two to three days ahead of time, and call reporters the night before or morning of the event to remind them.

➤ Begin the conference with a brief opening statement (3 to 5 minutes), and then spend the balance of the time answering reporters' questions.

➤ Bring and distribute copies of the opening statement and any appropriate background information (press kits, fact sheet, etc.).

➤ Check out the site of the news conference several days ahead of time.

➤ Make sure you have ordered any equipment or supplies you need, and that the equipment is in working order prior to the start of the news conference.

➤ Have a sign-in sheet for reporters so you can track attendance.

➤ If necessary, post signs in building lobbies, hallways, and so forth to direct reporters to the site of the news conference.

➤ Arrive early to ensure that all arrangements are in place and that everything is in working order.

As a former press secretary to several members of Congress and PR adviser to hundreds of companies, I know that many business executives and government officials have a common interest in generating news coverage about their respective projects, activities, and accomplishments.

To help call public attention to one of the least known programs within the National Park Service, I worked with the U.S. Department of the Interior to stage a news conference about the Rivers, Trails and Conservation Assistance program (RTCA).

RTCA serves as a facilitator to help communities set goals, resolve difficult issues, and reach consensus about the conservation and management of important land and water resources that are outside the control of the federal government. It's also one of the smallest programs within the National Park Service: its 80 employees work in 22 offices across the country with a budget of about $7 million a year. In the past 10 years, RTCA has helped over 1,000 communities across the country implement an estimated 400 locally guided conservation projects without the use of federal funds, management, or ownership.

Why take the time, trouble, and effort to arrange a news conference? Why not simply issue a news release instead?

D. Thomas Ross, assistant director of Recreation and Conservation for the National Park Service, said, "We thought the news conference would generate more news coverage if there was an opportunity for some interaction between the media and the Secretary of the Interior than if we just distributed a news release. In this instance, the news conference was also an opportunity for him to discuss his interests in local conservation efforts, and to meet with local leaders and supporters of our program."

The purpose of the news conference was to have Secretary of the Interior Bruce Babbitt announce that the National Park Service would help local communities in 46 states with $250 million worth of locally controlled conservation projects over a 12-month period.

■ YOUR NEWS CONFERENCE CHECKLIST

Of all the tools of the trade you may use to generate news coverage about yourself or your organization, a news conference will likely be the activity that will require the most time, resources, and planning.

To give you a better idea about the work that can be involved and the attention to detail that is required to successfully stage one of these events, following are highlights of the 60-point task list I prepared as I worked with the National Park Service to hold a news conference in Charleston, South Carolina, for Interior Secretary Bruce Babbitt:

- ☐ Finalize/approve date, time, location, staging, and details of event.
- ☐ Finalize/approve target audiences.
- ☐ Finalize/approve the geographic focus of the desired news coverage.
- ☐ Finalize/approve themes and messages to be communicated to the target audiences.
- ☐ Finalize/approve list of participants and speakers.
- ☐ Prepare draft press materials, including:
  - ☐ News advisory.
  - ☐ News release.
  - ☐ Fact sheet.
  - ☐ Press kit.
- ☐ Draft suggested soundbites for participants.
- ☐ Research/obtain media lists.
- ☐ Script event (who will say what, where they will stand, etc.).
- ☐ Issue invitations to participants and speakers.

☐ Approve all press kit materials.

☐ Distribute news advisory via mail and fax.

☐ Distribute news release via U.S. Newswire.

☐ Post news advisory on RTCA Web site.

☐ Finalize/approve draft press materials.

☐ Finalize/approve RTCA soundbites.

☐ Finalize/approve script of event.

☐ Prepare/finalize remarks for participants.

☐ Confirm attendance of invited participants.

☐ Obtain copies of remarks to be made by speakers.

☐ Place follow-up calls to selected editors and reporters to encourage them to attend.

☐ Retain print and TV media monitoring services.

☐ Retain local photographer to document event.

☐ Produce/assemble press kits.

☐ Confirm that event is listed on wire service daybooks and TV and newspaper listings of scheduled news events.

☐ Visit site of news conference.

☐ Confirm physical arrangements (podium, PA system, signage, etc.).

☐ Finalize staging and visuals.

☐ Conduct walk-through of event with participants or their representatives.

☐ Deliver all press materials, charts, graphs, and so forth to local hotel.

☐ Place reminder calls to key news organizations in the Carolinas about the event.

☐ Arrive two hours early to set up site.

☐ Hold news conference.

☐ Distribute press materials to media at event.

☐ Distribute news release via mail and fax immediately after the event (budget permitting).

☐ Distribute news release via U.S. Newswire.

- [ ] Seek to arrange press interviews with RTCA and National Park Service officials.
- [ ] Post news release and fact sheet on RTCA Web site.
- [ ] Clean up site after event.
- [ ] Document news coverage of event.
- [ ] Send thank-you letters to speakers and representatives of participating organizations.
- [ ] Prepare follow-up report about the news conference.

The weeks of planning and hard work leading up to the news conference paid off. Several local news organizations in Charleston attended the event, including a local TV station and a daily paper. The Associated Press carried a story about the announcement; and an article about the news conference, together with a large color photograph, made the front page of the *Post and Courier* daily newspaper in Charleston.

The text of the news release that was issued by the Department of Interior About Babbitt's Announcement is on page 190.

■ A NEW WRINKLE

Thanks to the Internet, it's now possible to have a successful news conference without having a single reporter show up. By holding an "e-conference" at your Web site, you can invite and have any number of reporters and editors see and hear the event, show them a video, slides, or other graphics to help illustrate your points, allow reporters to ask questions via their computer keyboards, and provide them with all the information they need to file stories about your news conference. For more information on how to stage an e-conference, see the listing for Medialink in the Resources section of this book.

BABBITT ANNOUNCES $250 MILLION WORTH OF CONSERVATION PROJECTS

WASHINGTON—Secretary of the Interior Bruce Babbitt announced today that the National Park Service will help local communities in 46 states with $250 million worth of locally-controlled conservation projects this year.

The 209 projects will be started, continued or completed through the NPS Rivers, Trails and Conservation Assistance (RTCA) program. National Park Service Director Robert G. Stanton joined Secretary Babbitt at the announcement to begin National Park Service Week.

The conservation projects include 1,100 miles of new trails, 1,200 miles of additional river corridors and 35,000 acres of expanded parkland and open spaces. Eighty-seven projects will begin this year, work will continue at 52 other sites and 87 projects will be completed.

The RTCA, one of the smallest programs in the National Park Service, facilitates local communities in helping conserve and manage important land and water resources which are outside the federal government. More than 1,000 national and local partners have worked with RTCA on the projects in the past decade. Partners include nonprofit organizations and local, county and state governments.

"This program is one of the best examples we have of making government work better and more efficiently. It helps local communities and provides recreation opportunities for millions of people," said Babbitt.

At the news conference, Babbitt presented the RTCA program with a Hammer Award from Vice President Gore, in support of the vice president's principles of reinventing government.

"I am pleased to announce this Hammer Award for the RTCA program," said Vice President Gore. "This program is a great example of the federal government working in a partnership with local governments to help our communities."

56 Say Cheese!

Photo Ops

A step below formal news conferences (see Chapter 55), photo ops (short for photo opportunities) are events or pictures that are staged for the benefit of photographers and TV news crews. The goal is to identify, create, or provide the media with attention-getting visuals that will be shown on TV news programs or used in wire service, newspaper, or magazine photos.

While photo ops require as much careful planning as news conferences, they can be faster to arrange or schedule, don't require the preparation or delivery of formal remarks, and can be much more effective by letting you demonstrate your point, rather than just talking about it (see Chapter 13).

HALL OF SHAME: TOO MUCH FIREPOWER

It's no secret that public officials like to stage "photo opportunities" to help get their picture in the paper and on the television. But sometimes the pictures may not send the message they want to convey.

Vice President Dan Quayle wanted to demonstrate his concern for human rights in San Salvador, and his staff arranged for him to meet with officials in the country to discuss the matter.

At the meeting, Quayle was handed and held up a Soviet-made flamethrower that had been captured from the guerrillas. The result was a photo at odds with the message he and his staff wanted to convey.

Photo ops are often used by politicians to help show their concern for victims of floods, fires, and other disasters by touring the devastated areas and meeting with survivors; by celebrities and athletes who want to illustrate their compassionate side by visiting with hospitalized children or residents of nursing homes; by corporations who seek to create news coverage about their products, such as a new car model rolling off the assembly line for the first time; and by entrepreneurs who try to publicize new technologies or inventions by demonstrating them at trade shows.

57 How to Be in Two Places at Once

Satellite Media Tours

Thanks to modern science, it's possible for you to be interviewed by television reporters in scores of different cities across the country or around the world on the same day without having to get on an airplane to see them. The technology that lets you do this is not a transporter from *Star Trek*, but a satellite media tour (SMT).

An SMT is a series of one-on-one interviews with television reporters or the anchors of a news show either for live broadcast or later use in a news story. While you sit in the comfort of a television studio or remote location, technicians bring online journalists who had previously agreed to participate in the tour and to interview you for a few minutes.

Depending on the topic and the interest among television stations, it's possible for you to be interviewed by as many as 20 stations within the course of a typical three-hour tour. To make your story as interesting as possible, stations often ask that you demonstrate or send videotape that shows your product or service being used.

Ross Products, a division of Abbott Laboratories, used an SMT to great effect to publicize the introduction of its new snack food for diabetics, Ensure Glucerna Bars. Targeting both English and Hispanic TV stations, the two company spokespersons conducted 30 interviews, 17 in English and 13 in Spanish, resulting in more than 100 stories. The SMT was produced by DS Simon Productions in New York.

Bill Wolfson, Ross' marketing communications manager, told *PRWeek* that an SMT is an effective PR tool because "you can control the message with a higher degree of precision. In a live situation, the producer can't edit out our brand references."

He said he was so pleased with the results of the SMT that "we plan to do this again with other products. And not just with new products, but with nutritionally related healthcare issues. The bang for the buck is obvious."

■ CHECKLIST

Medialink Inc., which has arranged numerous SMTs for companies and organizations, offers the following advice for those who arrange or do these tours. This advice is also applicable to live or taped interviews with individual television stations. (See Chapter 38.)

Define Your Message

☐ Determine the major points you want to make during each interview.

☐ Make sure you or your spokesperson understands the objectives of your tour, what to stress and which points should be answered delicately.

Dress the Way You Want Your Peers to See You

☐ Blues and grays always work best, giving an aura of professionalism.

☐ Avoid herringbone and other patterns in suits because they can cause electronic confusion for the camera.

☐ A simple stripe or muted design is acceptable but solids work best. Women should wear a jacket or a blouse with buttons to allow for a lavalier microphone. Never wear black or white clothing on camera.

The Natural Look Always Applies

☐ If you wear glasses, wear glasses on-camera. Chrome or metal frames sometimes cause problems as do certain lenses.

☐ Angle your glasses down slightly and try to use simple frames like light tortoise shell.

Avoid Elaborate Jewelry

☐ Avoid fancy bracelets and necklaces since they may cause flash or noise interference with microphones. A tailored look is preferable.

Simple Makeup

☐ Makeup is vital for any on-camera appearance. Medialink's experts recommend keeping it simple and making sure the makeup is well blended.

☐ Be certain to check your entire look before the tour and make certain your makeup is retouched if there are a number of "takes."

Don't Wear New Clothes

☐ You should be comfortable in your outfit, so try never to wear anything new to an on-camera appearance.

☐ Check the mirror before your appearance to make sure you look the way you want to appear during a session.

☐ If your appearance requires you to sit, be certain you have checked your appearance in the mirror in that position.

58 If It's Tuesday, This Must Be Cleveland

Multicity Media Tours

The proliferation of and our dependency on telecommunications technology such as phones, videoconferencing, and satellite tours (see Chapter 57) have almost rendered obsolete the need to hopscotch between cities to meet with the media.

I say "almost" because there are people who still depend on multicity media tours to help tell their stories to the widest possible audience. The list includes:

➤ Politicians seeking election.

➤ Authors touting their books.

➤ Experts on sundry topics explaining their views.

➤ Business executives unveiling new products or services.

➤ Hollywood stars seeking to publicize their latest movie.

For them, there is no getting around the need to travel from city to city to appear as a guest on regional or national television interview news programs and local talk shows; make in-studio appearances on radio stations; hold a news conference; or meet with a magazine or newspaper writer who is working on a personality profile.

For some, the multicity media tours are a necessary evil, since the visits can be:

➤ Time consuming (a day of travel between each city, depending on your destination).

> Expensive ($1,000–$2,000 or more per city, including airfare, lodging, meals, car rental, taxis, etc.).

> Physically exhausting (10- to 12-hour days of travel, meetings, and interviews).

If this kind of media tour is the best or only way for you to tell your story, then it is important that you:

> Plan and coordinate your appointments for maximum effectiveness.

> Prepare an adequate budget that covers all possible expenses.

> Purchase airline tickets as soon as possible to take advantage of any cost savings.

> Get as much rest as you can beforehand.

> Be in good physical shape.

HALL OF FAME: MEDIA TOURS ON THE INTERNET

The Internet may have as big an impact on media tours as it is beginning to have on news conferences (see Chapter 55). To help promote his new book, Michael Dell, CEO of Dell Computer, used a Cyber Media Tour™ (CMT) to conduct a series of online interviews with print and broadcast journalists. Sitting in a studio in Dallas, Texas, Dell answered questions that had been previously submitted from reporters. His answers were broadcast live over the Internet so news organizations and consumers alike could learn more about his new book. CMT is a service offered by Medialink, Inc. (see Resources).

59 Extra! Extra! Read All about It!

Getting the Word Out

Over the years, I've received more news coverage for clients from reporters I did not know, than from those I did. That's because a good story is like bait: it will encourage reporters to come to you.

While you cannot know every editor or reporter at every news organization (see Chapter 5), you can learn how to put that "bait" in front of as many journalists as possible who are likely to be interested in your story.

You can either take care of this important task yourself, or pay someone else to do it for you.

If the number of news organizations on your press list is manageable (say, under 100) then perhaps you will decide to do the mailing labels, copying, folding, stuffing, and mailing yourself.

Targeting 100 news organizations may be overkill however, depending on your news.

If, for example, you want to invite the media to a news conference, then all you may need to do is simply call the assignment editors of the major TV stations, radio stations, and newspapers in your area. And don't forget to give a call to the daybook editors of the nearest wire service bureaus, who can place information about your event on their daily or weekly calendar of listings, which they send to all the major news organizations in the region.

For help in compiling your media lists, or at least to get an idea about how many news organizations you might want to put on your mailing list, you can consult several good reference sources, including:

➤ A series of newspaper, magazine, radio, and TV directories published by Bacon's Information, Inc. (see Resources).

➤ Hudson's, which publishes a variety of guides to the media (see the Resources section).

But if you need to notify as many news organizations as possible about your news or event, several companies and services can help you get the job done:

➤ Private news wire services such as PR Newswire, U.S. Newswire, and Businesswire who, for a fee, will send your release electronically to the different categories of news organizations you specify, or nationwide to thousands of editors and reporters (see Resources).

➤ Full-service mailing houses, including PIMS and Media Distribution Sevices, who will send your press materials to their own constantly updated media lists, and handle everything, from printing to mailing for you (see Resources).

Whichever way you decide to go, keep the following points in mind:

➤ Since the features and costs for these and other services are always subject to change, be sure to contact them or their Web sites for the latest and most up-to-date information, and cost-compare to decide which is best for you based on your needs and budget.

➤ Use a heavy dose of common sense in determining how much time, effort, and money to spend in distributing your news release. If you send releases to people who, common sense would tell you, will have absolutely no interest in reading it, then you are wasting both your time and theirs. And remember that different reporters have different preferences for how they like to receive information—phone, fax, e-mail, or snail mail.

One of the best "do it yourself" examples I know of paid off in not one, but several newspaper stories about Ronald

L. Culberson, self-described "director of everything" of Funsulting, Etc., a business consulting firm in Herndon, Virginia. Culberson, a former social worker at a hospice, shows corporations and organizations how to use humor and fun in the workplace to help increase morale, creativity, and productivity.

To generate news coverage about his services, he mailed a press kit to the attention of the "Business Editor" at *The Washington Post*. The kit was accompanied by the following self-effacing, almost apologetic letter that was addressed to no one in particular:

> *Dear Sir/Madam:*
>
> *I know you get swamped with information on a daily basis. If you think this is one more bit of information that you don't need, please feel free to throw this packet into the trash immediately.*
>
> *If, however, you are in need of someone with an expertise in the value of humor and fun, please feel free to contact me or file this information where you can find it for future reference.*
>
> *I appreciate your taking the time to review my materials and I look forward to the opportunity to talk with you about my work.*

Shortly after Culberson sent the press kit to *The Washington Post*:

➤ The letter led to an interview by a reporter from the paper.

➤ That interview resulted in a flattering profile and several photos of Culberson in the business section of the *Post* with the following headline and subhead: The Cheerman Reports to the Bored: Ron Culberson Gets Attention with His Funsulting Tips to Make Work More Enjoyable.

➤ The story in the *Post* was picked up and reprinted by several daily newspapers in California, Florida, Kansas, and Minnesota.

HALL OF SHAME: DON'T GO OVERBOARD

Sometimes the best (and least embarrassing) way to get information to the media is to simply deliver it yourself. This thought probably occurred to the staff of Sen. Barbara Boxer (D-Calif.) after they tried to send an announcement promoting a news event to reporters at the *Los Angeles Times*.

Even though the newspaper is located only two blocks away from the senator's office in downtown L.A., the lawmaker's staff sent the announcement by Federal Express. Unfortunately, the package did not arrive at the offices of the *Los Angeles Times* until two hours *after* the event was held.

Under the headline "The Wonders of Technology," Steve Harvey did a story about the delivery snafu in his "Only in L.A." column. He asked whether the announcement traveled hundreds of miles across the country "by way of Memphis, the company's home base" before it could be delivered only a few minutes' walking distance from where it was sent in the first place. After all of that, it didn't even get there in time to be of any help in promoting the event.

60 Do I Have a Story for You!

Story Pitch Calls and Letters

As important as news releases are to tell your story to the media (see Chapter 45), some people are more comfortable sending a letter or making a phone call to editors and reporters instead. And sometimes the relatively dry aspects of the who, what, when, where, why, and how of a traditional news release may not do justice to the drama, action, emotion, or unusual human interest angle of your story.

In these instances, consider sending a story pitch letter to the media or making a story pitch call to journalists.

These one- or two-page letters or brief phone calls explain the importance or significance of news hooks, story angles, announcements or events, and encourage the reporters to do stories about them.

Some organizations, to generate as much news coverage about their activities and causes as possible, ask their members to contact local editors and reporters who may be interested in a local angle to a national story. For example, the National Alliance for the Mentally Ill (NAMI) posted a generic story pitch letter on its Web site, and urged people to help place local stories tied to its nationwide effort to end discrimination against people with severe mental illness.

NAMI provided its members with advice and guidance along with the following story pitch letter. (Used with permission.)

Consider replacing one or both of the success stories below with the story(ies) of a local individual who has been treated for a brain disorder. If possible, offer to introduce the reporter or news director to the individual(s) for the development of a feature on the treatments available for brain disorders. You may also want to supplement this letter with one or more of the fact sheets on individual brain disorders that are provided in this kit.

[Date]
[Name]
[Title]
[Media Outlet]
[Address]
[City, State, Zip]

Dear [Name]:

Daphne has experienced schizophrenia for ten years and once even attempted suicide. After two years of treatment with a new medication, she is teaching public school part-time and living independently.

(continued)

Alex, who has obsessive-compulsive disorder (OCD), was obsessed with the idea that the CIA was following him. Treatment helped him control his thoughts. He is now studying accounting in college.

These are just two of the many success stories that have been made possible by recent advances in the understanding, diagnosis, and treatment of brain disorders.

In any given year, about 2.8 percent of adults in the U.S., or five million Americans, suffer from a severe form of one of the following brain disorders—schizophrenia, panic disorder, OCD, bipolar disorder (manic-depressive illness), and major depression.

In [city/town] alone, [number] people suffer from brain disorders. Left untreated, disorders of the brain may profoundly disrupt a person's ability to think, feel, and relate to others and to his or her environment.

Fortunately, treatment of brain disorders is available, and it works. In fact, there are impressive success rates for the treatment of severe forms of brain disorders with medications and other therapies. According to the National Institute of Mental Health, the current success rate for treating schizophrenia is 60 percent; panic disorder is successfully treated 70 to 90 percent of the time; treatment of OCD is successful 75 percent of the time; bipolar disorder (manic-depressive illness) has an 80 to 90 percent treatment success rate; and major depression has a 70 to 80 percent treatment success rate. And, as illustrated above, people who are treated for brain disorders can lead healthy, productive lives.

For the millions of Americans affected by brain disorders, it is vital that the public be made aware that brain disorders are biologically based physical disorders that can be treated. I would very much like to meet with you to introduce you to the [city/town] affiliate of the National Alliance for the Mentally Ill (NAMI) and provide you with additional background information on science and treatment issues related to brain disorders.

Enclosed for your information are [fact sheets on brain disorders as well as background information on NAMI]. I will call you in a few days to see if we can set up a time to meet. In the meantime, if you have any questions, please don't hesitate to call me at [insert your phone number].

Sincerely,

[your name]

61 All Your News That's Fit to Print

Newsletters

If your company or organization sends a newsletter only to clients and customers, then you're omitting an important audience from the distribution list: the media.

Most editors, reporters, and columnists are always on the lookout for new story leads, article ideas, and reliable sources of information about the topics and issues they cover. That's why it makes sense to send a copy of your latest printed or e-mail newsletter to the journalists who have done stories about you in the past, who follow developments in your industry or profession, or who might want to write about you in the future.

Sending newsletters to the media is a good way to get "more bang for the buck" out of the work you or your staff have put into the newsletter in the first place. The information in your newsletter may also be perceived by reporters as being less intrusive than sending story pitch letters or "pestering" them with story ideas over the telephone (see Chapter 60). If you have a Web site, consider posting the text of the newsletter, as well as an archive of past issues, but only if you are willing to share the contents with the rest of the world!

All newsletters are not created equal, so carefully review your publication to determine whether its content will be of interest to journalists in the first place. Go over the copy with a fine-tooth comb to ensure that it does not contain anything you don't want reporters to see, such as company gossip, embarrassing or questionable photos, information about your competitors, and so forth.

HALL OF SHAME: IF IT'S TOO GOOD TO BE TRUE, THE PRESS WILL SHOW THAT IT ISN'T

The credibility of your research is just as important as any facts or figures that research comes up with.

A newsletter issued by the Princeton Dental Resource Center reported the results of a study that found that chocolate might help fight cavities. Reporters at *The New York Times* discovered that the study had been financed by the Mars candy company, and the newsmaking cavity fighting claims quickly lost their credibility.

Finally, if you have any doubts whether reporters would be interested in receiving your newsletter in the first place, just ask them. And always remove them promptly from the distribution list if they say they want to stop receiving it.

62 Your Own Crystal Ball

Editorial Calendars

Wouldn't it be wonderful if you could find out in advance when a newspaper or magazine was planning to run a story, special issue, or supplement about a particular topic in which you had expertise?

Armed with that information, you could then:

➤ Decide whether being included in that story would be a good fit with your own efforts to get your 15 minutes of fame.

➤ Contact the appropriate editor or reporter to let them know about your interest and availability in being interviewed for their story.

➤ Offer to provide them with a copy of your news releases or other background information they may need for their article.

➤ Seek to arrange to be interviewed by the reporter for their story.

Well, you're in luck!

All that information and more is available in the so-called editorial calendars that thousands of publications issue on a regular basis or post on their Web sites.

The calendars, which are used to help sell advertising in that particular issue, include such details as a brief description of the story opportunity; when the article is scheduled to run; how much lead time you have; name, contact, and Web site information; and an overview of the newspaper or magazine.

The two easiest ways to obtain this information is to either pick up your phone or surf the Internet:

1. If you already know which publications you'd like to be quoted in, then it is a simple matter of calling the news organizations and asking them to send you a copy of their editorial calendar.

2. If you want to cast a wider net for story opportunities, however, simply enter the words "editorial calendar" on your favorite Web site search engine, then click your way through the results.

As usual, there are those who will, for a fee, be glad to do this homework for you.

There is, for example, www.edcals.com on the Internet, a service of Bacon's Information Service and Media Map. Using your keywords, it can search thousands of upcoming issues of publications within a few seconds, and report back to you with the deadline, contact, and other information you need to help take advantage of each story opportunity (see Resources).

Part V

First, You Have to Get Their Attention

News Hooks and Story Angles

63 Grand Openings

Start a Company or Organization

Generating news coverage about the start of your new company or organization can help ensure that potential customers, clients, or investors know that it is or soon will be open for business. And since they're the lifeblood of any commercial enterprise, the sooner you get noticed, the better!

Considering the number of new businesses that are started each year—900,000 new ones in 1998 alone, according to the Small Business Administration—you'll need all the help you can get to make sure the public knows you exist. There are thousands of local, business, and trade news organizations across the country who regard entrepreneurs and their new companies as an important source of stories and articles for their consumer and business audiences.

Since you'll face lots of competition for news coverage from other entrepreneurs, there's no guarantee that just because you send out a release, the media will cover you in return. To help ensure that your new venture is the one news organizations decide to cover, as appropriate, be sure to include the following information in your press materials (for more advice on preparing effective news releases, see Chapter 45):

➤ A description of the products, services, and expertise you'll offer.

➤ The primary target audience for your products, services, or expertise.

➤ Any particular benefits or advantages you'll offer to clients or customers.

➤ When it began or will be open for business.

➤ Any special incentives, sales, and so forth, you'll offer to help attract customers or clients.

➤ Why you started the company or organization in the first place.

➤ Where it's located.

➤ How your start-up is different from or better than your competitors.

➤ Background information about yourself and your partners, investors, or founders.

➤ If appropriate, your projections for revenue, profits, sales, and so forth.

➤ If relevant, how many people you will employ or have hired.

➤ How to contact you or the company for more information.

➤ How people can receive more information about the company's products, services, or expertise.

What you say and the order in which you say it will depend on the details on your new venture, and the information that is most important in capturing the attention of the media.

■ HOW I GOT THAT STORY

The box on page 211 includes excerpts from a news release I prepared and distributed to publicize a new Internet company I helped start. (The full text of the release is on my Web site at www.edwardsegal.com.)

■ RESULTS

News coverage about the launch of Internetlobby.org included studies by *The Washington Post* and other daily newspapers across the country.

FIRST GRASSROOTS ADVOCACY GROUP TO FIGHT FOR THE POLITICAL AND LEGISLATIVE INTERESTS OF INTERNET USERS IS ESTABLISHED; NOW ON-LINE AT WWW.INTERNETLOBBY.ORG

WASHINGTON—Organizers today announced the establishment of Internetlobby.org, the first grassroots advocacy group whose sole purpose is to monitor and fight for the legislative, regulatory, and political interests, needs, and concerns of tens of millions of adult Internet users in the United States.

Internetlobby.org is now on-line at www.internetlobby.org. It will monitor and speak out on Internet-related matters including e-commerce, credit card fraud, privacy, children's access to on-line pornography, spamming, and taxation. Internetlobby.org will also prepare and publicize ratings on the votes politicians cast on matters that are of concern to members.

Spokesperson Edward Segal said Internetlobby.org will "serve as the eyes, ears and voice of Web surfers and on-line consumers throughout the country. High-tech, Internet and software companies are well represented in Washington, and now Internet users will have a place to turn to help ensure that their best interests are protected."

64 Now at Stores Everywhere!

Introduce a Product

As difficult as it may be for a new company to compete for media coverage (see Chapter 63), the competition to gain public notice may be many times harder for an established organization that's introducing a new product. While there are hundreds of thousands of start-up companies each year, millions of existing businesses already have their products in the marketplace or, as in the computer and software industries, bring out new or improved versions all the time.

Don't be discouraged by these numbers, however. In fact, there's every reason to be optimistic for news coverage if you can convincingly and effectively tell the media:

➤ How your product is different or better than all the rest.

➤ Its benefits and advantages.

➤ Why people will want to buy it.

➤ Exactly how it will help them.

➤ Who's used it already and why they're happy with it.

➤ How it works (but don't go into too much detail).

➤ When, where, and how people can buy or order it.

➤ Cost or pricing information.

➤ If appropriate, estimated or projected sales.

➤ Relevant warranties, guarantees, or money-back offers.

➤ Your background or qualifications in developing, introducing, or selling the product.

With so much potential competition, why on earth should you possibly believe that you might be able to get news coverage for your product? Because so few companies actually provide or properly present this important information to editors and reporters, that's why. Rather than sending a newsmaking news release, they may give the media instead:

➤ Copies of newspaper and magazine ads, or a television commercial of the product.

➤ A copy of the company's marketing plan for the new product.

➤ A brochure of the product.

➤ A news release that fails to describe the product or include some of the key information listed above.

➤ Information that is too detailed or complicated to understand or full of jargon and industry buzzwords that few reporters have the time or patience to wade through or decipher.

You can dramatically increase your chances of capturing the attention of the media and receiving the news coverage you want if you:

➤ Provide reporters the information they need to understand and do stories about the product.

➤ Eliminate the barriers that prevent journalists from understanding the importance and significance of your product.

This is not rocket science. But it is common sense.

If it's such a simple formula, why doesn't everyone follow it?

Don't look a gift horse in the mouth! If everyone did it the right way, then your opportunities for press coverage would be even more competitive than it already is. Just be sure that you do it the right way yourself, and be happy that your competitors haven't read this book (yet).

■ HOW I GOT THAT STORY

Dr. Bruce Kehr, a national authority on medication compliance technology, invented a new device that reminds people to take their medicine. Kehr, who introduced and demonstrated a prototype of the unit at a national trade show, wanted to generate as much news coverage as possible about his invention.

Following are the opening paragraphs of the news release that was sent to news organizations about the introduction of the invention (for the full text of the release, visit my Web site at www.edwardsegal.com).

ROCKVILLE, MD (April 9)—InforMedix, Inc. today announced the introduction of Medi-Monitor, the first in a series of portable interactive telemedical devices to help doctors monitor the condition of patients at home.

The device will ensure that an estimated 100 million Americans who are on one or more prescriptions take their medications on time, in sequence, with proper instructions, and in their proper dosage.

The portable Personal Medical Assistant(sm) (PMA), about the size of a videocassette, will save lives, help reduce the nation's skyrocketing healthcare costs and improve the health of patients. Three different models of the device will be produced for managed care organizations, clinical drug trials investigators, healthcare providers, pharmacists, and consumers. [Used with permission]

■ RESULTS

The news release led to several stories in local business publications, the medical media, and an invitation from a local television news show for Kehr to demonstrate his device to their audience.

65 Keep Ahead of the Competition

Provide a New Service

Generating media coverage about a new service offered by your company can be a faster and more effective way to promote it to the public than advertising or other marketing activities (see Chapter 10). The challenge is to find ways to make your service stand out from your competitors, and get the media to take notice of the difference.

To "break through the clutter," be sure to highlight the following aspects of your new service to news organizations:

➤ An attention-getting headline (see Chapter 45).

➤ How the new service is different from or better than your competitors.

➤ A brief description of the service in layperson's language.

➤ Why you are qualified to provide the service.

➤ Price or cost information.

➤ Sales projections.

➤ Contact information so the public can learn more about it.

➤ Testimonials from those who may already have tried the service.

➤ Plans for rolling out, marketing, or promoting the service.

■ HOW I GOT THAT STORY

Getting local news coverage for a new service was the challenge faced by the Executive Office Club, a traditional commercial real estate management company that operates several executive suite locations in the Washington, DC, area. President Mark Wiatrowski asked me to prepare the following release about the company's new "offices by the hour" service (to read the entire release, visit my Web site at www.edwardsegal.com).

> *WASHINGTON—Executive Office Club, a commercial real estate management company, today announced it has opened the nation's first "offices by the hour" facility in downtown Washington, DC. For only $7.95 an hour, entrepreneurs, home-based workers and mobile professionals can have access to a full range of traditional office facilities on an as-needed basis.*
>
> *Over the next five years, the Executive Office Club plans to build a nationwide network of 50 "offices by the hour" facilities in targeted metropolitan areas and "edge cities" across the country. The company plans to issue an initial public offering of stock to help finance the expansion.*

President Mark Wiatrowski said the Executive Office Club has taken the concept of traditional executive office suites to a new level. He said the "offices by the hour" approach "provides all the support, advice and expertise anyone needs to help launch, run or expand their business. It is a cost-effective way for entrepreneurs, home-based workers and mobile professionals to keep their overhead costs to a minimum while achieving maximum productivity and efficiency."

For more information about Executive Office Club's "offices by the hour," contact Mark Wiatrowski by phone (800-784-2484) or e-mail (markhw@attmail.com). [Used with permission]

■ RESULTS

The news release led to stories in *The Washington Post, Washington Business Journal, The Washington Times, Inc.,* and *Home Office Computing* magazine.

66 According to . . .

Serve as a Spokesperson

Each year thousands of individuals across the country are interviewed by news organizations not because of who they are, but because of what they do: They are the spokespersons for the corporations or organizations where they work and are the principal liaison between their employer and the media.

Corporate spokespeople can command the instant attention of an editor or reporter when they call, and are often the first people journalists contact for information or a quote on a story involving the spokesperson's company or organization.

Serving as a spokesperson can be an important and sensitive job, since everything the public knows or believes about your company's products, services, expertise, or reputation can hinge on your ability to faithfully and accurately convey information to the media and maintain good working relationships with reporters.

Burke Stinson, who serves as the spokesperson for AT&T, says "being a spokesperson is much like singing. Everyone can do it, but few do it well." So few, in fact, that he estimates that less than 25 percent of all companies have people in those positions who can represent them effectively to the media.

Whether you are the best person to serve as the spokesperson can depend on the size and structure of your organization or company, your background and experience in dealing with the media, and the nature of your job and responsibilities.

Who makes the best spokesperson? That can depend on the size and structure of the organization.

In smaller companies, the typical spokesperson is usually the president or founder of the company, a senior partner, or high-ranking corporate officer.

At larger organizations, the spokesperson is typically an individual specifically hired to serve as the liaison with the media. He or she will probably have had previous experience as a working journalist or press secretary for a politician or other public official.

Many colleges and universities offer courses or degree programs in public relations, journalism, or communications. But employers may feel more comfortable hiring a spokesperson who has real-world experience in the "school of hard knocks" working with the media—or a combination of academic credentials and practical knowledge.

Potential spokespeople should be as selective about the companies they decide to work for as the organizations that hire them. To be effective and credible in their role, spokespeople should:

➤ Have the full trust, faith, and confidence of senior officials.

➤ Be "in the loop" to receive the information they need to do their job and to have an early "heads-up" of any potential issues or problems that may affect the organization's reputation or bottom line.

➤ Be involved in the decision-making process for the approval of press materials and statements to the media.

➤ Have the resources and technology necessary to do the job, from monitoring the news to distributing press materials.

➤ Be guaranteed immediate access to the people who can help them answer questions from the media.

A 1999 study by the Public Relations Society of America (PRSA) and the Rockefeller Foundation showed that the credibility of a spokesperson could help or hurt the company or organization they represent. The five-year, nationwide poll of 2,500 individuals found that of the 44 categories of leadership the top 15 most credible people are:

1. Supreme Court Justices.
2. Teachers.
3. National experts.
4. Members of the armed forces.
5. Local business owners.
6. Ordinary citizens.
7. Local religious leaders.
8. High-ranking military officers.
9. School officials.
10. National leaders of people with shared traits.
11. National religious leaders.
12. Network TV news anchors.
13. Governors.
14. Representatives of a local business or trade association.
15. Reporters for local newspapers or TV stations.

Bringing up the rear, the study found that the four least credible spokespeople are political party leaders, public relations specialists, famous entertainers, and TV or radio talk show hosts.

But being the spokesperson for an organization may not hold much job security or make you immune from criticism. As *Investor Relations Business* noted in reporting the results of the PRSA survey, "If a company's communications strategy isn't successful, it might be time to shoot the messenger."

■ PRESCRIPTIONS FOR SUCCESS

But not everyone may have the temperament necessary to serve as a company's liaison with the media, according to William Harlow, the spokesperson for the Central Intelligence Agency. He notes, "It's important to take your work seriously, but not yourself too seriously. If you are a perfectionist and insist on everything coming out perfectly, then you are in the wrong line of work. No matter how great a job you do (in dealing with a reporter on a story), something is going to be lost in the translation, and at best the story will have a couple of lines that you would have written differently yourself. You just have to roll with the punches, otherwise you'll be very frustrated in this line of work."

Harlow says that the most important qualifications for a spokesperson is that he or she:

➤ Is honest.
➤ Has credibility.
➤ Never guesses at the answer to a question.

Each of the people I interviewed for this chapter had their own criteria for what makes a good and effective spokesperson.

Becky Madeira, senior vice president of public affairs for PepsiCo, lists the following characteristics:

➤ Can distill clearly and succinctly key messages that must be communicated to the media and the public.

➤ Helpful to have worked for a news organization and understand how a newsroom operates, or to have been on the staff of a public official and know what it's like to work under pressure.

➤ Has access to information and officials within the company.

➤ Must be trusted by the media and his or her employer.

Burke Stinson, spokesperson for AT&T, says a spokesperson should be able to:

➤ Write concisely.

➤ Think objectively and clearly.

➤ Speak memorably.

➤ Be proactive with the media, not just reactive.

➤ Have reporters think you are an honest person.

➤ Have a good working knowledge of how the media operates.

Joyce Oberdorf, vice president, corporate public relations, for Aetna, Inc., says her list includes:

➤ Integrity.

➤ Credibility.

➤ Statements that have believability and resonance.

➤ Honesty.

➤ Fundamental understanding of the operations of your company or organization, its goals, and how it works.

➤ Having the ear of the management.

➤ Journalism background important but not essential; awareness of how the media works is critical.

➤ Ability to speak the language of those you work with.

David Quast, a former spokesman for Phillip Morris, says the most important qualities are:

➤ Honesty.

➤ Passion, and a firm belief in what your company is doing.

HALL OF SHAME: THE MOUTH THAT ROARED

While the media has an insatiable appetite for interviews, don't feel that it's your responsibility to fill the void all by yourself.

William Ginsburg, Monica Lewinsky's first lawyer, set some kind of record when he appeared on all five Sunday morning national interview programs, including *Fox News Sunday, Face the Nation, Meet the Press, This Week,* and *Late Edition*. The attorney's willingness—some might say over-eagerness—to talk to the media about his client made him the butt of jokes by Jay Leno and other comedians, and soon earned him a reputation as a publicity hound. Ginsburg certainly did not help matters when he bragged, "I'm the most famous person in the world."

When Ginsburg left the case, *The Washington Post* noted, "It is difficult to accept that no television network, no media organization of any kind, will likely have any interest in anything this avuncular friend ever says again. But the Grim Reaper of Fame will not be denied: the time has come for William Ginsburg to shut up."

The moral to the Ginsburg saga is that when it comes to doing interviews with the media, moderation is better than overindulgence.

➤ The ability to deliver your message in the clearest possible manner so you can reach the largest number of people.

➤ A belief in what you are doing and saying.

➤ Having a real understanding of the company you work for.

➤ Being a true communications partner with the management of your organization.

■ IN THEIR OWN WORDS

Beyond the Call of Duty

Among the mistakes I made as a corporate spokesman was not wearing an overcoat on a cold January morning outside

AT&T's offices in New Jersey. Network and cable TV crews wanted one-on-one interviews with me to explain the company's plans to cut 40,000 jobs. By the time CBS spoke to me, the reporter removed her scarf and placed it sympathetically around my neck.

Burke Stinson
AT&T Spokesperson

67 We're Proud to Announce . . .

Tell the World about New Clients, New Employees, or Staff Promotions

Sometimes you don't have to look too far to find news hooks that, without much trouble or effort on your part, can be quickly and easily turned into short news releases about your company or organization.

One of the most common sources of story angles for any size company can be to announce your new clients, recently hired employees, promotions that you've given to your staff, or your own appointment to a committee, commission, or leadership post. While these stories are not likely to make it onto the front page of the local paper, they often will show up in its business section, or may be placed with other brief announcements in a "digest" or "movers and shakers" column. And don't forget to send a copy of these releases to any appropriate trade, business, or professional newsletters, magazines, newspapers, or local radio or TV business-oriented shows.

These stories are an effective way to help maintain top-of-mind awareness about your company, show a continued level of activity, and keep your name in front of the public.

When announcing a new client, tell the media:

➤ The name of the client.

➤ Where they are located.

➤ What they do.

➤ What you will do for them.

➤ When you'll start work for them.

➤ How long the contract will last.

➤ Whether you beat out any other companies to win the job and, if so, who they were.

➤ If appropriate, the dollar value of the contract, who on your staff will work on the account, and so forth.

➤ Other recent new client "wins" that may show additional momentum for your company.

To publicize new hires, include the following details in your news release:

➤ Their names and titles.

➤ Areas of responsibility.

➤ Any special skills or expertise they bring to your organization.

➤ Special accomplishments, awards, or professional recognition.

➤ Brief overview of previous employment.

It's also important to:

➤ Keep the news release short, since the story will likely be dramatically shortened or condensed by the news organizations that receive it.

➤ Include a current black-and-white head-and-shoulder photo of the person you are writing about; be sure his or her name is printed on the back of the photo in case it gets separated from the news release. [For more advice on how to prepare a news release, please see Chapter 45.]

For staff promotions, the media will be most interested in:

➤ The person's new position.

➤ His or her old position.

➤ A quote from you about why the individual was promoted.

➤ A brief description of his or her new duties or responsibilities.

➤ A black-and-white head-and-shoulder photo.

To read a sample news release announcing new clients, visit my Web site at www.edwardsegal.com.

68 Show *and* Tell

Demonstrate or Discuss Your Expertise

No matter what you do for a living or avocation, whether it's accounting or zoology, you've probably developed some level of skill or knowledge on matters related to your job, hobby, industry, or profession. In fact, you may be one of the country's leading authorities on whatever it is you do for a living, teach, study, or enjoy as a pastime.

Presenting yourself to the media as an expert on those topics is a time-tested way to help get your 15 minutes of fame. Why? Because editors, reporters, and columnists are

HALL OF FAME: THIS IS A TEST.
THIS IS ONLY A TEST (MAYBE)

There are several ways for experts and authorities to generate news coverage on their expertise and viewpoints. Two of the most effective ways are to either claim there is a problem, or prove it.

To show how easy it is to smuggle biological weapons into the United States, William C. Patrick II carried a small plastic bottle containing deadly anthrax powder into the Pentagon, the CIA, and several major airports without being detected. Patrick, a biological weapons expert, later testified about his experiences and safety concerns before a congressional committee—after he'd just gone through a Capitol Hill security checkpoint without being stopped.

But sometimes your tests may not turn out the way you expect.

The Associated Press reported the following:

"The FBI is investigating whether former federal transportation chief Mary Schiavo violated any laws when she checked a suspicious bag at an airport here to test security measures, officials said Sunday.

"Ms. Schiavo, a former inspector general of the Department of Transportation checked a bag Friday at Port Columbus International Airport as part of a story WCMH-TV was doing on airline security. The bag's discovery led to a shutdown of a runway for four hours Friday, but no flights were delayed." [Used with permission]

Finally, United Parcel Service of America (UPS) found out the hard way that even the best-planned tests can go awry.

In 1996, UPS, which handled the delivery of packages to the Olympics in Atlanta, tested its own security system by sending a fake bomb to one of the facilities at the games. The package went through without being detected until it was discovered by the Olympics' own security staff. Olympic officials evacuated the building and blew up the suspicious package. Among those who were forced to leave their offices were several journalists, who later wrote stories about the mishap.

always looking for experts to interview and quote in their stories. Your soundbites or inkbites can help enliven their reports, add perspective or color to their articles, and provide important insights and information to their audiences (see Chapter 28). According to the Dow Jones News Retrieval database, between 1998 and 1999, the word "expert" showed up in almost 250,000 newspaper, magazine, and wire service stories on a broad range of topics and subjects.

But for you to be interviewed about your expertise by reporters for their stories, you have to do four things:

1. Know what you are talking about and be, in fact, an expert in your field.
2. Know how to talk in soundbites or inkbites.
3. Let reporters know you exist and are available for interviews.
4. Return their calls immediately.

Assuming you are an expert and have mastered the art of soundbites, your biggest challenge may be to let reporters and columnists know who you are and how to reach you (see Chapter 33).

69 Blow Out the Candles

Celebrate an Anniversary or Milestone

One of the toughest stories to get the media to cover can be an anniversary or other milestone being celebrated by a corporation or organization. Most reporters regard them as nothing more than self-congratulatory events that their audience will not be interested in or care about.

Since entire books could be and have been written about how to plan and stage special events to mark these corporate milestones, I won't try to duplicate them here. However, the most effective way to grab the attention of the media is to ensure that the events:

➤ Are easily accessible to reporters.

➤ Have good visuals.

➤ Have a local tie-in to the community.

➤ Are well organized.

➤ Are planned far enough in advance.

➤ Are staged so that it will be as easy as possible for news organizations to cover and photograph the festivities.

➤ Involve employees and customers in some way.

➤ Are consistent with the image, reputation, or history of the company or organization.

■ HOW I GOT THAT STORY

An example of a successful corporate anniversary celebration is the project I worked on for the Roy Rogers restaurant chain, which wanted to generate consumer awareness that it was celebrating its twentieth anniversary in business in major metropolitan areas where most of their restaurants were located.

Instead of simply bragging about its twentieth anniversary, Roy Rogers restaurants agreed to give something back to the community instead.

The project included:

➤ Planning and coordinating a series of special events at which officials of the restaurant chain presented remote-controlled robots to the police or fire departments at mock swearing-in ceremonies at its restaurants in Baltimore, Washington, Philadelphia, and New York. The four $8,000 robots—each standing four-feet tall and weighing about 100 pounds—were to be used by the departments to help educate nearly 1.5 million schoolchildren each year about street safety, the dangers of drugs, and fire prevention.

➤ Arranging for representatives of the police or fire departments to preside at mock swearing-in ceremonies at a Roy Rogers Restaurant in each city. The robots, called Officer I.M. Aware or Firefighter I.M. Aware, were customized for each department with a special hat, badge, and shirt displaying the Roy Rogers logo.

➤ Choreographing and scripting the ceremonies so they emphasized that Roy Rogers was donating the robots to the department as a goodwill gesture to mark its twentieth anniversary in business.

➤ Preparing press materials, including news releases, press kits, news advisories, and remarks for use by company officials at each event.

■ RESULTS

News coverage about the donation of the robots—and the fact that Roy Rogers was celebrating its twentieth anniversary—included 20 minutes of television and radio air time on seven television stations and five radio stations in Baltimore, Washington, Philadelphia, and New York. The coverage reached a combined audience of two million households in those cities.

The text of the news release that was used by the restaurant to generate news coverage about the donation of the robots in Baltimore can be found on my Web site at www.edwardsegal.com.

70 This Program Is Brought to You By . . .

Sponsor or Participate in a Conference or Trade Show

Trade shows and industry conferences are great backdrops against which individuals, corporations, and organizations can generate public awareness about their products, services, or expertise.

For the organizations that sponsor them, trade shows provide the perfect news hook to encourage reporters, editors, and columnists who follow the industry to:

➤ Attend the event.

➤ Interview officials and authorities in the field.

➤ Report to their audience the latest news, developments, or trends.

The companies who exhibit or participate at these shows and conferences can use the events as:

➤ A setting to announce a new product or service.

➤ A way to establish or maintain working relationships with the journalists who cover the event.

And the speakers and other experts who are invited to address conference sessions or workshops can take advantage of the shows to:

➤ Establish or reinforce their credibility in the topics in which they have expertise.

➤ Cultivate relationships with editors and reporters.

➤ Seek to generate news coverage about their company, remarks, opinions, observations, or predictions.

Despite all that these events have to offer, there can be special challenges in generating the news coverage you want. My client, the Society of the Plastics Industry, sought to create maximum favorable news coverage about its triennial exposition in Chicago. But show officials knew that most of the products and services to be displayed by the 1,800 exhibitors would be of little interest to anyone outside the plastics industry.

I tried to answer the questions of "who cares and why" (see Chapters 5 and 8) by talking to show officials and exhibitors and walking the aisles of the event to find examples of products and services that would directly affect and benefit consumers. Among my discoveries: a graffiti-resistant plastic stop sign that reflects light more effectively, a prototype fire truck made with plastic parts, and new heat-resistant roofing material.

I prepared and distributed a news release about the most interesting consumer angles at the show, and pitched the story to assignment editors at TV stations in Chicago and national news organizations such as CNN and Fox News.

In researching news hooks to promote the show, I discovered the event would be held during the anniversary of the movie *The Graduate,* in which one of the characters provides Dustin Hoffman with this pithy advice: "Just one word: Plastics." I used that anniversary to help increase interest among news organizations in the event. Later, several network TV news programs used that scene from the movie in their stories about the plastics exposition.

The news release (see my Web site at www.edwardsegal .com) and story pitch calls hit a responsive cord with the media, resulting in scores of stories in the international, national, and local press, including CNN, Fox News, *Time* magazine, the *Chicago Tribune,* and the *Chicago Sun-Times.* The news coverage was seen by an estimated 30 million people in the United States and around the world.

71 And in Conclusion . . .

Make a Speech

For the thousands of people who are invited each year to make remarks or presentations to conventions, workshops, or other meetings, public speaking represents an opportunity to help spread the word about their own accomplishments, activities, opinions, or expertise. Speeches are also an excellent way to position yourself as an expert on any number of topics or issues, and to help attract the interest of editors, reporters, and columnists to interview you for stories in which you may have some expertise.

Every speech has the potential to help you become famous in front of two audiences: those who hear your speech when you deliver it, and those who read about it before or after you make it. Here are some steps you can take to make sure you are taking full advantage of every speaking opportunity that comes your way and that you make your speech work for you long after you've delivered it.

➤ Prior to your speech, send a news release announcing your appearance to the editors of appropriate newsletters, magazines, newspapers, or other news outlets.

➤ Ask the people who invited you to speak to place a story about your upcoming presentation in their organization's newsletter or on their Web site.

➤ If you will be speaking at a convention or conference where there is a pressroom for the reporters who are covering the event, drop off copies of your release and remarks at the room when you arrive at the site. If time permits, introduce yourself to any reporters in the room, tell them about your speech, and offer to be available for interviews if they are interested in doing a story about it.

➤ Immediately after your appearance, prepare and distribute a news release about your speech, whom you spoke to, and highlights from your remarks.

➤ Make your speech work for you long after you've delivered it.

Arnold Sanow has written four books about business development and personal effectiveness, and delivers scores of speeches and presentations across the country every year on topics including customer service, communication, presentation skills, and business development.

Every time Sanow is invited to give a speech, he provides his hosts with a computer disk of 50 different articles he has written on aspects of business development and personal effectiveness. The groups are free to use his articles in their newsletters, magazines, or post them on their Intranet or Web sites. At the end of the article, he includes contact information so others can book him for speeches, or the media can call him for interviews.

To date, his articles have been used or reprinted more than 60 different times by organizations ranging from the Texas Pest Control Association to the Glass Packaging Institute. And, combined with his efforts to publicize his speeches, he has parlayed his 15 minutes of fame into even greater public recognition through appearances on CBS's *Evening News with Dan Rather* and stories in *USA Today* and *The Wall Street Journal.*

An example of one of Sanow's generic articles on how to improve your personal communication skills is reprinted in the Resources section.

72 You Don't Have to Be Tom Clancy

Write a Book

One of the best reasons for the media to do a story on or about you is that you've written a book.

According to the Dow Jones News Retrieval database, between 1997 and 1999, there were more than 200,000 stories or articles about or that mentioned authors and their books. And it's a conservative estimate, since the database does not include thousands of daily or weekly newspapers, local television and radio stations, or small circulation magazines or newsletters.

Why all the fuss over authors?

Being a published author automatically confers on you instant credibility in the eyes of editors, reporters, and columnists. Journalists assume that since you wrote a book, you are an expert on the topic and therefore must know what you are talking about. Reporters reason that if you know what you are talking about, you can probably provide important information, insights, and perspectives on that or related topics for their stories.

But it doesn't have to stop there:

➤ Depending on the topic and current events, authors are frequent guests on the radio talk show and television news and interview program circuit.

➤ By turning chapters of your book into stand-alone articles, authors can often get extra mileage out of the work they did in writing the book, while receiving additional attention from the media.

And the more news coverage you can generate about your book, the more likely it is that you will sell more copies. The more copies you sell, the more credibility you'll have as an author.

Although there are tremendous opportunities for news coverage about you and your book, there is also a tremendous amount of competition for that coverage. According to publishing expert Dan Poynter, 100,000 different books are published each year (that's almost 275 new books every day), accompanied by nearly as many authors who are seeking to create as much news coverage about themselves and their books as possible.

To help stand out from this crowd, you have to answer the same questions posed by reporters to everyone else who wants to be famous: Who cares about your accomplishment (in this case, a book)? And why should they care (see Chapters 5 and 8)?

Another potential downside is that it can take months or years to write a book, and still longer to get the book published.

While a book may not be a guaranteed ticket to fame, it can certainly provide the news hook or story angle you'll need to help achieve public recognition.

73 Now on Newsstands Everywhere!

Publish or Be the Subject of an Article

It's always satisfying when a prestigious publication does a story about your work or accomplishments. The challenge, however, is to turn that one article into multiple news stories.

That was my assignment when the Research Institute for Genetic and Human Therapy (RIGHT) asked me to help publicize an article in *Science* magazine about the efforts of their scientists in finding effective ways to combat the AIDS epidemic.

The magazine reported that a study conducted by the scientists found that a new combination of antiviral drugs led to the early remission of HIV in a patient who had been infected with the virus for seven weeks. The patient went into remission during six months of treatment, and remained in remission nine months after he stopped taking the drugs.

Based on the news report in *Science,* I prepared a news release about the discovery and the fact that the publication had done a story about it. In addition to calling key editors and reporters to encourage them to do stories based on the news release, I had the release distributed by PR Newswire and faxed to a key list of selected journalists who were likely to be interested in the news.

■ RESULTS

The additional news coverage about the story in *Science* magazine and the work of RIGHT included stories by several news organizations, including Reuters and CBS News.

The text of the story that ran nationwide on the Reuters news service follows:

NEW COCKTAIL SENDS HIV PATIENTS INTO "REMISSION"

WASHINGTON (Reuters)—A new cocktail of drugs including hydroxyurea—not usually an AIDS drug—suppressed the HIV virus to undetectable levels in one patient, even after treatment stopped, the journal *Science* reported Friday.

He seemed to be free of infection nine months after he stopped taking the drugs, the report said. Astonished researchers are now trying the treatment in 20 patients.

Franco Lori and Julianna Lisziewicz, who founded the Washington-based Research Institute for Genetic and Human Therapy (RIGHT), said the virus was undetectable in the patient's blood.

"We are not saying this represents a cure for, or will lead to eradication of, HIV," they said in a statement.

"More patients need to undergo this particular therapy and be observed for a longer period of time before any conclusions can be drawn about this approach as a new source of treatment," they said.

They also warned people not to try the combination themselves. "Since these drugs are toxic if taken in the wrong dosage, this mixture should be used only under a doctor's strict supervision."

The patient, who lives in Berlin, was given hydroxyurea, Bristol-Myers Squibb Co.'s didanosine (ddI) and indinavir (Merck and Co. Inc.'s Crixivan).

Hydroxyurea has been around for a long time—it is used to treat disorders such as polychemia vera, which causes overproduction of red blood cells, and some types of leukemia.

74 50 Million People Can't Be Wrong

Commission a Public Opinion Poll

There is no such thing as a "sure thing" when it comes to trying to capture the attention of the media. But releasing the results of polls about what the public's opinion is on any number of topics comes pretty close.

How often does the media do stories about opinion polls? More than you might think.

According to the Dow Jones News Retrieval database, between 1997 and 1999, the phrase "public opinion poll" appeared in more than 1,300 newspaper and magazine stories around the world. Add to that radio, TV, and newsletter stories that report such findings, and the figure would reach many thousands.

The results of a newsworthy poll can provide a quick, easy, and legitimate news hook for reporters and columnists, who usually will give proper credit to the company or organization that commissioned the study in the first place. Often, the journalists call officials of the company or organization who sponsored the poll to interview them about the results and include their comments in the story.

A case in point is a survey I commissioned on behalf of a client, the Life & Health Insurance Medical Research Fund. The poll, conducted by Market Facts, Inc., contacted 1,000 randomly selected Americans by phone and asked them whether they thought the private sector should contribute more money to basic medical research.

Based on the results of the survey, I prepared and distributed to the news media a release about it. An hour after I had sent the release by fax and PR Newswire, a reporter with the Associated Press radio network called to interview my client. A few minutes after the interview,* the wire service broadcast the following story over hundreds of radio stations that carry its news service:

ANCHOR: Businesses looking to improve their corporate image might want to consider contributing more money to basic medical research. James Limbach has details.

REPORTER JAMES LIMBACH: A survey conducted for the Life and Health Insurance Medical Research Fund found ninety percent of those asked think the private sector should be doing more. And according to the Fund's executive director, Dr. Eve Katz. . . .

KATZ: Six out of ten consumers say they would think more favorably of companies that provide funds to support basic medical research.

LIMBACH: Dr. Katz said there is business funding for research but not in the basic medical area.

KATZ: Business in general, to the extent that it funds biomedical research, supports clinical research with the likelihood of profits.

LIMBACH: Dr. Katz says basic medical research is the foundation for all progress in science and medicine.

In addition to helping to generate news coverage about your company or organization, an opinion poll can be an excellent way to gather information you need to support or substantiate your credibility on an issue (see Chapter 74) and gain valuable insights into what the public thinks on a given topic.

There are several professional polling organizations that can prepare and conduct an opinion poll for you.

Humphrey Taylor is chairman and CEO of Louis Harris and Associates, an international market and opinion research firm. Taylor, who has had overall responsibility for

---

*Used with permission.

more than 5,000 opinion polls in 80 countries, lists several guidelines for a successful poll. Writing in the *Canadian Journal of Marketing Research,* Taylor said polls should:

➤ Be designed to have the maximum news appeal.

➤ Address a serious topic that is related to your business or organization.

➤ Be intellectually solid.

➤ Be objective, fair, balanced, and comprehensive.

Sid Groeneman, a polling expert with Market Facts, Inc., offers the following advice:

➤ Avoid sloppy methods of sampling; except in special circumstances, use randomly selected samples so the results are projectable, defensible (and thus credible).

➤ Avoid biased or "loaded" questions. Some readers will see through this, and any publicity may turn out to be of negative value.

➤ Avoid technical jargon and other language that might not be familiar to the average person.

➤ When respondents are not likely to have an opinion, make it easy for them to answer "don't know" or "not sure." Forcing people to provide opinions on issues they know nothing about, haven't thought about, or don't care about will produce "attitudes" that don't exist. Remember: The average person is not as close to your issues of concern as *you* are.

➤ Give careful consideration to the response scales/options offered to respondents. They should contain the full range of realistic anticipated answers to a question.

➤ In telephone surveys, pay attention to how many contact attempts the polling organization makes to each phone number in the sample before it is replaced. Making extra contact attempts is one important technique for improving the survey response rate.

➤ Ask how the survey interviewers are trained, supervised, and monitored—as well as their level of experience.

Reject any polling company that does not allow you to monitor some of your survey's interviews.

➤ Sample size or design is only one form of a potential survey error that can affect the accuracy of results. The wording of questions often plays a greater role. *It is impossible to spend too much time developing, reviewing, and testing the questions you want to use in a survey.*

➤ It is usually not possible to get any useful or interesting results asking only one or two questions. Try to address each topic or issue with at least several questions.

➤ Hire an expert for professional assistance.

75 We'll Be Back after This Commercial

Pay for Advertising

Earlier, I noted that the difference between advertising and news coverage is that you pay for advertising, but must pray for news coverage (see Chapter 10). But sometimes companies (and a few individuals with lots of money) will take out newspaper and magazine ads to communicate a purely noncommercial message to the public for a specific public relations reason.

The ads usually have nothing to do with the benefits or advantages of the company's products, services, or expertise. But they will have everything to do with the company's efforts to—in addition to using traditional PR strategies and techniques—help shape or repair its image or reputation, send a message to its customers, or apologize to the public for some snafu:

➤ Coca-Cola took out full-page ads in Belgian newspapers to say they were sorry about an incident in which some Belgians became sick after drinking Coke. In the ads, company chairman Douglas Ivester said, "To those people who suffered, especially the children, my colleagues and I want to express a very sincere apology. We strive to make sure that Coca-Cola always stands for good feelings, and regret that it resulted in feelings of illness."

➤ CVS, which operates a chain of pharmacies, placed ads to deny allegations that it sold information about their customers to other companies.

➤ The American Society of Composers, Authors, and Publishers bought full-page ads in major American newspapers to help refute allegations that it wanted to charge the Girl Scouts royalty fees for the songs they sing at camp.

➤ Sears took out an ad in *The Wall Street Journal* when the national newspaper did not run a chart that the retail chain wanted to accompany a correction to an article about the store's income. The ad noted in part:

> An article in The Wall Street Journal of Thursday, July 23, included a chart on Sears that was highly misleading. It showed net income steadily decreasing without explaining that Sears had divested several major businesses including Allstate and Dean Witter, Discover.
>
> Although the Journal has acknowledged its error through its corrections column, it declined to run the chart shown above. We are running this ad to make sure the correct information is seen by all readers. We do so on behalf of 300,000 dedicated associates who are transforming this great and profitable company.

Often the very fact that a company has taken out an ad to explain its views, justify some action, or make its case on a controversial matter, can become the basis of a news story in itself.

That's exactly what happened when Coke ran the apology ads in Belgium, and when Airbus Industrie (a consortium of European companies that manufacture airline passenger aircraft) ran a three-part print ad campaign in the United States. The Airbus ads sought to help combat a growing "antiforeign" sentiment in the United States that was hampering its ability to do business here. News coverage about the campaign included stories by ABC News, the Associated Press, United Press International, *The New York Times,* the *Philadelphia Inquirer,* and *Aviation Daily.*

Sometimes news coverage about an ad can have more of an impact than the actual ad itself. When Internet company Hotjobs.com Ltd., an on-line employment service, tried to buy a 30-second commercial during the Super Bowl on the Fox Network, TV executives rejected it on the grounds of poor taste. The final ad, and the controversy surrounding it, attracted the interest of the media. According to company CEO Richard Johnson, 450 publications and 180 broadcast outlets ran stories about the commercials. After the Superbowl, Johnson estimated that as many as six million people visited the Hotjobs.com Web site.

76 Nine Out of Ten Doctors Say . . .

Do a Survey

Conducting a survey or preparing a report about a problem can provide you or your organization with an effective and attention-getting news hook that will provide you with a forum for talking about the problem in the first place.

To help position itself as an advocacy organization for airline passengers, the Air Travelers Association prepared and released to the media the first-ever Airline Safety Report Card[SM] for 260 scheduled passenger airlines around the world. The report card was designed to serve as a single, authoritative source of safety data consumers need when deciding which airlines to fly.

It included airline safety ratings of 0–100 and grades of A through F for the fatal accident history of the 260 scheduled passenger airlines in 107 countries that used Western-built jet aircraft and operated at least 20,000 flights between January 1, 1987, and December 31, 1996.

The report card was prepared by David S. Stempler, the former executive director of the International Airline Passengers Association. Stempler, an aviation attorney, is an internationally known authority on airline passenger and travel issues.

After preparing a news release to announce the results of the report card, I called reporters at major news wire services and offered to provide the release to them on an embargoed basis so they could have more time to review and fully understand it.

When the embargo was lifted, we also faxed and e-mailed the release to contacts on a media list we had previously assembled, and distributed the release nationwide via PR Newswire, a private news wire service.

Working with Stempler, we came up with several soundbites that he agreed to use during his interviews with reporters. The soundbites included:

➤ "When it comes to airline safety, tens of millions of airline passengers have been flying blind because they do not have direct access to critical information about the safety record and accident history of airlines."

➤ "Ironically, it is easier for travelers to obtain advance information about in-flight meals or movies, than it is to find out about the safety record of the airlines they are going to fly."

The results exceeded even my own expectations for news coverage:

➤ Each of the national news wire services ran the story at about the same time soon after the embargo was lifted.

➤ We received dozens of interview requests from reporters who had received the release or had seen the story on the wire services.

➤ After all was said and done, more than 100 news stories about the report card were published or broadcast by newspapers, magazines, radio stations, and television stations across the country and around the world.

The text of the story that was carried by the Reuters news service follows:

> *WASHINGTON (Reuters)—A new organization representing air travelers has begun compiling safety ratings for airlines around the world and has failed 29 of them, its founder said last week. The Air Travelers Association issued its first Airline Safety Report Card based on the fatal accident history of 260 carriers in 107 countries.*
>
> *The worst crash-to-flight ratios were attributed to Aviateca (Guatemala), COPA Panama, Aero Peru, Lan Chile, Lauda Air (Austria), Aeroflot Russian International, ADC Airlines (Nigeria), Air Mauritanie (Mauritania), Ethiopian Airlines, China Northwest Airlines and Xiamen Airlines (China).*
>
> *"It is easier for travelers to obtain advance information about in-flight meals or movies, than it is to find out about the safety record of the airlines they are going to fly," said aviation attorney and association founder David Stempler.*
>
> *The safety report covers airlines that use Western-built jet aircraft and operated at least 20,000 flights between January, 1987, and December, 1996.*
>
> *The association, which will serve as an advocacy group, can be contacted on the Internet at www.1800airsafe.com. (Copyright Reuters Limited, 1997. Used with permission.)*

77 Hitch Your Wagon to a Star

Use Celebrities to Boost Your Visibility

Millions of people follow the latest doings of movie stars and other celebrities: witness the popularity of *People* and *Teen People* magazines, gossip columns, and TV shows such as *Entertainment Tonight* and *Access Hollywood*.

Involving a popular actor, actress, entertainer, or athlete in your cause, project, event, or activity can be an effective way to capture the attention of the media and make the task of generating news coverage that much easier.

The Lee Company, which makes a best-selling line of jeans for young women, sought to encourage them to wear more denim and thereby increase their spending on denim clothing. Lee's PR firm, Barkley Evergreen & Partners, devised and implemented the idea of an annual Lee National Denim Day™ on a Friday in October, when companies would let their employees come to work wearing denim. In exchange, participating employees would each donate $5 to the Susan G. Komen Breast Cancer Foundation.

Breast cancer is the most common cancer in American women, and the leading cause of death among women aged 35–54. Company officials say the Lee National Denim Day "is a way to fight breast cancer by raising funds to help fund a cure and raising awareness in the workplace."

Donations from Lee National Denim Day have funded research grants at university and teaching hospitals, as well as local screening and education programs in medically underserved areas of the country.

Among its publicity efforts, each year Lee enlists the support of celebrities who have lost loved-ones to the disease, and highlights their participation in news releases, fact sheets, press kits, and marketing activities. Well-known individuals, including basketball star Rebecca Lobo and actresses Josie Bissett, Yasmine Bleeth, and Patricia Arquette, have helped deliver the company's messages to millions of people through wide-ranging news coverage that featured:

➤ Stories in *The Wall Street Journal, Fitness,* and *Self.*

➤ Appearances on several national television programs and shows (The *Tonight Show, Live! Regis and Kathie Lee, Access Hollywood, The Rosie O'Donnell Show,* and the Fox News Network).

➤ A radio station interview tour of the 20 media markets across the country.

Arquette, whose mother died of breast cancer, said, "Losing my mother was terribly difficult because she was such an important part of my life. And it makes me think that every second that goes by that we don't have a cure, more mothers are dying. It's got to change, and Lee National Denim Day is helping to bring about this change."

In the first three years of the program, Lee National Denim Day raised more than $10 million for the Komen Foundation, all through individual donations of $5 each from two million women who work at about 25,000 companies across the country. The annual project is now the nation's largest one-day fundraising event for breast cancer research, treatment, and education.

Kathy Collins, director of strategic planning for the Lee Company, said the company decided to sponsor the project "because we felt it was a necessary thing to get involved with, as well as an opportunity to give something back to consumers. Our strongest consumer base is women and we thought that, in order to do something good as well as to be more competitive, we have to start speaking to these women on a more personalized level. We are committed to continuing the project until they find a cure for breast cancer."

Collins said the company decided to use celebrities because "they can help us get the message out about Lee National Denim Day, they can encourage participation, and they can get news coverage that we could not get otherwise."

Collins noted that having celebrities involved in the anti-cancer project "helps make people aware that breast cancer can happen to anybody. A celebrity really helps to put a face on the disease and makes people realize that 'Wow, it happened to her too!"

Lee Company's criteria for deciding which celebrities to use includes the following checklist:

➤ Close ties to someone who had breast cancer.

➤ High recognition, so it will be easier to place them as guests on TV talk shows.

➤ Ability to speak to our target audience of young women.

➤ Articulate, so they can speak intelligently about what we are doing.

➤ A high level of passion and commitment for the cause.

To build brand awareness for its retirement planning services for baby boomers, SunAmerica, Inc. hired not one, but several Hollywood spokespersons—a trio of former childhood actors who shared their stories about their financial difficulties. The former stars—Jon Provost, who appeared in *Lassie*; Paul Petersen, of the *Donna Reed Show*; and Brandon Cruz, who acted in *The Courtship of Eddie's Father*—were booked as guests on local and national TV talk shows across the country to discuss how they lost their money and urged viewers to call SunAmerica for retirement planning information.

You don't always need a Hollywood star to capture the attention of the public and the media. Sometimes local talent will do just fine, such as a well-known athlete, business executive, community leader, or entertainer.

To generate public awareness on a transportation issue for a client, I once commissioned the Capitol Steps, a satirical singing group in Washington, D.C., to write and perform a song about how bad the traffic on the Capital Beltway had become over the years. Taped copies of the song, a parody of country and western singer Willie Nelson's "On the Road Again," were sent to radio stations in the region, which played it for several days running. The music helped draw attention to growing traffic congestion in the area, made people smile, and helped deliver my client's message about the need to fix the problem.

Often, arranging for celebrities to appear or perform at your event is all that is needed to draw the attention of news organizations or your target audience:

➤ SkyCache, an Internet broadcast network, hired Penn & Teller, a well-known magic team, to perform at and attract crowds to its booth at a high-tech conference and trade show in Atlanta.

➤ When Sheraton opened a new hotel in Africa, it hired the band Cool and the Gang to give several performances on the hotel's grounds. News organizations around the world made note of the singing group's participation in the hotel's grand opening activities.

Using well-known people to publicize your project, cause, or activity is one of those classic "win-win" situations. A celebrity's involvement can enhance your own news hook or story angle, and provide news organizations with a story that is more interesting to their audiences.

78 Kill Two Birds with One Stone

Conduct a Study

Do you find yourself at a loss for words to tell reporters or columnists about what's new, interesting, or noteworthy in your industry or profession?

Have you run out of ideas for news angles and story hooks on issues related to your products or services?

Do you get the feeling that you've said everything that can be said about your area of expertise?

If so, then it may be time for you to do a study!

Commissioning or conducting a study on an appropriate or relevant topic, and announcing the results to the media via a news release, may be the answer to your prayers for news coverage. In addition to the news you'll make, you can use the results to position or reinforce your company or organization as an expert on the subject, validate or bolster your point of view, or call attention to an issue that you think deserves scrutiny, public debate, or some type of action.

Every year, newspapers, magazines, newsletters, and TV and radio stations report the results of the newest study or research project that has just been released on any one of hundreds of different topics. Invariably, reporters and columnists include in their stories the comments and observations of the organization's officials about the significance, impact, or meaning of the report's finding, conclusions, recommendations, or call for action.

In just a one-week period during the summer of 1999, news organizations across the country published or broadcast reports about the following studies:

➤ Rutgers University's National Marriage Project found that Americans are less likely to get married than ever before.

➤ A study by State Farm Insurance listed the most dangerous intersections in cities across the country.

➤ A report by McGladrey & Pullen, LLP, the nation's seventh largest accounting and consulting firm, named the best mutual fund Web sites.

➤ A study of children's TV viewing habits conducted by the Annenberg Public Policy Center found, among other things, that more children could name the Simpson TV program on the Fox Network than could name Hillary Rodham Clinton as the First Lady.

➤ A survey by the American Gaming Association, an industry trade group, showed that people who go to church think it's okay to gamble.

➤ A study for the California Board of Energy Efficiency and Pacific Gas & Electric Company showed that students who are exposed to more sunlight do better on tests in school.

➤ A study paid for by the National Cattleman's Beef Association found eating red meat can help reduce bad cholesterol, increase good cholesterol, and might reduce the risk of heart disease.

➤ A study found it's easier for people to deliver bad news via e-mail than to give the same news in person. The study was conducted by Stephanie Watts Sussman, an assistant professor at Case Western Reserve University, and her colleague Lee Sproull.

It's not necessary for the findings of your study to be profound, just interesting or unusual.

Caliper, a human resources consulting firm in Princeton, New Jersey, was the subject of a front-page story in *The Wall Street Journal's* "Business Bulletin" column about its survey of the reasons that more than 180 executives gave for quitting their jobs.

According to the paper, Caliper's list of the top ten strange reasons included:

➤ The building temperature is much too cold.

➤ I had a vision and was told to resign.

➤ I had to go to jail.

➤ There was a demon residing in our computer network.

79 The Envelope, Please

Sponsor or Win a Contest

From football to the lottery, the media always seems interested in reporting the results of different kinds of contests, competitions, or games of chance. No wonder: these events can be wonderful stories full of pathos, emotion, suspense, and drama. And who doesn't enjoy rooting for the home team, or fantasizing what it's like to be a winner?

Each year, corporations and organizations sponsor numerous competitions, from essay contests to athletic events, attracting the participation of thousands of people who hope lady luck will smile down on them.

And some people seem willing to do almost anything to win:

➤ At the National Capital Boat Show in Chantilly, Virginia, the person who could keep his or her lips on a 15-foot water ski boat the longest won the watercraft.

➤ During the annual Washington Auto Show, the concept was the same (the winner was the one who could touch a car the longest), but the prize was different: a new Mazda.

➤ In New York, Breath Savers sponsored the "Longest Kiss Challenge."

➤ In Atlanta, a radio station awarded automobiles to four people who lived in a Volkswagen Beetle for more than a month.

Even some high-tech companies have gotten into the contest business, including Dell Computer Corporation, which sponsored a nationwide effort to find the oldest personal computer in use by a small company. The winner received $15,000 worth of new computer equipment in exchange for donating his old machine to a computer museum.

At the other end of the spectrum, even a no-tech product like Crayola crayons can reap a public relations bonanza from a contest. Binney & Smith, Inc., which makes the crayons, asked the public to send in suggestions for a new name for one of its colors. More than 100,000 people responded with over 300,000 suggestions, and the contest made news across the country.

Sometimes a person can win a contest simply for being born with the right name, as was the case when American Movie Classics conducted a nationwide search for men with the same name as movie stars. The winners included Elvis Presley, a data center supervisor in Houston; Cary Grant, president of an investment banking firm in Chicago, and Sean Connery, a high school student in Oklahoma City.

Then there are the competitions that require more skill than luck.

Each year Ernst & Young, Massachusetts Mutual, Arthur Andersen, the U.S. Commerce Department, and the Small Business Administration sponsor awards programs that recognize the expertise and accomplishments of entrepreneurs across the country.

Some contests are more conducive to news coverage than others. The MOST electronic banking network wanted to increase consumer awareness through television and newspaper stories that its ATMs were easy and convenient to use, and to educate consumers that they could use their ATM cards to purchase various goods and services.

When I was on the staff of Earle Palmer Brown Public Relations, I helped plan and coordinate a competition designed to take advantage of the media's interest in covering contests. The contest, called the MOST Sweepstakes, encouraged people to use their ATM cards more often. As part of the sweepstakes, 32 consumers in eight different media markets were randomly selected to participate in a grand prize drawing where they had the opportunity to withdraw up to $5,000 in cash from a MOST ATM machine.

To encourage the media to cover each contest, we prepared and distributed news advisories about the events, made follow-up calls to news organizations, and issued news releases after each contest to announce the names of the winners.

HALL OF FAME: YOU MAY ALREADY BE A WINNER

Contests can be good PR for the companies that sponsor them. They can also be good PR for the people who win the contests.

Robert Sachs, a teacher at the Balboa Magnet Elementary School in Northridge, California, entered his fourth-grade class in the Erector Auto Design Challenge. The nationwide program asked students to design and build a model of their vision of a "car of the future" using Erector sets for parts.

Over 6,000 students from 41 states participated in the contest, and the top 25 entries were displayed at the annual International Auto Show in New York. Sachs's class was selected as one of the top 10 winners for a vehicle designed to run on solar-power and with a backup battery. The teacher and his class were praised by Erector officials for clearly demonstrating "an understanding of automotive history, design, and safety. We were all impressed with your originality, presentation, and hard work."

Sachs and the students received a letter of congratulations from the governor of California, and were the subject of stories in the *Daily News* (the local newspaper), KABC-TV (the Los Angeles affiliate of the ABC television network), and *Hot Rod* magazine.

An unanticipated side effect of all that press attention was that Sachs became very much in demand at his school. For several months after the contest, scores of parents clamored to have their children enrolled in classes taught by Sachs, the teacher who helped win local and national recognition for the achievements of his fourth-grade students.

The news coverage about the sweepstakes included nine television stories and 14 newspaper articles. The reports were seen or read by an estimated audience of one million people in the several media markets where the events were held.

80 For a Limited Time Only

Hold a Sale, or Give It Away

One way to capture the attention of the media and the public is for you or your company to do something unusual, unique, or unexpected (but legal!).

At Thanksgiving one year, Leedmark, a retail store near Baltimore, sold turkeys for 28 cents a pound. Within a matter of days, the store had sold more than 30,000 of the birds, and was featured on local TV stations and in the region's two daily newspapers.

The following month the same store had a sale on Christmas trees, selling them at the rate of one every 20 seconds. The store set a record for selling 20,000 trees that holiday season, more than any other single store east of the Mississippi.

The steps you can take to get the media interested in you are limited only by your imagination, standards of good taste, and the law:

➤ *The Toronto Sun* reported that a Mexican restaurant was offering a lifetime of free lunches to anyone who agreed to wear a tattoo of the restaurant's logo.

➤ In Vermont, ice cream manufacturers Ben & Jerry's sought to publicize the introduction of its new flavors by offering a $65 gift package of the new products. The unusual part of the offer, however, was that flavors were a surprise, since no one would know what they were until they received the ice cream. Mary Lou Kelley, Ben & Jerry's product marketing director, told the Associated Press, "For the first time in our history, we decided to give people the chance to get in on the secret and find out what the new flavors are before they hit the shelves."

➤ In the high-tech arena, several computer makers, including Compaq and Micron, gained national media attention by offering free computers to consumers.

Calling attention to corporate anniversaries, birthdays, or milestones has also been effective in generating news coverage when:

➤ McDonalds' restaurants celebrated the opening of its 25,000th store.

➤ Crayola marked its 40th anniversary by, among other things, donating the only known box of its original Crayons to the Smithsonian Institution, and noted that over the course of four decades it had sold more than 11 billion crayons.

➤ Bayer called attention to the 100th anniversary of Aspirin by turning its 400-foot tall headquarters building into a replica of a giant box of the product.

➤ Hasbro Games unveiled its first new Monopoly game token in four decades at a well-publicized event at the American Museum of Financial History in New York City that featured someone dressed up as Mr. Monopoly. The new token was in the shape of a bag of money.

➤ The Roy Rogers restaurant chain celebrated its 20th anniversary by donating four robots for use in school fire safety and drug education programs in the communities where its restaurants were located (for a behind-the-scenes look at how this activity was publicized, see Chapter 69).

81 I Don't Want to Say That I Told You So, But . . .

Issue a Warning or Raise a Red Flag

If you or your company have expertise or specialized knowledge about any of the issues or topics that affect the public (such as health care, transportation, drugs, or the Internet), then your comments, observations, or warnings on these subjects are likely to attract local and even international attention.

That's exactly what happened when:

➤ William C. Patrick II, a biological weapons expert, showed how easy it is to sneak a container of the deadly anthrax virus past security checkpoints in the nation's capital (see Chapter 68).

➤ David Lawrence, chief executive of the Kaiser health plans, told an audience of biotech industry executives that an estimated 180,000 hospital patients die each year because of problems associated with the use of prescription drugs. As reported by the *San Francisco Chronicle*, Lawrence called those deaths "the number one public health risk in the United States, ahead of tobacco, alcohol, drugs, or guns."

➤ In 1993, Canadian technology consultant Peter de Jager issued the first warning about the hazards posed by the so-called Y2K bug, which he said could cause computer systems around the world to crash on January 1,

2000. Toronto's *Financial Post,* in a article headlined "Turn of Century Poses a Computer Problem," reported de Jager's concern that the glitch "will affect such time-related calculations as life insurance, mortgages, and pension plans. But few companies have taken steps to head off the problem, he says." Thousands of ensuing news stories about his predictions helped convince companies, organizations, and governments around the world to spend hundreds of billions of dollars to fix and avoid the Y2K bug. News organizations later dubbed de Jager as a "Paul Revere" of the information age.

Any warnings, forecases, or predictions you or your company decide to issue to the media should be tempered by caution and restraint—and a clear understanding of their legal, moral, and ethical implications.

Your comments must be warranted and supported by the facts, not made just for the sake of seeing your name in the newspaper or your face on television. Otherwise, your effort will be like the story of the boy who cried wolf and your image and reputation will suffer accordingly (as well it should).

On the other hand, if you have strong opinions or feelings about a subject you think will interest or concern the public, then that publicity can accomplish two goals at once: provide an important public service while legitimately generating public recognition for your expertise.

HALL OF SHAME: BE SURE OF YOUR FACTS

Based on information provided by scientists with the Smithsonian Institution, *The New York Times* reported in a front-page story that an asteroid "is likely to pass within 30,000 miles of Earth on Oct. 28, 2028, a Thursday, and there is a possibility that it would hit the Earth." The prediction, understandably, made headlines around the world.

The next day, however, researchers at the National Aeronautics and Space Administration said that, based on updated information and calculations, the forecast was wrong, and that the asteroid would miss the planet by 600,000 miles.

82 Be a Good Samaritan

Do a Good Deed or Charitable Work

While you certainly can't buy positive news coverage, it may be possible to at least rent it for a few hours when you make a sizable donation or contribution to important, timely, or worthwhile projects and causes.

News coverage about the good deeds of others include the following:

➤ California Governor Gray Davis asked AirTouch Cellular to give free phones to high school teachers for use in emergency situations. Davis announced the donation of 10,000 cell phones worth $1 million, plus $6 million worth of connection charges, at a news conference in the state capitol.

➤ In Glendora, California, the Glendora United Methodist Church and First Christian Church bought and gave away hundreds of locks for gun triggers. The generous donation resulted in stories by the *Los Angeles Times*, the *Baltimore Sun,* and other news organizations.

➤ Mead Johnson Nutritional, in cooperation with the National Academy of Recording Arts & Sciences, scored a PR coup when it announced a $3 million campaign to donate compact disks of classical music to new mothers. Some experts believe the music helps spur the development of an infant's brain. *The Wall Street Journal* reported that more than one million of the CDs, together with a goody bag of Mead Johnson coupons and baby products, would be given to new mothers when they leave the hospital.

➤ Three employees of a Starbucks coffee shop were murdered during a robbery attempt at one of the company's stores in the Georgetown section of Washington, D.C. To help combat further violence, the company donated $25,000 in the memory of the workers to a non-profit group to operate a youth leadership program in several Washington neighborhoods.

➤ Bank of America Corp. established a $500 million equity investment fund to help stimulate additional private investments in central cities and rural areas in 21 states where the bank operates. The move, first reported by *The Wall Street Journal,* was formally announced by President Clinton during a three-day trip to promote public-private partnerships and the administration's New Markets program.

83 Put Your Money Where Your Mouth Is

Hold a Fundraising Drive

Raising money to help pay for worthwhile community projects or activities can be made that much easier by seeking public support through news stories about your efforts. And, for the companies or organizations that play a major role in raising those funds, news coverage about their generosity can help their own public image, positioning them as good corporate citizens who want to give something back to their neighborhood.

News organizations, from major daily newspapers and neighborhood weekly publications to local television and radio stations, report regularly on the beneficiaries and benefactors of these fundraising drives:

➤ Organizers of the International Gem & Jewelry Show in Houston melted down one of O.J. Simpson's football trophies. The metal was then made into angel-shaped pins that were given to people who donated $100 or more to support a battered women's program run by the Houston Area Women's Center. The unique fundraising angle resulted in more than a dozen newspaper stories in Houston and across the country.

➤ Outback Steakhouse restaurants sponsors a charity event to help mark the opening of each of its new facilities. The *Milwaukee Journal Sentinel* reported that one of the restaurants that was scheduled to open in its readership area would donate the profits from an open house to help build a local arts center.

➤ In Portland, Oregon, the Soroptimists (a volunteer service organization for business and professional women) donated $12,000 to the Children's Museum to help in its fundraising drive to renovate the building. In an interview with the *Portland Oregonian,* Colleen Lowery, a spokesperson for the service group, said, "Soroptimists International looks for projects that can provide a positive influence on children and the community. This is a perfect opportunity to work with other nonprofits to make a difference for the Portland area's youth."

➤ In Maine, the *Bangor Daily News* reported that The Neighborhood House community center had launched a $500,000 fundraising campaign to help pay for a new program and a renovation project.

➤ In a story headlined "Mock Arrests Benefit Muscular Dystrophy," the *Sun-Sentinel* daily newspaper in Fort Lauderdale, Florida, reported that more than 250 people were "arrested," had their mug shots taken, and were taken to a local jail. They were released after they posted a $1,500 "bond" that was donated to the charity.

➤ Finally, to raise money for the Special Olympics in Virginia, dozens of people competed in a contest to see which team could pull a 145,000-pound, Boeing 727 across the tarmac at Washington Dulles International Airport. Forty teams paid $1,000 each to see who could pull the jet the fastest. The winning team pulled the plane across 12 feet of runway in 5.9 seconds. According to *The Washington Post,* which ran a picture and article about the event, the Special Olympics sponsors similar "plane pulls" across the country.

■ CHECKLIST

To help publicize your own fundraising efforts, make sure the following items are on your checklist when you tell the media about your project:

- ☐ The name of the charity or charities you are supporting.
- ☐ Why you are supporting these specific charities.
- ☐ How much you hope to raise.
- ☐ How the charity plans to use the money.
- ☐ The interesting or unique way in which you will raise the money.
- ☐ When and where the fundraising event or activity will be held.
- ☐ If appropriate, how the public can participate in the campaign.
- ☐ When you will announce how much you've raised.
- ☐ When and where you will present a check for the money you've raised.

Part VI

From Fame to Infamy

When Bad Press Happens
to Good People

84 Bad Things Only Happen to *Other* People, Right?

Create Your Image Insurance Policy

As a famous or wannabe famous person, the image you project to the public is one of your most important assets. But what can you do to protect that image?

You probably don't think twice about buying all the health, life, or property insurance you need. But what will you do to guard against dozens of potential problems and disasters, any one of which could seriously damage or destroy your carefully cultivated reputation?

There is an effective two-step process you can begin using immediately. With little cost, it will provide the "image insurance" you need to help prevent these "accidents":

1. Study others in the public spotlight to see how well or poorly they have conducted themselves.
2. Using common sense, apply those lessons to yourself.

You don't have to spend a lot of time, resources, or money to find these examples. Pay attention to the stories in your local newspapers and national magazines, watch television, and listen to the radio. News outlets provide a constant, important, and low-cost continuing education on fame by showing you how well or how poorly those in the public spotlight—whether they are individuals or corporations—conduct themselves.

■ LESSONS FOR STUDY

➤ Don't Offend Your Customers

Vietnam refugee Troung Van Tran attracted more attention than he probably bargained for when, in an effort to spur a community debate about resuming relations with Vietnam, he displayed that country's flag and a picture of the late communist leader Ho Chi Minh on the wall of his video rental store. The store is located in the Little Saigon section of Westminster, California, where a large number of pro-American Vietnamese refugees live.

But instead of a debate, the flag and photo immediately inflamed the passions of the community: at one point, more than 15,000 people surrounded the store to protest the display. Dieu Phan, a computer programmer, told *The Washington Post,* "Our people died fighting communism in our country, or died at sea trying to escape it. These symbols he has in his store are just too much. People's hearts catch on fire when they see it."

➤ Don't Lie

Nineteen-year-old Riley Weston was profiled by several news organizations as a talented young writer who was working on *Felicity,* a youth-oriented drama on the WB network. Weston, an unemployed actress, was later discovered to be 32 years old, and claimed it is "an accepted practice for actresses to lie about their age."

Weston claimed that she never figured on becoming a writer, however, and decided to maintain the ruse when she landed a job on the other side of the camera. Her deception was widely reported in the media, and Weston apologized on television.

➤ Don't Make a Mountain out of a Molehill

A boy in the first grade who affectionately kissed a female classmate on the cheek was charged with sexual harassment and threatened with suspension by school officials. The incident, which generated national and international media interest and ridicule, forced the school board to revise its sexual harassment code to take age into account.

➤ Don't Sell Out

After retiring from broadcasting, veteran newsman David Brinkley agreed to become a television spokesperson for Archer Daniels Midland, one of the sponsors of the Sunday morning public affairs show he had hosted for more than 15 years. Many of his fellow journalists were appalled, and said he had exchanged his reputation for financial gain.

TV journalist Daniel Schorr told *The Washington Post,* "I frankly cannot understand it. He is a role model for young people. I was dismayed and shocked. He built his reputation on being this acerbic, no-nonsense guy who would never lie to you. What he is doing is giving his reputation for integrity to ADM for money."

➤ Make Sure Your Own House Is in Order before You Tell Others to Clean Up Theirs

➤ Los Angeles television station KCBS aired a highly publicized investigative series of reports about the unsanitary conditions of restaurants in the area. The Los Angeles County Health Department later found several health code violations at the station's own commissary and threatened to close it down because of an overdue payment on its public health license.

➤ The director of Washington DC's health department took action against two city forensic pathologists for working without medical licenses. The following week, it was discovered that the director himself was not licensed to practice medicine in the nation's capital.

➤ Standards of Good Taste Are Subject to Change

In 1996, news accounts reported that 10 years earlier the Republican Party produced a video for a Christmas party that, according to the Associated Press "featured top GOP officials in skits parodying cocaine use and lewd behavior."

The wire service noted that "the tape's disclosure comes at a sensitive time for the GOP, which is fending off a lawsuit that includes allegations from three female former employees that Republican National Committee headquarters in Washington is rife with lewd behavior, racism and gay-bashing."

GOP official Bill Greener told the AP, "I think what you see (here) is one more indication of why what many people would consider to be innocent humor is now something that lots of people give a very serious look at."

Sometimes even judges may have a hard time judging what's appropriate.

At the end of an annual conference for judges and lawyers in Virginia, Supreme Court Chief Justice William H. Rehnquist led attendees in a rendition of "Dixie, " a Confederate marching song. African American lawyers who attended the meeting told the media they were offended by the song, saying it recalled the days of slavery.

➤ No Detail Is Too Small to Worry About

➤ To encourage Canadian consumers to shop at its stores in upstate New York, Wal-Mart mailed promotional flyers to residents of the province of Quebec, where French is the official language. But Wal-Mart printed the flyers in English. The gaffe not only outraged the people Wal-Mart wanted as customers, the store also broke Quebec's language law.

➤ After months of promising improved customer service, the Internal Revenue Service mailed out a million tax forms that included an incorrect preprinted address label which sent completed returns back to the taxpayer instead of to the IRS.

➤ To mix metaphors, Hellman's got egg on its face after it arranged to have *The New York Times* insert packets of salad dressing in tens of thousands of the papers that were delivered to home subscribers. The newspaper received dozens of calls from irate readers complaining that the fragile product samples had burst open, exploding their gooey contents over all the news that had been fit to print.

➤ If You Can't Say Anything Nice, Don't Say Anything at All

According to the *Chicago Tribune,* the owner of the Skeleteens candy company had some harsh words for parents across the country who complained that the name and packaging of its Crave candy was similar to cocaine. In reaction to their concerns, company owner Steve Corri said: "These parents are like sheep. They're nothing but uptight, narrow-minded, self-righteous, mentally constipated hypocrites, afraid to have fun."

➤ The Devil Is in the Details

No detail is too small to ignore or worry about when planning a special event, especially when you've invited the whole world to watch.

When Queen Elizabeth II stepped up to the podium to make a speech on the south lawn of the White House, the only thing a TV audience of millions of people could see was her purple-and-white straw hat bobbing up and down as she spoke behind a bank of microphones. It turned out that no one had bothered to either raise the height of the podium or offer her a step to stand on after she was introduced by a much taller President George H. Bush.

There was a lot of finger-pointing after the embarrassing incident. The President blamed his protocol chief for the snafu, and admitted he should have stepped forward to fix the problem himself. The goof was the subject of stories and jokes around the world, with *The Washington Post* and the British tabloids headlining their accounts of the episode, together with a large photo of the snafu, as "Britain's Hat of State."

The Queen referred to the incident two days later when she began an address to Congress by saying, "I do hope you can see me today from where you are." They did, since this time someone had the good sense to place a riser behind the podium for her to stand on.

➤ Don't Offend Anyone, Not Even in Jest

When Scope mouthwash named Rosie O'Donnell one of the country's least kissable celebrities as part of a Valentine's

Day promotion, the talkshow host wasn't laughing. She told her national television audience that "I will teach them to mess with me," and went on to sing the praises of Listerine, Scope's arch rival.

Listerine in turn, named O'Donnell the "queen of kissing" and agreed to donate $1,000 to O'Donnell's charity for disadvantaged children each time she kissed someone on her show. Over a three-month period, O'Donnell kissed hundreds of people on the air, raised more than $500,000 for her favorite cause, and was the subject of dozens of favorable news stories about the slight. Each story, of course, mentioned Scope's insult and positioned Listerine as the knight in shining armor who came to O'Donnell's defense.

A Scope official later admitted the promotion had backfired. "It was intended in fun. We didn't mean to inadvertently hurt anyone. We've offered our apologies and they've been accepted." O'Donnell said she thought the episode "taught (Scope) a lesson in negative advertising. People don't like it when you're mean."

➤ Don't Put It in Writing if You Don't Have To

Is there a business or personal document on your desk or in your files that, if it were printed on the front page of the local newspaper, would cause you or your company grief, embarrassment, or humiliation? The easiest way to prevent that from happening is not to put it in writing in the first place.

The *Daily News* in New York City reported that Amcasts, an advertising sales firm, had sent a memo to companies that made disparaging remarks about blacks and Hispanics. Among other things, the memo said recipients should limit the number of commercials they purchase on Hispanic and black radio stations, since "advertisers should want prospects, not suspects."

A spokesperson for Amcasts told the *Daily News* that the memo "is a year old and virtually everything in it is obsolete." The company said the embarrassing memo was not meant to be seen by advertisers or anyone else.

No kidding!

➤ Never Claim More Than Your Fair Share of Credit

Asked to explain how his record differed from that of former Democratic Sen. Bill Bradley of New Jersey, Vice President Al Gore said, "During my service in the United States Congress, I took the initiative of creating the Internet." In fact, the Internet was created in 1969, several years before Gore was first elected to the House of Representatives.

The gaffe led to sarcastic newspaper editorials about Gore seeking more than his fair share of credit for the Internet, and prompted rival politicians to poke fun at the vice president. In a tongue-in-cheek news release, Senate Majority Leader Trent Lott of Mississippi claimed credit for creating the paper clip.

➤ Take Responsibility for Your Actions

It's amazing how quickly people can change their mind when they find out the media is looking over their shoulder.

Even though U.S. Senator Robert C. Byrd (D-W. Va.) had rear-ended a van in Washington's Virginia suburbs, police said they would not charge him because he was a member of Congress.

But Byrd apparently changed his tune when he found out that *The Washington Post* was looking into the incident. The lawmaker insisted that he not receive any special treatment, and asked that he be charged in the accident. He was.

Ironically, in an editorial in the Capitol Hill newspaper *The Hill,* Byrd was complimented for setting "a commendable example by refusing to use congressional immunity to escape punishment. . . . By accepting reasonability for his action, Byrd has demonstrated his respect for the all-important democratic principle that no citizen is above the law. It's a lesson that other high officials, especially President Clinton, would do well to heed."

When his day in court arrived, Byrd pleaded "no contest." Since it was his first offense, the judge did not fine Byrd, but the senator did pay $30 in court costs.

➤ Don't Buy Trouble

According to a story by the Associated Press, Wyth-Ayers Laboratories, which makes a portion of the fen-phen diet drug, "hired ghostwriters for articles promoting obesity treatment and then used prominent researchers to publish the works under their names." A lawsuit charged that the company "allegedly tried to play down or remove descriptions of side effects from the articles."

While company officials defended the articles as "a common practice in the industry," medical experts and journalists were critical. Stories about the incident were carried by several news organizations, including the *Dallas Morning News,* which first reported the story.

➤ Be Prepared for Success

When the Encyclopaedia Britannica converted its paid printed reference work to a free on-line service, the overwhelming public response was more than it could handle. Soon after its debut, Britannica's Web site received more than 10 million hits a day.

Unfortunately, the company had not anticipated how popular the Internet-based service would be, and did not have the necessary software or hardware to accommodate everyone who tried to visit the site. Millions of people were turned away from www.britannica.com, and newspapers across the country published stories about what the Associated Press called "a real fiasco.com."

➤ Weigh Your Words Carefully

News events can be important opportunities for you to be quoted by the media—but only if you know what you are talking about, since your off-the-cuff remarks may send the wrong message to the media and the public, and you may wind up eating your words. After professional basketball star Latrell Sprewell was fired by the Golden State Warriors for choking and threatening to kill his coach, San Francisco Mayor Willie Brown defended the player, saying "His boss may have needed choking. It may have been justified. . . ."

In an editorial titled "Hold On, Mr. Mayor," the *San Francisco Chronicle* noted, "The same mayor who claims to abhor workplace violence denounced the public reaction to Sprewell's offense—and his year-long suspension by the NBA—as 'overkill.' Brown is a powerful and persuasive communicator. In this case, he is sending a mixed message. The wrong message."

After a public outcry about his remarks, Brown issued a statement saying, "Violence in the workplace, or any place else, cannot be condoned under any circumstances."

Throughout this book, I've included a series of anecdotes like the ones above that demonstrate how well or poorly others in the public eye have conducted themselves—lessons that are reported by the national and local media on a daily basis. The lessons, and the chapters where you can read more about them, include:

➤ If it's too good to be true, the press will show that it isn't (Chapter 61).

➤ Soundbites can bite back (Chapter 28).

➤ You might not be able to control what the media says, but sometimes you can decide when they say it (Chapter 24).

➤ Good deeds can get good press (Chapter 82).

➤ Tell your side of the story (Chapter 85).

➤ Contests can be as good for the winners as for the sponsors (Chapter 79).

➤ Don't just say it . . . show it (Chapter 13).

➤ If PR people are so good, why do they have problems (Chapter 16)?

➤ Sometimes a news interview can have unexpected consequences (Chapter 27).

➤ Watch what you say (Chapter 22).

➤ You don't have to fill the media void all by yourself (Chapter 66).

For the latest examples of how well or poorly those in the public spotlight are handling themselves, visit my Web site at www.edwardsegal.com.

The bottom line is this: learning from others is easier and less costly than experiencing these problems yourself. You can take three simple steps to ensure that you do not repeat the mistakes of others and keep your "image insurance policy" up to date:

1. Consider all the possible consequences of anything you, your company, or your organization may say or do.

2. Identify everything that could go wrong in your professional life or business; take steps to guard against those potential hazards.

3. Pay close attention to the successes and failures of others as reported by the media.

Here's hoping that the only examples you set are good ones.

85 Just in Case You Need It . . .

Prepare Your Crisis Communications Plan

Your worst business nightmare has just come true: a crisis that threatens your professional reputation, your relations with clients or customers, the bottom line of your corporation, or the image of your organization.

What can you do now to help prevent your nightmare from becoming a reality?

Be prepared.

The best way to deal with a crisis is to prevent it from happening in the first place:

➤ List everything that could go wrong in your organization.

➤ Take every step possible to guard against it.

➤ Make sure that you have a workable plan in place that can be quickly and effectively implemented to handle any problem situation.

Several well-known corporations have found out the hard way the consequences of being unprepared, ranging from Sears for the way it handled charges of auto repair fraud to Exxon for its clumsy response to the Valdez oil-spill disaster.

How you handle a problem can have a direct impact on what the public thinks about you and your company or organization. According to a survey by National Family Opinion, 95 percent of people feel more offended by a corporation that lies about a crisis than by the crisis itself.

Here are some guidelines to prepare and implement a communications plan for dealing with the media and the public during a crisis.

Since no crisis communications plan can ever cover all possible situations, this generic plan is intended to serve as an outline for the basic procedures and policies that should be followed when handling an emergency. *These recommendations should be customized to meet the needs, concerns, and situation of your own organization.*

■ STRATEGIES

The strategies behind these recommendations are based on the fact that appearances and perceptions about how a crisis is handled can be more important than reality. During a crisis you should:

➤ Control the crisis instead of letting the crisis control you.

➤ Immediately provide accurate and up-to-date information—and your point of view—to the media and the public.

➤ Make sure you are available to and accessible by the media.

Your plan should include the following components.

■ CRISIS TEAM

Procedures

➤ Establish guidelines for what constitutes or will trigger a crisis.

➤ Establish a reporting process to transfer responsibility for the handling of a crisis to a designated team leader.

➤ Establish guidelines to determine when a team leader should activate a crisis team.

Team Leader

➤ The team leader should be an individual who is intimately familiar with the organization and can be reached 24 hours a day, 7 days a week. In case of illness, travel, or vacation, a backup team leader should be appointed.

➤ The team leader should have the authority to deal with the highest ranking officials in the organization.

Team Members

➤ Members of the team should include a representative from each major component of the organization.

➤ In addition, a list should be prepared of the names, phone numbers, and fax numbers of specialists who would know how to handle the specific details of a particular kind of crisis or emergency.

➤ All members of the crisis team should be required to carry pagers, and to appoint backups in case of illness, vacation, or travel.

➤ When activated, the team should have access to all relative information about the situation, including the who, what, when, where, why, and how of the crisis.

➤ Before it is needed for an actual crisis, the team should meet to come up with the worst-case scenarios, and determine what, from a theoretical standpoint, the options or most appropriate response should be.

➤ While actual decisions will be based on real situations, a list of potential alternatives that could be discussed and considered during an emergency will help save valuable time.

➤ These scenarios and responses should be written down and kept as a ready reference for when the team meets.

➤ Decide who else should be notified about a particular crisis, such as political or elected leaders.

➤ Determine ahead of time where the team will work, access to communications, secretarial support, and so forth.

Spokesperson

A spokesperson should be designated who, during a crisis, will:

➤ Communicate and advance the organization's viewpoint.

➤ Release only that information which is needed to inform the media and the public. Initial announcement of a crisis should be limited to giving out basic details about the location, type of incident, when it happened, why it happened (if known), and who is involved or affected, and what is being done about it.

➤ Give updates as appropriate to the media.

➤ Respond to all press calls.

➤ Have access to top officials of the organization 24 hours a day. All members of the leadership of the organization must have access to the spokesperson around the clock; and in case of illness or vacation, a backup spokesperson should be designated.

➤ Provide appropriate organizations in the community with the spokesperson's name, telephone number, and pager number in case they need to reach him or her about a crisis situation that officials of the organization have not yet heard about.

■ GENERAL GUIDELINES

Do

➤ Demonstrate the organization's concern and show that it is in charge of or on top of the situation.

➤ Prepare a chronology or fact sheet about the crisis. Distribute it as a handout for use by the crisis team, the media, and as a historical account of the incident.

➤ Gather and centralize all information in one location.

➤ Have access to facilities, staff, and resources to prepare, print, and distribute information when needed.

➤ Refer to written statements that have been approved for release to the press when answering or giving out information.

➤ Get the crisis out in public as soon as possible.

➤ Put the matter behind you as soon as possible.

➤ Be honest and candid without violating any confidences.

➤ Go to the scene of the crisis immediately.

➤ Find ways to cut red tape.

➤ Release only verified information.

➤ Explain and inform the employees or members of the organization about what happened.

➤ Provide information from the viewpoint of public interest instead of from the organization's interest.

➤ Tell employees or members of the organization what they should say to the press (e.g., "I'm sorry, but you will have to talk to [insert name] about that").

➤ Notify officials of the organization prior to the release of information.

➤ Take appropriate steps to communicate information directly to the public (e.g., the Internet, letters, signage, advertising).

➤ Keep a list of all calls received during the crisis.

➤ Thank staff and others in writing immediately after the crisis for a job well done.

Do Not

➤ Speculate on the cause of the emergency.

➤ Speculate on the resumption of normal operations.

➤ Speculate on the outside effects of the emergency.

➤ Speculate on the dollar value of the losses (if any).

➤ Place blame.

➤ Leave the press unattended at the scene of the emergency.

➤ Be defensive.

➤ Minimize the problem.

➤ Let the story dribble out.

➤ Release information about people if it will violate their privacy or legal rights.

➤ Say "no comment." Instead, explain why you cannot comment.

■ IMPLEMENTATION

➤ Distribute copies of the finished crisis communications plan, including phone numbers of people to be contacted in case of an emergency, to those likely to need them.

➤ Meet with and circulate an abbreviated version of the plan to others in the community who would most likely be called in a crisis.

■ TEST, TEST, TEST

After your crisis communications guidelines and policies
are in place:

➤ Stage a mock crisis to identify any potential problems and revise or modify these guidelines as needed.

➤ Stage an annual mock crisis to evaluate the state of
readiness of the organization to an emergency, evaluate
procedures, and make changes as necessary.

HALL OF FAME: TELL YOUR SIDE OF THE STORY

As soon as allegations surfaced that syringes had been found
in the aluminum cans of Diet Pepsi, PepsiCo assembled a crisis communications team to handle the situation and ensure
that its denials of any possible product tampering were included in news reports.

According to Becky Madeira, PepsiCo's senior vice president for public affairs, the company:

➤ Joined forces with the Food and Drug Administration to
investigate the allegations.

➤ Arranged for corporate officials to conduct interviews
with dozens of news organizations.

➤ Produced and distributed a video news release to assure
the public its product was safe to drink and showed the
procedures in place that made it impossible to tamper
with cans during the manufacturing process.

➤ Publicized the fact that a shopper had been caught by a
store's video surveillance camera trying to insert a sy-
ringe into a can of Diet Pepsi.

➤ Ran newspaper ads telling consumers, "Those stories
about Diet Pepsi were a hoax. Plain and simple. Not true.
Drink all the Diet Pepsi you want."

Within days, the public's concerns about the safety of the
product were alleviated. PepsiCo's handling of the situation
later received high marks from several crisis management
experts.

Part VII

"Thanks for Having Me Back, Oprah."

Now That You're Famous . . .

86 Don't You Know Who I Am?
Find Out How Famous You've Become

In Chapter 14 you completed an exercise in which you set certain goals for achieving fame or recognition for yourself or company.

Go back now to that chapter to review your plan and objectively answer the following questions:

➤ How well did I implement the plan?

➤ How close did I come to attaining my goals?

➤ How famous have I become?

While only you can answer the first two questions, there are measurements, tools, standards, and resources to help paint a complete picture of how famous you are, and whether and how that recognition has affected your job, career, company, products, services, expertise, or reputation.

The sources of this information can include:

➤ Print, radio, video, and Web site monitoring services (see Resources).

➤ Computer databases.

➤ Public opinion polls.

➤ Focus groups.

➤ Business or sales figures.

➤ Feedback from your friends, colleagues, coworkers, clients, and customers.

Elements of your "fame portrait" may include:

➤ The number of times you've been mentioned or featured in newspapers, magazines, wire service stories, and television and radio reports.

➤ The number of times you've appeared on radio and TV talk shows as a guest.

➤ Circulation or viewership figures of the news organizations that have done stories about you or your company.

➤ Name recognition or reputation as measured by public opinion polls or focus groups.

➤ Sales figures for your products or services.

➤ Number of new clients or customers.

➤ Hits on your Web site.

➤ Raises or promotions at work.

➤ Comments from employers, clients, or colleagues.

If you are searching for the best, most effective way to measure the success of your efforts, then you have a lot of company.

A study conducted in June 1999 by CARMA International for *PR Week* found that professional public relations practitioners at PR agencies, corporations, and government agencies depend on many techniques—from press clippings to Web site hits—to help measure the results of their PR activities. Those surveyed included 301 readers and subscribers of *PR Week* who were randomly selected to be interviewed for the study.

The following list shows, in order of frequency, how often the pros used various techniques to gauge the success of their most recent PR campaign:

➤ Analyzing the content of stories and articles (69%).

➤ Anecdotal feedback and gut feelings (58%).

➤ One-on-one interviews with the target audience (48%).

➤ Consumer surveys (47%).

➤ Media reach (47%).

➤ Attendance at conferences or events (45%).

➤ Focus groups (28%).

➤ The equivalent value in advertising dollars of the news coverage that resulted (25%).

➤ Pretesting campaign themes (21%).

➤ Industry awards or prizes that their efforts receive (18%).

➤ Polling (18%).

➤ Increases in sales or the prices of shares of stock (18%).

A significant portion (31%) did not do any follow-up evaluation of the effectiveness or impact of their work.

How much will you have to spend to determine the success of your efforts? Again, it depends on what your goals were to begin with. If you just wanted a letter to the editor to be published in the local daily paper, then all you have to do is read the paper to see if they used your correspondence.

But if you've waged an aggressive nationwide campaign to promote your expertise, product, or service, it could cost hundreds or thousands of dollars to document your success. Various media monitoring services are listed in the Resources section.

87 Be Careful What You Wish for . . .
Don't Let Fame Go to Your Head

If you've successfully followed all the advice in this book, it's possible that by now you've achieved some level of fame or recognition.

If so, the good news could be that:

➤ All the stories about you or your company are positive.

➤ The quotes used by the media are accurate.

➤ Your picture looks good in newspapers and magazines.

➤ You have a winning personality on television.

➤ You sound good on radio.

➤ People recognize you when you walk down the street or attend industry conferences or workshops.

➤ You get the best table at restaurants and tickets to the most popular shows.

➤ Because of the news coverage about your company, more people are buying your products or services.

The bad news is that you'd better not get used to it, because that fame will not last forever.

One of the reasons I called this book *Getting Your 15 Minutes of Fame* was to emphasize that fame is temporary. Of course, depending on why you wanted to be widely known in the first place (see Chapter 6) and the goals you hoped to achieve by implementing your plan (see Chapter 14), your fame may not need to last any longer than 15 minutes anyway. When it's over, you can get on with the rest of your life. And like any other pleasant experience, you may have some nice memories that you'll be able to recall and relive over and over again.

Psychologists say that too many people get used to and believe that their fame and the good times and good feelings that can come with it will last indefinitely, and that all the wonderful things people say and believe about them must be true.

It can be quite a shock when they find out otherwise. Sooner or later the public recognition can turn to indifference, the adulation can turn to apathy, and reporters will stop calling for quotes or interviews.

For some people, achieving and maintaining the level of fame they've lusted after can be a mixed blessing. That's because fame can act like a drug to distort your perception of reality and lead you to do or say things that are completely out of character, and even self-destructive.

These and other aftereffects of fame can linger for days, months, or years, and wind up alienating you from your friends, family, coworkers, and colleagues.

Dr. Carole Stovall is a licensed psychologist and executive coach in Washington, DC who has counseled hundreds of executives over the years. She explains that when people concentrate on achieving fame to the exclusion of everything else in their lives, "Often when they look up all they have is recognition, money, or power. But they don't have a good marriage, if they have a marriage at all. Their health is shot and they don't know their children.

"And when they finally do get some down time and want to spend it with their family, they discover that their family is no longer there and that their life is empty. It's very sad but it is also very common."

She adds, however, that it is possible to come back from the brink. "Go back to your core values, return to what's important in your life. Anyone who has ever received a tremendous amount of fame will tell you that the most important things to them are their relationships with people and having a balanced life."

"I've found that when executives place more importance on their family than on achieving fame, they feel happier and more contented and their success means even more to them."

If you are just starting out on your road to fame (see Chapter 2), Stovall says it's important to remember to share your experience with others along the way.

"People who have someone to share their fame with are less likely to become isolated or turn into workaholics. When they are in balance with their family and core values, they are more likely to take better care of themselves and be in better physical shape. For them, the problems associated with money, power, and sex that can bring people down are not an issue."

There are several steps you can take to make your experience in the public spotlight a good one not just for you, but for your family, friends, and colleagues.

Stovall recommends, "Don't confuse who you are with what you do. What you achieve as an individual or do for a living is not who you are as a person. Your self-esteem has to be kept separate from the work that you do or the fame that you achieve."

She points to the famous inventor Thomas Edison, noting that he had 10,000 failures before he came up with a lightbulb that worked: "If his identity was based on his ability to do something terrific within the first five tries, then he would never have been able to keep going."

Dr. David Clayman is a clinical psychologist and CEO of the Process Strategies Institute in Charleston, West Virginia, which provides employee assistance and managed care programs.

Although Clayman points out, "No one has a school on how to deal with fame," he offers the following advice for those who are or who want to be in the public spotlight:

➤ Remember where you came from, because you may have to go back there tomorrow.

➤ Don't believe your own press clippings.

➤ Don't think you are any better than anyone else.

➤ Ask yourself whether the impact your fame will have on you, your friends, and family will be worth the cost.

➤ Ask yourself how you'd feel if, having been famous one day, you lose it all the next. Remember that today you may be a superstar, but tomorrow you can be a has-been.

➤ Share your experiences and feelings about being in the public spotlight with your friends, spouse, or significant other so they know what its like and why you are doing it.

➤ Keep yourself grounded by holding on to old friendships.

Former Congressman Michael Barnes, who used to be in the news all the time because of his political and congressional activities, has this word of advice for wannabe-famous people: "Don't get used to it." He notes, "Fame is very fleeting.

HALL OF FAME: INSTANT FAME

Michael Barnes knows what it's like to go from nobody to somebody overnight.

As a freshman congressman from Maryland, he served as the spokesperson for a group of Democratic members of Congress who believed that the renomination of President Jimmy Carter would be suicidal for the Democratic Party. The legislators and other Democrats waged an unsuccessful three-week effort to allow delegates to the National Democratic Convention to vote for any presidential candidate they wanted.

Barnes was catapulted virtually overnight into the national limelight:

➤ He was a guest on TV interview shows such as *Meet the Press* and *Face the Nation.*

➤ He was the subject of stories in every major newspaper and news magazine in the country.

➤ Reporters eager for interviews camped out in front of his house.

➤ Because of his support for an open convention, Barnes faced both political criticism from the Carter White House and pressure from would-be Democratic presidential candidates.

Barnes compared the brief but intensive experience to being "on a roller coaster ride that is out of control. You are flying through the air being tossed about by forces over which you have no say or influence. It was both scary and exhilarating. It was just insane."

He also had mixed emotions about the situation he found himself in.

"Here I was a freshman member of Congress challenging a sitting President for the renomination of his party. On the one hand, I had some regret that I had allowed myself to get into this predicament. On the other, I knew that politicians could go through their entire careers and not receive this kind of attention."

Barnes said that, on balance, the experience was a plus for his political career since his colleagues in Congress thought the young politician had handled the challenges of the situation in a mature and responsible manner.

There were times in my life when I would walk down the streets of the Nation's Capital and virtually everyone I passed recognized me because I was so much in the news. Today, I can walk into any restaurant in downtown Washington and probably be recognized by less than 10 percent of the people in the place."

Not only is fame fleeting: it's no place for fakes or pretensions. Pat Croce, owner and president of the Philadelphia 76ers professional baseball team, cautions, "A person in the public eye must be true to themselves. You have to come across as real and legitimate or else the public will see right through you. Never try to fool your clients, customers, or fans."

■ IN THEIR OWN WORDS

What's Important

Fame is not about me, it's about the fans who follow the team. Do I want to sell tickets? Yes! Do I want people to applaud the team? Yes! Do I want them to come to games? Yes! Do I want them to buy the team's merchandise? Yes! But I want the fans to know that this is their team and hope they will support it because it's fun for them, not for me.

Pat Croce, Owner and President
Philadelphia 76ers professional basketball team

Glossary

Audio News Release   The audio version of a video news release, which is sent to the news directors of radio stations (see Chapter 54).

Biographical Profile   Provides editors and reporters with key background information about an individual (see Chapter 50).

Fact Sheet   Describes essential, complex, or background information reporters may need to fully understand or accurately report an event or news announcement. May include information that is too long to put into a news release (see Chapter 46).

Interview   An opportunity for editors and reporters to talk directly with a person who is the subject of a news release or who is making news for some reason. Comments made during interviews are often used as quotes or background information in news reports and articles (see Chapter 27).

Letter to the Editor   Usually written by a reader in response to a story published in a newspaper or magazine about events or developments in the news (see Chapter 52).

Media Event   A staged event or activity that is designed to provide a backdrop or news hook for news announcements (see Chapters 55, 69, and 79).

Media Monitoring Service   Commercial service that monitors newspapers, radio stations, magazines, and television news programs for stories that include specified key words. Copies of the news coverage can be used in press kits to provide additional background information to editors and reporters, measure the effectiveness of a public relations campaign, and demonstrate to the media that your story is newsworthy (see Resources).

Media Training   Professional advice and mock interview sessions that prepare you to deal with editors and reporters in a variety of situations with confidence and authority. The training includes how to ensure that your themes and messages are reported by the media, how to conduct news interviews, how to prepare and use soundbites/inkbites, what to wear and how to stand or sit during interviews, how to handle negative questions, and so forth (see Resources section).

Multicity Media Tour   Traveling from one city or region to another to meet with editors and reporters in person or to appear live or taped on locally broadcast news programs or shows (see Chapter 58).

News Advisory   Serves as a notice or invitation to the media about a planned event, activity, or scheduled news announcement (see Chapter 48).

News Conference   A gathering of reporters that enables a newsmaker to meet with as many members of the media as possible at one time and in one place. These events include an opening statement, the distribution of a news release or other press materials, and a question-and-answer period (see Chapter 55).

News Hook   The basic element of news behind an announcement, activity, or project that will convince editors, reporters, or columnists to do stories about it. The most effective news hooks affect the most people, impact a news organization's audience, and address the audience's interests, needs, or concerns. News hooks vary depending on the nature, needs, and audience of each news organization. The best news hooks answer the question of "who cares?" in a direct, forceful, timely, and compelling manner (see Chapters 63–83).

News Release   The cornerstone of most public relations efforts, a one- to two-page document explaining the who, what, when, where, and why of a news announcement (see Chapter 45).

Op-Ed and Bylined Article   Opinion pieces published by newspapers and magazines that explain and discuss personal viewpoints, observations, or experiences (see Chapter 51).

Opinion Poll   An effort to determine what the public thinks or feels about an issue or topic. The results of the poll can be used as a news hook to help generate media coverage about a project or cause (see Chapter 74).

Photo Op   A step below a formal news conference, a photo op is usually staged for the benefit of television cameras and photographers (see Chapter 56).

Photo and Cutline   A black-and-white or color photo of a person, product, or event, accompanied by a caption that identifies or explains the picture (see Chapter 49).

Press Kit A complete package of information that provides the media with everything they need to know about a news announcement. The kit often includes photos, fact sheets, news releases, and related news clippings (see Chapter 47).

Press Lists Alternative methods for identifying and targeting news organizations, finding the right editors and reporters who may be interested in your story, and different ways of distributing news releases and news advisories to the media. These methods may include consulting various media directories and using commercial newswire, press release distribution, and fax broadcasting services (see Chapter 59).

Resource to the Media Establishing and maintaining ongoing working relationships with editors, reporters, and columnists who cover topics or activities in which you have knowledge, experience, or expertise. By providing them with good quotes and worthwhile story ideas, journalists may come to rely on you as a source of information for other stories and interview you for those articles or news reports (see Chapter 33).

Satellite Media Tour The use of video and satellite technology to enable a newsmaker to be interviewed in a short time frame by reporters in different cities across the country (see Chapter 57).

Soundbite/Inkbite The nine seconds or 30–40 word excerpt from an interview that may be used in newspaper, radio, television, or wires service stories; the amount of time it takes to read this sentence aloud (see Chapter 28).

Story Pitch Letter One- or two-page letter to editors and reporters explaining the importance or significance of an announcement or event, and encouraging them to do stories about it (see Chapter 60).

Video News Release A complete 90-second news report about an event, activity, or news announcement. It is sent to television stations that broadcast local news programs. According to surveys, 75 percent of all television stations accept and use video news releases in some way (see Chapter 53).

Visual The picture or action symbolizing the new hook that will most likely capture the attention of newspaper photographers and television camera crews (see Chapter 13).

Resources

This section includes a sample news release and magazine column that were mentioned earlier in the book, as well as a list of useful vendor services and sources of information. For additional sample press materials, please be sure to visit www.edwardsegal.com.

SAMPLE NEWS RELEASE

IMPROVED STOP SIGN, SELF-HEATING BEVERAGE CONTAINER, AND PROTOTYPE FIRE TRUCK ARE AMONG NEW PRODUCTS ON DISPLAY THIS WEEK AT WORLD'S LARGEST PLASTICS EXPOSITION

CHICAGO, June 18—A revolutionary graffiti-resistant plastic stop sign that reflects light more effectively, a prototype fire truck made with plastic parts, and new heat-resistant roofing material are among the more than 1,000 new products and services on display this week at NPE 1997, the world's largest and most influential plastics show to be held this year.

NPE 1997, the triennial exposition and conference for the plastics industry, is sponsored by The Society of the Plastics Industry, Inc. (SPI). The show runs through June 20 at McCormick Place in Chicago, Ill., North America's largest exhibition center.

More than 1,700 companies from 26 countries representing every sector of the plastics industry are exhibiting the latest innovations in materials, machinery and controls, as well as the state-of-the-art in auxiliary equipment, moldmaking, robotics and automation.

SAMPLE NEWS RELEASE *(Continued)*

Among the consumer-related products on display at the show this week are:

➤ A prototype stop sign. The traffic sign incorporates new plastics technologies that provide greater reflective capability and improved durability in harsh weather conditions. It also features an anti-theft device and a graffiti-proof face. The 10-pound sign is believed to be the world's first all-plastic, retroflective stop sign.

➤ A new self-heating beverage container that can warm liquids by 75 degrees within five minutes and keep fluids warm for at least 20 minutes. The device, which holds 10.5 ounces of liquid, features a trigger button on the bottom of the container that, when pushed, activates a mix of two natural heating materials. Beverage makers are expected to use the new container to market coffee, tea, soup, and baby formula.

➤ A prototype fire truck made with plastic panels. The plastic panels make the truck lighter, thus enabling the vehicle to carry more water, equipment and firefighters.

➤ Flame resistant plastic roofing material, featuring a new cedar shake replica that is resistant to wind, hail, rain and extreme temperatures and is tough enough to walk on.

Visitors will also see the latest developments in computerization, including computer-integrated manufacturing (CIM), computer-aided design (CAD), computer-aided manufacturing (CAM) and computer-aided engineering (CAE). All in all, more than 80 product categories are on display.

Attendees include professionals from all segments of the plastics manufacturing and processing industry, representatives of end-use markets, and participants from government, academic, and research organizations.

NPE 1997 Chairman David Hahn said that this week, "NPE serves as the world's stage for the unveiling of the newest and most advanced products and services that the plastics industry has to offer. The show reinforces the fact that NPE continues to set the standards for the introduction and display of new equipment and services for the global plastics industry."

(continued)

SAMPLE NEWS RELEASE *(Continued)*

Hahn said the show is the "the biggest, the best, and the most successful in NPE history," with more than 1,700 exhibiting companies, over one million new square feet of space, and more than 75,000 visitors registered to date.

SPI President Larry L. Thomas said that "the steady growth of the exposition since the first NPE was first held in 1946 is an important barometer of the health of the plastics industry. Compared to that first show, NPE 1997 boasts more than 40 times the exhibit space and more than 10 times the number of exhibitors."

NPE is sponsored by The Society of the Plastics Industry, Inc. (SPI) a trade association of nearly 2,000 members representing all segments of the plastics industry in the United States. SPI's business units and committees are composed of plastics processors, raw material suppliers, machinery manufacturers, moldmakers and other industry-related groups and individuals. Founded in 1937, SPI serves as the "voice" of the plastics industry.

Used with permission.

SAMPLE MAGAZINE OR NEWSLETTER COLUMN

COMMUNICATE LIKE A PRO

By Arnold Sanow

From the time we're young children, we're taught how to talk. All through school we take classes in English to help us speak and write properly. What we aren't taught is the art of interpersonal communication.

Being an effective communicator is especially important in the sales process. To move your sales to the next level follow the guidelines below:

Good Communication Skills Can Be Learned. Many people believe good communicators are "born with" the skill—and

SAMPLE MAGAZINE OR NEWSLETTER
COLUMN *(Continued)*

only a few "lucky people" possess outstanding communication ability. In reality, those excellent communicators who you admire either had superior role models, or they made a deliberate effort to learn. For example, Winston Churchill, one of the greatest orators of all time, grew up with a severe stuttering problem. It took him three years to get through the 8th grade because of his poor communication skills. But with practice and determination he became a great speaker.

To help you with your interpersonal communication skills, I would recommend Toastmasters International. Toastmasters programs can be offered at your workplace. They focus on all aspects of communication and the program allows you to get positive constructive feedback. To get more information, call 1-800-9-WE-SPEAK.

You Have Two Ears and One Mouth. Many people assume that good communication only deals with how well you talk. This couldn't be further from the truth. Most of the communication mishaps happen because of poor listening habits.

To become an active listener follow these 6 rules:

➤ Limit your own talking. You have two ears and one mouth. The more you listen the more opportunity you'll have to find and understand the wants, needs and aspirations of your employees.

➤ Don't interrupt. By interrupting your clients, sensitivity, rapport and commitment are all killed. Although at times it seems expedient to interrupt, this perceived lack of respect for others helps to deteriorate the relationship and makes it harder to develop rapport.

➤ Notice nonverbal communication. Only 7% of the message we are communicating is through the words we use, 38% is through the tone of our voice and 55% is through our body language. This means that 93% of the message that someone communicates is conveyed by body language and tone of voice. Therefore, if you're talking to another person and they start doing things like, crossing their arms, crossing their legs away from you, yawning, leaning back, looking bored or avoiding eye contact, you

(continued)

SAMPLE MAGAZINE OR NEWSLETTER
COLUMN *(Continued)*

need to "listen" to their body language. By being sensitive to their body language you pick up the real underlying messages and feelings that are being conveyed. In addition, you can encourage others to communicate with you by softening your body language. Follow the key points in this acronym: S-smile, O-open posture F-forward lean T-touch in a friendly way, such as shaking hands, E-eye contact, N-nodding to show you're listening.

➤ Don't only think about what you're going to say next. Too many times we are so concerned about what we want to say that we don't hear what the other person is really saying. By not paying total attention, we focus on what we think is important to them and not what they're really concerned about.

➤ Talk in a conducive setting. To get others to listen to us and have them focus on the substance of our message, distractions must be minimized. Is your office too hot? Too cool? Is the phone ringing all the time? Are you answering the phone while talking to them? Are there other people around? Do you have distracting habits? To make sure active listening takes place, you must eliminate all distractions.

➤ Paraphrase what has been said—To avoid misunderstandings, it's important to repeat back what you have heard. The problem is that when you talk, how you say something and the words you use may have a different meaning. Many times we say, "do you understand? or does that make sense?" In most cases the other person will say, "yes." The question we really need to find out is, "what did they understand?" And since it may seem rude to ask that question, we need to repeat back what they said to make sure we are both hearing and understanding the same thing.

Arnold Sanow, MBA, CSP, is the author of four books, including "Marketing Boot Camp." He is a professional speaker and trainer with more than 2,000 speaking engagements to his credit. His keynotes, breakout sessions, and seminars focus on marketing, sales, customer service, communication, and presentation skills. You can reach him at 703-255-3133 or visit his Web site at www.arnoldsanow.com.

➤ Vendors, Services, and Sources of Information

You can make the task of achieving and managing your fame or public recognition much easier by considering the use of the following vendors or services. (While I have used many of them in the past, I do not endorse them or guarantee their information, services, prices, or performance. You should evaluate each of them on their own merits, request and review their costs or estimates, and decide for yourself whether to use them.) For your convenience, I've noted the chapters in which their expertise could be of assistance in helping you to implement the advice, activities, or recommendations in that part of the book.

To ensure you receive the help you need from these resources, be as specific and detailed as possible with them about the type or level of assistance you are seeking and the kind of information you are after. When dealing with consultants or PR firms, there are no stupid questions or too many questions you can ask, so be sure you find out as much as you need to know before you make an intelligent decision about their services or fees.

For an updated list of resources, please visit my Web site at www.edwardsegal.com.

Audio News Releases (see Chapter 54)

Medialink, Inc.
708 Third Avenue
New York, NY 10017
Phone 800-843-0677
Web site www.medialink.com

North American Network, Inc.
Corporate Offices
7910 Woodmont Avenue
Suite 1400
Bethesda, MD 20814
Phone 301-654-9810
Fax 301-654-9828
Web site www.radiospace.com

Become a Resource to the Media (see Chapter 33)

Experts magazine
6852 Skyline Drive
Delray Beach, FL 33446
Phone 561-637-7912
Fax 561-498-7316
Web site www.expertsmagazine.com

ProfNet
Phone 800-PROFNET
Fax 516-689-1425
E-mail info2profnet.com
Web site www.profnet.com

Radio-TV Interview Report
135 East Plumstead Avenue
Lansdowne, PA 19050
Phone 800-989-1400
Web site www.rtir.com

SpeakersVoice Association
E-mail info@speakersvoice.com
Web site www.speakersvoice.com

Yearbook of Experts, Authorities and Spokespersons
2233 Wisconsin Avenue, NW
Washington, DC 20007
Phone 202-333-4904
Fax 202-342-5411
E-mail editor@yearbooknews.com
Web site www.yearbooknews.com

Cyber Media Tours™ (see Chapter 58)

Medialink, Inc.
708 Third Avenue
New York, NY 10017
Phone 800-843-0677
Web site www.medialink.com

Editorial Calendars (see Chapter 62)

Edcals.com
(A subscription-based Web site that enables you to search thousands of continually updated editorial calendars of major magazines and newspapers featuring more than 100,000 planned upcoming stories and special issues. Edcals.com is a joint service of Bacon's Information and MediaMap.)
Web site www.edcals.com

Bacon's Information, Inc.
332 South Michigan Avenue
Chicago, IL 60604
Phone 800-621-0561
Fax 312-922-3127
Web site www.baconsinfo.com

MediaMap
215 First Street
Cambridge, MA 02142
Phone 888-624-1620
Fax 617-374-9345
Web site www.mediamap.com

Media Information Directories and Services (see Chapter 59)

Bacon's Information, Inc.
(Publishes a series of directories with contact information for newspapers, magazines, radio stations, TV stations, cable outlets, and Web sites.)
332 South Michigan Avenue
Chicago, IL 60604
Phone 800-621-0561
Web site www.baconsinfo.com

Burrelle's Media Directory
(Publishes a series of directories with contact information for newspapers, magazines, newsletters, and broadcast news outlets.)
Burrelle's Information Services
75 East Northfield Road
Livingston, NJ 07039
Phone 800-876-3342
Fax 800-898-6677
Web site www.burrelles.com

Hudson's Directory
44 West Market Street
P.O. Box 311
Rhinebeck, NY 12572
Phone 914-876-2081
Fax 914-876-2561

Media Map
Corporate Headquarters
215 First Street
Cambridge, MA 02142
Phone 617-374-9300
Fax 617-374-9345
Web site www.mediamap.com

News Media Yellow Book
104 Fifth Avenue
New York, NY 10011
Phone 212-627-4140
Fax 212-645-0931
E-mail info@leadershipdirectories.com
Web site www.leadershipdirectories.com

Media Monitoring Services (see Chapter 86)

Bacon's Information, Inc.
332 South Michigan Avenue
Chicago, IL 60604
Phone 800-621-0561
Fax 312-922-3127
Web site www.baconsinfo.com

Dow Jones News Retrieval
Phone 800-369-7466
E-mail djinfo@wsj.dowjones.com
Web site www.djinteractive.com

Luce Press Clippings
420 Lexington Avenue
New York, NY 10710
Phone 800-528-8226
E-mail clip@lucepress.com
Web site www.lucepress.com

Video Monitoring Services of
America (VMS)
Phone 800-VMS-2002
E-mail news@vidmon.com
Web site www.vidmon.com

Media Training (see Chapter 9)

Edward Segal
Edward Segal Communications
E-mail edwardsegal@aol.com
Web site www.edwardsegal.com

Karen Friedman Enterprises
P.O. Box 224
Blue Bell, PA 19422
Phone 610-292-9780
Fax 610-292-9781
E-mail karen@karenfriedman.com
Web site www.karenfriedman.com

News Release Distribution Services (see Chapter 59)

Bacon's Information, Inc.
332 South Michigan Avenue
Chicago, IL 60604
Phone 800-621-0561
Fax 312-922-3127
Web site www.baconsinfo.com

Businesswire
Corporate Headquarters
44 Montgomery Street
39th Floor
San Francisco, CA 94104
Phone 800-227-0845
Web site www.businesswire.com

Media Distribution Services
307 West 36th Street
New York, NY 10018
Phone 800-MDS-3282
Fax 212-714-9092
Web site www.mdsconnect.com

North American Precis Syndicate,
Inc.
Chrysler Building
59th Floor
New York, NY 10174
Phone 212-867-9000

PIMS
1133 Broadway
New York, NY 10010
Phone 212-279-5112
Fax 212-645-5217
Web site www.pimsinc.com

PR Newswire
Corporate Headquarters
810 Seventh Avenue
New York, NY 10019
Phone 800-832-5522
Web site www.prnewswire.com

U.S. Newswire
National Press Building
Suite 1272
Washington, DC 20045
Phone 800-544-8995
Web site www.usnewswire.com

Presentation Skills Training (see Chapter 19)

Arnold Sanow
2810 Glade Vale Way
Vienna, VA 22181
Phone 703-255-3133
Fax 703-255-4668
E-mail speaker@arnoldsanow.com
Web site www.arnoldsanow.com

Public Opinion Polls (see Chapter 74)

Louis Harris and Associates, Inc.
111 Fifth Avenue
New York, NY 10003
Phone 212-539-9600
Fax 212-539-9669
Web site www.harrisinteractive.com

Market Facts, Inc.
Corporate Offices
3040 West Salt Creek Lane
Arlington Heights, IL 60005
Phone 847-590-7000
Fax 847-590-7010
Web site www.marketfacts.com

Public Relations Agencies and Consultants (see Chapter 16)

*O'Dwyer's Directory of Public
    Relations Firms*
J.R. O'Dwyer Co.
271 Madison Avenue
New York, NY 10016
Phone 212-679-2471
Fax 212-683-2750
Web site www.odwyerpr.com

PR Central
(Includes report card for the 100
largest public relations agencies.)
Web site www.prcentral.com

Public Relations Society of America
33 Irving Place
New York, NY 10003-2376
Phone 212-995-2230
Web site www.prsa.com

Understanding and Working with Reporters (see Chapter 26)

Bulldog Reporter
(Reports on media placement
opportunities and features advice
on how to work with reporters.)
5900 Hollis Street
Suite R2
Emeryville, CA 94608-2008
Phone 510-596-9300
Fax 510-596-9331
Web site www.infocomgroup.com

Interactive Public Relations
(Strategies and tactics for Internet
public relations campaigns.)
316 North Michigan Avenue
Chicago, IL 60601
Phone 800-878-5331
Fax 312-960-4106
Web site www.ragan.com

Editor & Publisher
(Weekly news and information
about the newspaper industry.)
11 West 19th Street
New York, NY 10011
Phone 212-675-4380
Web site www.mediainfo.com

Jack O'Dwyer's Newsletter
(Reports on trends and
developments in the public
relations profession.)
271 Madison Avenue
New York, NY 10016
Phone 212-679-2471
Fax 212-683-2750
Web site www.odwyerpr.com

Partyline
(Information on media placement
opportunities.)
35 Sutton Place
New York, NY 10012
Phone 212-755-3487
Fax 212-755-4859
E-mail byarmon@ix.netcom.com

Phillips International, Inc.
(Publishes several newsletters
about trends and developments in
the public relations profession:
*Interactive PR & Marketing News;
PR News; PR News Media Hotsheet.*)
7811 Montrose Road
Potomac, MD 20854
Phone 301-424-3338
E-mail clientservices.pbi@phillps.com
Web site www.phillips.com

PRWEEK
(A weekly magazine that covers
news and developments in the
public relations industry.)
Phone 800-722-2346
Fax 212-532-6733
E-mail prweek@prweekus.com
Web site www.prweekus.com

Ragan Communications, Inc.
Publishes a variety of newsletters
and magazines having to do with
the public relations industry:
Ragan's Media Relations Report
(information on media placement
opportunities); *Public Relations
Journal* (a strategic focus on issues
facing public relations
practitioners); *Interactive Public
Relations* (advice on Internet public
relations campaigns); *Ragan Report*
(a weekly report on ideas and
methods for communications
executives and the latest trends in
the field of corporate
communications and public
relations).
316 North Michigan Avenue
Suite 300
Chicago, IL 60601
Phone 800-878-5331
Fax 312-960-4106
Web site www.ragan.com

Research (see Chapter 12)

Dow Jones Interactive
(Access to the text of stories in
more than 6,000 publications
around the world.)
Phone 800-369-7466
E-mail djinfo@wsj.dowjones.com
Web site www.djinteractive.com

My Virtual Reference Desk
(A portal to 16,000 Web sites that
you use to help find a wide range
of information, facts, and figures.)
Web site www.refdesk.com

Television News Archive
Vanderbilt University
E-mail tvnews@tvnws.vanderbilt.edu
Web site www.vanderbilt.edu.

Satellite Media Tours (see Chapter 57)

Medialink, Inc.
708 Third Avenue
New York, NY 10017
Phone 800-843-0677
Web site www.medialink.com

Video News Releases (see Chapter 53)

Medialink, Inc.
708 Third Avenue
New York, NY 10017
Phone 800-843-0677
Web site www.medialink.com

About the Author

Edward Segal is president of Edward Segal Communications, a full-service public relations agency in Washington, DC. Segal has:

➤ Helped generate thousands of stories about the products, services, activities, and expertise of more than 500 clients in dozens of industries and professions. The list includes Marriott Corporation, MCI, American Red Cross, The Society of the Plastics Industry, Air Travelers Association, National Park Service, TeleCon West (the world's largest trade show on teleconferencing products, systems, and services), the American Council of Life Insurance, and numerous Internet and software companies.

➤ Written more than 1,000 news releases, op-eds, and bylined articles that have resulted in stories by news organizations including *The Wall Street Journal, The New York Times, USA Today, The Washington Post, Time, U.S. News & World Report,* the Associated Press, Reuters, Bloomberg News, Dow Jones, CNN, CBS News, and trade publications in dozens of industries and professions.

➤ Provided media training to hundreds of corporate executives and government officials on how to conduct successful interviews with reporters. Among those he's trained are officials of the Ford Motor Company, Cable & Wireless, Air Travelers Association, U.S. Census Bureau, National Park Service, National Immigration Forum, U.S. Public Health Service, ClickAction, Humana, Society of Manufacturing Engineers, and Group Health Association.

➤ Served as an expert to the media on effective public relations techniques, and has been interviewed by various news organizations including *BusinessWeek,* the *Los Angeles Times,* Gannett News, Fox News, and nationally syndicated television news programs.

➤ Worked as a media relations consultant to the clients of major PR firms and advertising agencies, including Ogilvy Public Relations Worldwide, Earle Palmer Brown, and Adworks.

■ I WANT TO HEAR FROM YOU

I'd appreciate hearing from you about:

➤ Your comments on this book.

➤ Stories, examples, or anecdotes you'd like to share about how well or poorly people, companies, and organizations have done in the public eye, and what others can learn from their successes or failures.

➤ Any recommendations or changes you'd like to see in future editions of the book.

➤ Your experience in implementing the advice within these pages.

➤ Copies of news coverage you've generated about yourself, company, or organization using the advice in this book.

➤ Comments or observations you'd like to share with readers.

Please send them to me by e-mail at edwardsegal@aol.com. And be sure to visit my Web site at www.edwardsegal.com for updated information, news about activities related to this book, and the text of news releases and other press materials referred to in earlier chapters.

EDWARD SEGAL
Washington, DC

YOU'RE ONE CLICK AWAY FROM RECEIVING YOUR FREE "15 MINUTES OF FAME" NEWSLETTER

Now that you've read *Getting Your 15 Minutes of Fame—and More!* visit www.edwardsegal.com to receive your free e-mail newsletter on fame.

The Web site and newsletter feature:

> ➤ Information on how to contact Edward Segal about speaking to your organization or company.

> ➤ The latest examples on the best or worst ways to achieve or manage fame.

> ➤ More "Hall of Fame" and "Hall of Shame" anecdotes about the successes or mistakes of people, companies, and organizations in the public eye.

> ➤ Updates on the strategies, tactics, and techniques you can use to become famous.

> ➤ Success stories from people who have implemented the advice in the book.

> ➤ Information about Edward Segal's speaking appearances in your area and book-related events and activities that are planned for the future.

> ➤ Answers to questions from readers of the book and subscribers to the newsletter.

Visit www.edwardsegal.com to begin your free subscription to the *Getting Your 15 Minutes of Fame—and More!* e-mail newsletter, or send an e-mail to edwardsegal@aol.com.

Index